Brick City
Grudge Match

Brick City Grudge Match

*Tony Zale and Rocky Graziano
Battle in Newark, 1948*

ROD HONECKER

McFarland & Company, Inc., Publishers
Jefferson, North Carolina

Excerpts from *Sugar Ray* by Sugar Ray Robinson and Dave Anderson, copyright © 1969, 1970 by Sugar Ray Robinson. Used by permission of Viking Books, an imprint of Penguin Publishing Group, a division of Penguin Random House LLC. All rights reserved.

Library of Congress Cataloguing-in-Publication Data

Names: Honecker, Rod, 1962– author.
Title: Brick City grudge match : Tony Zale and Rocky Graziano battle in Newark, 1948 / Rod Honecker.
Description: Jefferson, North Carolina : McFarland & Company, Inc., Publishers, 2023 | Includes bibliographical references and index.
Identifiers: LCCN 2022057330 | ISBN 9781476689432 (paperback : acid free paper) ∞ ISBN 9781476647722 (ebook)
Subjects: LCSH: Graziano, Rocky, 1922–1990. | Zale, Tony, 1913–1997. | Boxing—New Jersey—Neward—History. | BISAC: SPORTS & RECREATION / Boxing
Classification: LCC GV1132.G62 H66 2023 | DDC 796.83092 [B]—dc23/eng/20221219
LC record available at https://lccn.loc.gov/2022057330

British Library cataloguing data are available

**ISBN (print) 978-1-4766-8943-2
ISBN (ebook) 978-1-4766-4772-2**

© 2023 Rod Honecker. All rights reserved

No part of this book may be reproduced or transmitted in any form or by any means, electronic or mechanical, including photocopying or recording, or by any information storage and retrieval system, without permission in writing from the publisher.

Front cover: (left) Rocky Graziano (Stanley Kubrick/Library of Congress); (right) Tony Zale (William C. Greene/Library of Congress)

Printed in the United States of America

*McFarland & Company, Inc., Publishers
Box 611, Jefferson, North Carolina 28640
www.mcfarlandpub.com*

To Maureen

Acknowledgments

This book would never have been possible without the extraordinary efforts of my loving wife, Maureen. Beyond supportive, she served as my first editor, research assistant, and sage advisor. My daughter Molly heard more about Zale and Graziano than any teenager should be forced to endure, yet my musings were always met with earnest interest.

I must offer a special thanks to Paul Cavaliere, Jr., for his insights regarding his father, referee Paul Cavaliere. Ted and Deborah Zale were extraordinarily generous with their time and memories regarding Ted's uncle, and by sharing photographs for use in the book. Moreover, Ted's biography of Tony Zale, coauthored with boxing historian Clay Moyle, was a primary source for this book. Jeffrey Sussman's biography of Rocky Graziano (especially concerning Graziano's postboxing career), along with the Rock's classic autobiography (written with Rowland Barber), Scott Deitche's book on the Jersey mob, and Brad Tuttle's book on Newark, all served similar sourcing roles. Brad Tuttle, New Jersey sportswriting legend Jerry Izenberg, and boxing historian Springs Toledo are owed special thanks for their generous granting of permissions. I encourage readers of this book to review the bibliography section for references to the many excellent books that were read with much benefit to this author.

In addition, I received invaluable support and assistance from the Newark Public Library, even when faced with the unprecedented challenge of the COVID pandemic. I would be remiss if I failed to give credit to the excellent service I received from Newspapers.com.

Finally, I wish to express my thanks to friends and family who were all, without exception, enthusiastically supportive of this book.

Table of Contents

Acknowledgments   vi

Preface   1

1. The Precinct Captain and the Redhead   5
2. Noir City   11
3. From the Open Hearth   20
4. Black Sheep   32
5. A Fighting Champion (Zale Graziano I—Yankee Stadium, September 27, 1946)   43
6. Never Lay Down for Any Man   51
7. Blood and Thunder (Zale Graziano II—Chicago Stadium, July 16, 1947)   58
8. Born Dead with a Black Eye (Jersey Pugilistica)   63
9. Landing the Big Fight   77
10. Racing Head-On into the Night   90
11. Newark Grudge Match (Zale Graziano III—Ruppert Stadium, June 10, 1948)   108
12. Postfight Analysis   119
13. Last Round in Jersey City   126
14. Trial of the Redhead   132
15. Somebody Up There Likes Me   140
16. Brick City   148
17. Requiem for a Middleweight   155

Table of Contents

Appendix: Career Records of Tony Zale and Rocky Graziano   163

Chapter Notes   171

Bibliography   185

Index   189

Preface

This time Jersey would be in the spotlight. There was no question the eyes of the sports world would be locked on that minor league ballpark carved out of the mean streets of Newark.

Early on a bitter March morning I made my way east on Route 78. Although downtown Newark was closer, Manhattan's imposing skyline dominated the horizon. I took the exit for Routes 1 and 9, which feed into the Pulaski Skyway, that Depression-era engineering marvel snaking over the dank marshes and connecting Newark's East Ward to Jersey City. The off-ramp for Wilson Avenue and the Ironbound Section is shortly before the Pulaski starts in earnest.

I was in search of a plaque commemorating a minor league ballpark that had once stood on Wilson Avenue. Internet searches of a "missing ballpark" website, old newspaper articles, and a memoir by New Jersey sportswriting legend Jerry Izenberg indicated a plaque had been dedicated in 2007 by the Newark Preservation and Landmarks Committee. Try as I might, I could not locate it. At the corner of Wilson and Avenue K, where the plaque should have been located, I found instead a "PRIVATE PROPERTY" sign threatening to tow anyone who dared park their car.

As I expanded my search down Wilson Avenue toward Avenue L, a burly guard dog trotted up on the other side of a chain-link fence. The big fella did not bark but gave me a good looking over. I got the message and moved on—nothing to see here.

My interest in the site concerned a legendary boxing match that took place there in 1948. I was a boxing fan in my youth, when the sport was still among the most popular. Great champions like Muhammad Ali, Sugar Ray Leonard, and Alexis Arguello filled the headlines and airwaves. A history buff, I had read about the bout, the rubber match in one of the most famous trilogies in boxing history. I was curious about

Preface

why a fight of such magnitude took place in Newark, and I filed that thought away. Although I was born in Newark and attended law school there, I felt little connection to the place. My mother's family, which had deep roots in Newark, relocated to Ocean County in the early 1960s when the Jersey Shore was opened to residential development with the completion of the Garden State Parkway. Only years later, when I read that Newark reached its peak population in that same year of 1948, did the urge to find an answer to the "why Newark?" question return.

The men who met in the ring that night, middleweights Tony Zale and Rocky Graziano, were two of the most famous sports figures of their time. They were central characters during the Golden Age of boxing, when tens of thousands of men—mostly second-generation immigrants and African Americans—pursued professional careers in that most dangerous and corrupt sport. Like the others, Zale and Graziano had been buffeted by the Great Depression. Their lives were disrupted and altered, albeit in different ways, by the Second World War. Both men suffered more than their fair share of personal tragedy. These midcentury Americans had to fight for their place in the world. Boxing was their way out.

Neither man was the most talented fighter to step into the ring. But they both toughed their way to the top in the roughest racket out there. Both were sluggers, Zale with more polish and known as a body puncher; Rocky more crude and powerful, a headhunter. Their styles "meshed like gears."[1] The first two fights of the pair were instantly considered classics for their concentrated violence, brutality, and heroics. The public loved it and they drew record gates. As recently as the 1990s, the first two matches were ranked among the top ten greatest ever.

The names of Zale and Graziano became virtual appendages of each other.[2] The highly literary sportswriters of the time, men like Jimmy Cannon, W. C. Heinz, and Red Smith, did much of their best work covering Zale and Graziano. Newark's two leading newspapers had their own respected boxing writers: Anthony Marenghi of the *Newark Star Ledger* and Willie Ratner of the *Newark Evening News*. Much of what is presented here was seen through the eyes of these men.

As the popularity of boxing waned, the epic of Zale and Graziano faded. Even among some knowledgeable fans of the sweet science, the reputations of Zale and Graziano as fighters have suffered with shifts in modern perceptions. A Wikipedia page devoted to the sports history of Newark, which includes a subsection on boxing, makes no reference to the third Zale Graziano bout.

Preface

The Newark of 1948 was at its zenith, with its population peaking at 450,000. It maintained a reputation as a manufacturing powerhouse, a retail giant, and a brewing capital. The largest city in New Jersey, Newark flexed outsized political clout. President Truman campaigned in Newark that year as part of his uphill reelection bid.

Most Newarkers chose to downplay or ignore long-standing problems of political corruption and organized crime. For decades, they had gone hand in hand in Newark. Some say life imitates art, and the city of Newark in 1948 was like a real-life noir film, that genre then at its peak and characterized by dark shadows, cynicism, and betrayal (often sexual). As Zale and Graziano prepared for their third scrap, the story of a sensational killing with a real femme fatale filled Newark's newspapers. Some of the most powerful figures in organized crime made Newark their base of operations. Perhaps even more serious—and ominous—for the city's future was the start of deindustrialization as war contracts burned off and good-paying, working-class jobs began relocating to the South and West.

The big fight offered a respite. It was a point of civic pride. The city's most prominent politicians, from the mayor on down, associated themselves with the event. Journalists and everyday Newarkers dreamed the fight foreshadowed a more hopeful future. There was no question the eyes of the sports world would be locked on that minor league ballpark carved out of the mean streets of Newark—Zale and Graziano, it was said, could "draw in Siam."[3] This time Jersey would be in the spotlight, hosting the headline event. The big shots from the Big Apple would be traveling west through the tunnels under the Hudson River.

On that raw winter morning, in the darkness on the edge of town, I searched unsuccessfully for a plaque commemorating the site of the famous clash more than seventy years ago. Yet I left determined to tell the story of the final battle between Zale and Graziano against the backdrop of a gritty city staggering precariously at its peak.

1

The Precinct Captain and the Redhead

At 4:00 a.m. on May 21, 1948, Newark Police Captain Thomas Rowe, a thirty-three-year veteran of the department, appeared at his First Precinct station house. It was obvious to his brother officers that the fifty-seven-year-old captain had been drinking. He was also in the company of a much younger woman. The shapely redhead was not his wife. Lieutenant Henry Ville was manning the information desk. Ville noted Rowe's visit on the precinct house log but failed to mention his female company.

The couple went toward Captain Rowe's private office. Prior to entering, Rowe stopped and spoke to plainclothesman Raymond Poquette in the detective's room adjacent to Rowe's office. Poquette heard the redhead call out to Rowe: "Come in and close the door." When Rowe objected, the redhead replied with an obscene remark in French. Poquette spoke French and interpreted for Rowe, who laughed and then went into his office and closed the door.[1] Ten minutes later a pistol shot rang out.[2]

Poquette and Ville were startled by the blast. Poquette entered Rowe's office and observed a jarring scene. The captain was hunched over his desk, clutching his stomach as blood gushed through his fingers. "The bitch got me,"[3] Rowe said, adding, "Quick, get me a doctor."[4] He rapidly went into shock and became unresponsive. Today Rowe may have survived, but in 1948 there were no paramedics so he did not receive medical care en route to Newark City Hospital. Upon arrival, the trauma surgeon treated Rowe with morphine, Adrenalin, and a blood transfusion (five hundred cubic centimeters) to no avail. Captain Rowe died at 5:52 a.m.[5] The autopsy revealed that Rowe was killed by a hemorrhage started by a bullet that entered the right side of his abdomen, made three holes in his intestines, and passed through his left kidney, where the hemorrhage occurred.[6]

Brick City Grudge Match

The cops' attention turned to the redhead. She was an uncooperative witness. The "sultry" woman, "stylishly dressed and high heeled," was coolly confident and completely defiant. Chain-smoking cigarettes, she refused to provide her name and address: "You're the policeman. You find out."[7] Refusing to believe Rowe was dead, she challenged the cops to prove it. The police took her to the hospital and displayed Rowe's inert body.[8] She remained unmoved, blurting, "It's a frameup."[9] When a detective got smart with her, the fiery redhead cursed and slapped him across the face with her handbag.[10]

Word of the shooting spread quickly. As the sun rose, agog Newarkers began gathering outside police headquarters hoping to get a glimpse of the mysterious suspect. The *Newark Star Ledger* ran a series of photos of the captain's office "still splattered with blood."[11] New York's *Daily News* ran a headline "Spitting Tigress Is Caged," accompanied by a photo of the redhead covering her face with a burning cigarette clamped between her thumb and forefinger.[12] The more staid *Newark Evening News* took a different tack, expressing appall at the spectacle and deep concern about the shooting of the highest ranking officer in "the most important precinct of the city involving extremely questionable circumstances."[13] Indeed, the First Precinct encompassed the downtown business area. The station house, located at Washington and Court streets, was the "nerve center" of the precinct.[14] The *Newark Evening News*, the paper of record for the entire state of New Jersey, demanded an independent investigation of the incident and the conditions at the First Precinct.

The cops closed ranks. Reporters found First Precinct officers glum and closed mouthed.[15] The *Newark Evening News* criticized "the higher ups of the Newark Department" for their less than zealous hunt for the facts of Rowe's death. Equally troubling was a spike in crime, specifically "vicious" and audacious muggings in the heart of downtown.[16] The authorities felt the pressure. Essex County Prosecutor Duane E. Minard and his detectives were tapped to take over the investigation and provide independent oversight.

Rowe's colleagues in the department had good reason to remain loyal to his reputation. Captain Thomas "Tim" Rowe's record was as colorful as it was stellar. He joined the force in 1915. After a stint in the Navy during the First World War, the brawling Irishman became recognized for his fearlessness. In 1920, Rowe rushed into a gang fight and disarmed an assailant. In 1923, he rescued a brother officer when, despite being shot himself, he crashed into a room and overpowered a

1. The Precinct Captain and the Redhead

gun-toting hoodlum. Rowe was assigned to investigate the Lindbergh kidnapping and logged thousands of miles tracking down clues.[17] In 1939, Rowe was promoted to captain after finishing first on the civil service exam. And in 1946, Rowe took over as head of the First Precinct where he had started his career.[18] By 1948, Rowe was Newark's best-known policeman.[19]

Rowe's outstanding record, however, was marred by a single but significant blemish. On August 2, 1937, Rowe was involved in another very public shooting incident, this time with twenty-two-year-old Effie Rallie. The young woman was shot in the thigh while sitting with Rowe in his car. At the official review of the incident, Rallie testified that she was waiting at a bus stop when Rowe offered her "a ride." She "brushed up against [Rowe's] automatic pistol which discharged as she slid into the seat."[20] The shooting was deemed an accident, and Rowe was cleared by the Board of Public Responsibility.[21]

But the man's interest in extracurricular activities was not satiated. He bought off one lover's silence with a fur coat.[22] Reports of another affair seemed more relevant: one year prior to the 1948 shooting, Rowe was said to have broken off another relationship by offering his paramour his gun and defying her to "use it if you have the nerve."[23] Prosecutor Minard, however, promptly and emphatically shot down this particular report.[24]

Prosecutor Minard's gumshoes quickly tracked down the identity of the mysterious redhead. Ann Seamons was one of thirteen children. She came from a mining town in Pennsylvania. Weary of her grimy surroundings and fascinated by fancy clothes and the fast life of the city, Ann quit school at sixteen and traveled to Newark to work as a domestic.[25] At twenty-one, she married Newark undertaker Henry Powers. But she became bored with the embalmer and booted him out of the marital residence with nary but the clothes on his back. "One day she told me she did not want me around—just like that," said the rebuffed ex.[26] But she never divorced the mortician, and Ann's legal name remained Powers at the time of the shooting.

The "stately" woman (she was 5'9" tall) resided in an attic apartment in Bloomfield at the time of the shooting. A "closed book" to her neighbors, she occasionally worked as a waitress but otherwise had no visible sources of income. Powers went by the name "Ann Neff." George Neff was a former lover who was then serving time at Rahway Prison. Neff was locked up for check kiting, a crime that came to light after Ann accused him of trying to kill her at the close of an all-night drinking party.²⁷ After George Neff was imprisoned, Ann was frequently seen in the company of different men.²⁸ Her landlady slut-shamed the woman by chastising her for having "too many boyfriends." Unperturbed, Ann frequented local watering holes where she imbibed scotch and sodas. A local bartender recalled that she never appeared to get drunk and never caused any trouble.²⁹

Further investigation revealed that Captain Rowe and Ann Powers struck up a "close association" starting in January 1948. The couple met at a tavern on Halsey Street in the First Precinct.³⁰ They became "frequent companions" and openly cavorted during drinking binges through Newark taverns and higher-end establishments.³¹ A hotel register was found bearing the name of "Tim Rowe" and listing a fictitious address.³²

Eventually the affair caught the attention of high-ranking members of the department. Captain James Bell of the Third Precinct, a close friend of Rowe, urged him to break off the relationship.³³ Rowe initially procrastinated, but a few days before the shooting resolved to "unload Ann so I will never see her again."³⁴ Prosecutor Minard settled on a theory of the case that Powers became enraged and shot Rowe while he was in the process of jilting her. "Like hundreds of men he had put behind bars, [Rowe] found himself on a dead-end street with a thirst for hard liquor and a yen for beautiful women."³⁵

There were problems with the theory. As the detectives pieced together events leading up to the shooting, they discovered that Rowe and Powers had been on a pub crawl. They were seen at 10:30 p.m. on the night of May 20 at Mayfair Farms and later at Pal's Tavern (where Frank Sinatra got his start) in West Orange. The couple was then seen at a Newark tavern at 2:00 a.m. on May 21.³⁶ In each instance, the couple was observed engaging in congenial conversation.³⁷ There was no sign of trouble.

The firearm involved added to the mystery. Ballistics pointed to a .38-caliber sawed-off revolver as the source of the fatal shot. The weapon was not Rowe's standard .38 police special, but rather an untraceable ghost gun. The identification number had been filed or burned off.³⁸ Powers's fingerprints were not on the weapon, which was found neatly placed on Rowe's desk. If Powers did shoot Rowe, she displayed remarkable composure in wiping the gun clean. Given the copious amount of alcohol they were seen consuming (Powers acknowledged drinking six or seven scotch and sodas), there is little doubt both Rowe and Powers were inebriated, heightening the possibility of an accidental

1. The Precinct Captain and the Redhead

shooting—just like Rowe's prior incident with the twenty-two-year-old. There were no living eyewitnesses, other than perhaps Powers who could not be compelled to testify. Moreover, Powers had been through many tumultuous relationships and had never shown a violent streak. Why would she choose to murder a police captain, of all people, especially while in the precinct house?

On May 30, an alternate theory of Rowe's death splashed across the *Newark Star Ledger* in a blaring headline: "DID ROWE TOY WITH SUICIDE PACT?" Powers had told investigators that Rowe raised the possibility at a downtown Newark bar.[39] Supposedly, Rowe had a serious heart condition and knew he did not have long to live.[40]

Prosecutor Minard moved promptly to squelch talk of suicide. On June 1, 1948, Minard was quoted as saying that Rowe was not suffering from any illness, contrary to "irresponsible reports."[41] Pointing to the ballistics analysis, Minard claimed the shot was fired from two feet away, with no powder burns on Rowe's clothing. These facts, coupled with the trajectory of the bullet as it traversed Rowe's midsection, convinced the state's experts that the fatal shot could not have been self-inflicted.[42]

Powers was arraigned on the charge of murdering Captain Thomas Rowe and ordered by Superior Court Judge Pellecchia to be held without bail in the Essex County Jail on Newark Street. On June 3, 1948, Powers was deemed sane to stand trial after a half-hour examination by a psychiatrist.[43] One week later, Powers would be cooling her high heels in the county jail when champion Rocky Graziano squared off with challenger Tony Zale three and a half miles away in the biggest sporting event in Newark that anyone could remember.

If the case against Powers had a few holes, the other aspect of Minard's mandate—investigating the conditions at the First Precinct—had gotten nowhere. Minard's sifting through Rowe's bank accounts for suspicious transactions turned up nothing. Rowe was not corrupt. He was broke at the time of his death.[44] For a married man, juggling girlfriends has always been an expensive proposition.

Minard seized the First Precinct's blotters. Rowe's visit on the night of his death was noted, but Powers's tandem visit was not recorded.[45] Powers told investigators that she had visited the precinct house on prior occasions, but the ledgers reflected nothing of the kind. None of the First Precinct officers admitted to seeing Powers prior to the shooting, or any other "suspicious characters."[46] Minard complained about "carrying the ball alone" in "determining the conditions" at the First

Precinct.⁴⁷ The hectoring of the press for full disclosure and transparency were going unheeded.

Then things took a dark turn. On June 3, Detective Lt. Benjamin Schaeffer of Minard's staff received a death threat scrawled on a postcard. It depicted a scalping and Native American motif, and read: "This man asks too many questions; now he gone dead…. Warning to men who want to know too much."⁴⁸ Perhaps even more disturbing, reports surfaced of Newark police cruisers trailing Minard's men as they prowled the city conducting the investigation.⁴⁹

Newark's organized crime element was humored by the cops' embarrassment and the authorities' infighting. Taunting their enemies, illegal bookmakers laid ten-to-one odds that Powers would beat the rap.⁵⁰

2

Noir City

In 1948, Newark hit the peak of its population, just under 450,000.[1] Strategically located between New York and Philadelphia, the city had always been an industrial powerhouse and prime transportation hub. Newark's natural strengths had been buoyed further by wartime production contracts. But the city remained dogged by a reputation for political corruption and as a nest for organized crime. And ominous clouds were gathering that would lead quickly to a shocking collapse characterized by extreme violence, hatred, and hopelessness.

Newark was founded in the mid–seventeenth century by Puritans in search of a religious community devoted to God's work.[2] The Puritan founders would be the first of many to have their dreams bedeviled by the challenge of governing Newark. At a time when transportation relied heavily on access to free-flowing water, the site appealed to the founders because of the wide and fish-stocked Passaic River and easy access to Newark Bay. The relative remoteness of the site was a bonus for the Puritans who did not want their spiritual harmony disrupted by meddlesome bureaucrats.[3]

Newark's fathers chose their site too well for their purposes. Located directly west of Manhattan, the village became a colonial-era stopover for travelers heading to Philadelphia. Commercial and population growth followed.[4] Conflict was not far behind. Angered at violations of the sabbath, oldline religious groups began harassing non-observant businesses. By the post–Revolution era, they threatened to tar and feather federal officers carrying the mail.[5] Enraged by the consumption of alcohol on Sunday, religious zealots erected stocks on Broad Street, only to have them torn down by a mob of irate drunks.[6]

The rout of the temperance forces ended Newark's phase as a theocratic village. Newark embarked on a period of rapid industrialization and, ultimately, urbanization. The challenges associated with the transition—crime, poverty, and disease—followed apace. By 1836, reports circulated of widespread consumption of alcohol, and spousal and child abuse.[7]

Public health suffered as infrastructure lagged behind factory and population growth. Newark lacked paved roads and adequate drainage systems leading to outbreaks of disease, including malaria.[8] "The stench of coal dust, animal dung and raw sewage was everywhere."[9] Newarkers even died of rabies as packs of wild dogs roamed the streets.[10]

In pre–Civil War Newark, public officials tended to come from the business world. These businessmen were tightfisted with public expenditures and favored a laissez-faire approach to government. Long-term investments got shortchanged.[11] Civic leaders failed to set aside public space for rest and recreation.[12]

Business interests also affected the response of the city to the election of Abraham Lincoln. Newark's businessmen had long cultivated strong ties to the South, as Newark's factories produced much of their products for southern customers. These men were less than enthused about the prospect of Lincoln's election and war with the Confederacy. New Jersey was the only northern state to not give all of its electoral votes to Lincoln.[13] On his famous journey from Springfield to his inauguration, Lincoln's train pulled into Newark from Jersey City. Honest Abe could not have helped but notice the subdued, almost somber reception he received in Newark. He may have even caught a glimpse of his effigy hung from a Newark lamppost.[14]

But predictions of economic doom from the Civil War proved wrong. Business lost from the South was more than made up for with government war contracts. By 1872, Newark was a "monster workshop" and boasted the third highest industrial output in the nation, making virtually everything manufactured and consumed at the time.[15] Public investment, however, still lagged. By 1890, Newark was the nation's most unhealthy big city, the worst in infant mortality, typhoid, malaria, and tuberculosis.[16] Disrespect for the living was matched by desecration of the dead. In the 1880s, the city sold off the Old Burial Ground on Broad Street, the remains of the Puritan founders dug up and the lot converted to a public urinal.[17]

The Progressive Era finally ushered in long overdue changes. As the immigrant population of the city surged, political power shifted to the newcomers. German immigrant Julius Lebkuecher took over as mayor and proved to be an energetic executive. Cutting through red tape and axing deadweight patronage jobs, Lebkuecher set about installing a long overdue sewer system and paving streets.[18]

2. Noir City

By the turn of the twentieth century, Newark had become a popular shopping destination and center for entertainment. The completion of the imposing City Hall on Broad Street in 1906 seemed to augur a bright future.[19] But this same era saw the advent of two disturbing trends that would come to define Newark's reputation: rampant political corruption and the rise of organized crime. Corruption "evolved into something of a tradition in Newark dating back to at least the late 1800s. It has survived in Darwinian fashion, adapting and taking new shape in response to reformers' efforts and swings in voter populations." A grim joke goes, "Newark politicians leave office in only one of two ways: death or conviction."[20]

Political corruption in the "Soprano State" has been closely linked with the rise of organized crime. And no place in New Jersey is more closely associated with organized crime than Newark.[21] During the immigration boom in the early part of the twentieth century, Italians migrated to Newark's First Ward. Wary of the police, the new immigrants were particularly vulnerable. Newark's rough neighborhoods would serve as incubators for wise guys throughout the twentieth century.[22]

The roster of notable Newark mobsters reads like it was dreamed up by a Hollywood screenwriter: Charlie "The Blade" Tourine. Anthony "Tony Pro" Provenzano. Joe "The Indian" Polverino. Nicholas "Joe Bones" Bufania.[23] Stefano Badami. Tony "Bananas" Caponigro. Anthony Rotando. Louis Larasso. The LeConte Brothers. Joe Stassi. Otto "Abbadabba" Berman. Charles "The Bug" Workman. Joseph "Doc" Stacher. Max "Puddy" Hinkes. Albert Anastasia. Kayo Konigsberg. John "Big Pussy" Russo. Sam "Big Sue" Katz. Angelo "Gyp" DeCarlo.[24]

Mob hits in Newark were distinguished by brazenness and elements that eventually made their way to the big screen:

    a. November 3, 1930—Dominic "The Ape" Rosselli was shot twice in the head in Room 33 in Newark General Hospital. Two gunmen ignored hospital protocol and entered without checking in with the information desk. The Ape, described as a "Beer Gangster," was killed instantly. His assailants, who bowled over nurses while making their escape, were never identified.[25]

    b. November 26, 1930—Richie "The Boot" Boiardo (named for "da phone boot" he used because his home line was tapped) was machine-gunned on Broad Street. Although shot eleven times in his head and body, the Boot survived and lived to 1984 and the ripe age of ninety-three. His assailants were never prosecuted.[26] However, shortly after the brazen assassination attempt, two teenage boys spotted a body floating in the Passaic River. The dead man was Adam Dresch, former Newark police officer. The authorities concluded Dresch's killing—his body was riddled with bullets and there were signs he had been bound and severely beaten—was in retaliation for the attempt on the Boot's life.[27]

 c. September 15, 1931—The bodies of Sam Monaco and Louis "Babe Ruth" Russo were fished out of the Passaic River. Their heads were beaten in and their bodies weighted down. Known for shaking down other racketeers, these two embarked on a particularly dangerous career path. Their killers were never identified.[28]

 d. August 22, 1935—Vincent Troia, Joseph Troia, and Frank Longo were gunned down in broad daylight at a candy store at 317 South Sixth Street. The authorities concluded the shooting resulted from a dispute over illegal lottery operations.[29]

 e. February 22, 1937—Gaspare D'Amico and his father were shot in broad daylight while packing macaroni at the family factory. Gaspare survived but fled the city and quit mob life. No arrests were made.[30]

The situation grew dire. The federal judge for the District of New Jersey complained to FBI Director J. Edgar Hoover about "conditions in Newark, as the gangsters and racketeers ... were running wild and nobody seemed able to stop them."[31] Judge Clark had "given up all hope of legal officials ever accomplishing anything insofar as crime" was concerned. "Not only the police force but higher officials in the City, including the Mayor, are corrupt."[32]

Newark's chaotic underworld was ripe for an organizational mastermind. That force would come in the form of one Abner "Longie" Zwillman. Born in the Jewish Third Ward of Newark, Zwillman got his name, not from his sexual equipment as rumored (Hollywood's "blonde bombshell" Jean Harlow was one of many conquests[33]), but because he reached his 6'2" height by the time of his bar mitzvah.[34] When Irish and Italian hooligans harassed Jewish merchants, they would yell *"Ref der Langer"* (Fetch the tall one).[35] Naturally cunning and manipulative, Zwillman pawned off tough assignments to younger boys by convincing them it was an honor to be trusted with the job.[36] Other than a six-month stint for assault and battery in the twenties, Longie avoided jail his entire life.[37]

2. Noir City

Depression-era Newark (photograph by Arthur Rothstein; Library of Congress).

Zwillman would come to be known as the "Al Capone of Newark." He may have been more accurately described as a real-life hybrid of Vito and Michael Corleone. Smart, polished,[38] and tough, Zwillman, like the fictional Godfathers, had the talent to operate both as a mobster and as a legitimate businessman.[39] He understood, like John D. Rockefeller, that cooperation was better for business than endless conflict. It was Zwillman who formed the "Commission" with infamous New York mobsters Frank Costello, Lucky Luciano, and Meyer Lansky. Zwillman formed a long-lasting and lucrative Newark partnership with Richie "The Boot" Boiardo, ceding control of the Italian First Ward to the Boot.[40] At his peak, Longie controlled Newark politicians "like nickels and dimes carried around in his pocket."[41]

Zwillman, like many infamous gangsters, initially made his mark during Prohibition. Longie and his partners made approximately $50 million and supplied 40 percent of all the illegal liquor consumed in the United States during the dry time.[42] The booze was dropped at remote spots on the Jersey Shore, cut with water, and then brought to Newark. Bribing the cops and probation agents to look the other way was a cost of doing business.[43] Newark's citizens, by 1920 heavily infused with Irish, German, and Italian immigrants, had no tolerance for the temperance movement.[44] Other relatively harmless vices such as gambling and prostitution were profitable lines of business for Zwillman.[45] Longie eventually crossed a line that Don Corleone refused: dealing in heroin. The white powder was being handled at the Casablanca Club, located on Broad Street in Newark, ostensibly owned by Zwillman's chauffeur.[46]

Zwillman had a deft political touch. While avoiding the spotlight and maintaining an air of mystery,[47] he cultivated the image of a civic-minded Robin Hood. He offered a reward for the return of the kidnapped Lindbergh baby and donated $250,000 to a Newark slum-clearing project.[48] Zwillman set up soup kitchens during the Depression and donated Christmas and Passover baskets to needy Newark families.[49] He ingratiated himself with Newark politicians on both sides of the aisle.[50] Zwillman exerted control over the Third Ward and then "influenced" political appointments.[51]

Longie's public persona masked a rougher side. One businessman made the mistake of competing with Longie's sideline in coin-operated washing machines. When the competitor pushed to get his machines into public buildings ostensibly owned by the Newark Housing Authority, he ran into a brick wall. It finally dawned on the poor man who he was dealing with and he backed off, not wanting find himself "in the Passaic River."[52]

Zwillman bared his teeth in a more well-known bit of mob folklore. New York City Mayor William O'Dwyer linked Zwillman to "Murder, Inc.," the enforcement arm of the Italian and Jewish mobs.[53] Zwillman is generally considered to have given the order, or at least the go-ahead, for the most infamous Newark mob hit. Arthur Flegenheimer, a.k.a. Dutch Schultz, was a notorious New York mobster. Schultz relocated to Newark when pressured by Prosecutor Thomas Dewey, later a GOP presidential candidate (of "DEWEY DEFEATS TRUMAN" fame). When Schultz made noise about having Dewey killed, Murder, Inc., decided Dutch had become too much of a loose cannon.

On October 23, 1935, Schultz was enjoying his regular meal of steak and fries at the Palace Chop House in downtown Newark. Hitmen Charles "The Bug" Workman and Emanuel "Mendy" Weiss blasted Schultz and his bodyguards. Incredibly, Schultz and his guards initially survived the attack. They even managed to wound the Bug, who was abandoned by the getaway car and consigned to fleeing on foot.[54]

The first police officer on the scene was Captain Thomas Rowe—the

2. Noir City

same man later killed in his office at the First Precinct.[55] Schultz was still alive when Rowe arrived, slumped in his chair. Dutch, who had been hit with a rusty slug, began to incoherently spout off. Hoping to capture something of value, the police summoned a court stenographer. The resulting transcript is a bizarre ramble ("I know what I am doing here with my collection of papers, for crying out loud. The Chimney Sweeps. Talk to the Sword...."). Fiction writers and musicians have found inspiration in Dutch's oration, including hip-hop performers.[56] Schultz lingered for a day before succumbing to peritonitis.

Zwillman was brought in for questioning by the Newark Police. He was seen arguing with Schultz at the Robert Treat Hotel the Saturday before the massacre.[57] Longie absurdly denied any knowledge of the Schultz hit. Zwillman, always a step ahead of the law, had several high-ranking members of the Newark Police Department on his payroll (a 1940 reorganization of the department was said to be a "reorganization by Zwillman"[58]). He deftly maneuvered his way out of further scrutiny.[59]

Longie remained in control of Newark's underworld throughout the 1940s, manipulating city officials, judges, and police.[60] Zwillman was said to be in charge of all rackets in the Newark area.[61] Longie was the "biggest power on the waterfront."[62] He was even said to have handpicked Newark's Mayor Meyer Ellenstein and other high-ranking city officials. Later, Zwillman's public pawns ended up facing federal charges for shady real estate transactions.[63] But Longie himself seemed untouchable. An internal FBI memo explained the difficulty in nailing him: "Zwillman's operations are extremely circumspect. He has a highly organized operation and commands unusual loyalty and prestige among his associates. He has top-flight lawyers and accountants advising him on his extensive business operations."[64]

By midcentury, the FBI began focusing on rooting out corruption in Newark. In 1948, the mayoralty was in the hands of Vincent Murphy, a reformer. Mayor Murphy helped create a Central Planning Board (CPB), which formulated aggressive plans for urban renewal, including slum clearing and construction of public housing.[65] With its population never higher, Newark seemed to be moving toward a brighter future.

The Newark of 1948 was probably one of the most ethnically diverse places in the country. The immigrant waves of Irish, German, and Italian people were supplemented by African Americans emigrating from the South. The population of Newark grew by more than 26 percent between 1910 and 1950. Drawn by relatively high-paying factory jobs, largely desegregated schools, and an established African American community,[66] the black population increased more than 700 percent in those four decades. According to the 1950 census, Newark's white population stood at 363,000, still approximately 83 percent of the total population.

Downtown Newark offered major retailers such as Bamberger's and Hahne's. Newark Airport, the first in the metropolitan area, was one of the busiest. Newark's nightclubs featured some of the finest jazz and big band performers going. The First Ward's Italian restaurants drew celebrities from New York City, including none other than the Yankee Clipper, Joe DiMaggio. Rumor had it that DiMaggio was friendly with Longie Zwillman and Richie the Boot. Joe's driver and bodyguard, Jimmy "Peanuts" Ceres, was said to be on the Boot's payroll.[67]

Midcentury Newark, enveloped in fog. (Newark Public Library).

Peanuts and Newark even played a supporting role in Joltin' Joe's immortal fifty-six-game hitting streak. In the middle of the streak, DiMaggio's favorite bat was stolen between games of a doubleheader in Washington. Peanuts made it his business to find the missing bat. He was reported to have investigated for five days in Washington and then, mysteriously, tracked "the prized bludgeon" to New Jersey. Reports conflicted as to whether Peanuts purchased the bat or traded Yankee tickets or simply took back the bat from the hapless thief. No one seemed to care about the details as everyone wanted the bat restored to its proper owner.[68]

Midcentury Newark was a great baseball town. The mighty Bronx Bombers maintained their top Triple A farm team in Newark. The

2. Noir City

Newark Bears played their home games at Newark's nineteen-thousand-seat Ruppert Stadium located in Newark's East Ward. Referred to as "Down Neck" because of a bend on the Passaic River, the ward is also known as the Ironbound Section because it was once bounded by railroad tracks. Many stars of the Bronx Bombers played for the Bears on their way up, including Hall of Famers Yogi Berra and Joe Gordon. The 1937 Newark Bears, with a record of 109–43, are widely considered the greatest minor league team ever assembled.[69]

The Negro leagues featured a prominent franchise: the Newark Eagles. One year prior to Jackie Robinson's debut with the Brooklyn Dodgers, the Eagles won the 1946 Negro leagues championship. The Eagles also played their home games at Ruppert Stadium and featured legendary players, including Larry Doby, the first African American to play in the American League. Monty Irvin, Leon Day, and Biz Mackey were other Hall of Famers who played for the team. The Eagles' owner, Effa Manley, holds the distinction of being the only woman ever elected to the National Baseball Hall of Fame.[70]

New Jersey sportswriting legend Jerry Izenberg wrote nostalgically about the connection between the city and its ball clubs: "These two teams wrote the history of this town. They won world championships of their social sets, and a dozen Hall of Famers played for them. They were kings of a city where every 8 year old could explain the infield fly rule—where you could walk down the city's streets when the Bears played and through open windows hear radio broadcasts of the games."[71] Ruppert Stadium "was more than a ball park to us. It was youth and magic and a place where hope was never defeated by nine bad innings." This "happiest and busiest place" put the city "on the national sports map."[72]

Another sport also captivated Newark's citizens, as it did the rest of the county. Second only in popularity to the national pastime, this other sport—less savory than baseball and often relegated to the fringes or even outlawed—was at its peak of popularity in 1948. In June of that year the eyes of the sporting world would settle on a boxing ring constructed on the infield of Newark's Ruppert Stadium.

3

From the Open Hearth

The man the world came to know as Tony Zale was born Anthony Florian Zaleski on May 29, 1913. He was the sixth of seven children of Josef and Kataryna (Catherine). The Zaleskis emigrated from Poland, desperate to escape that war-torn country. They settled in Gary, Indiana, home to the industrial-age behemoth United States Steel. A true company town, the manufacturing of steel was the very reason for the city: Gary is named after United States Steel founding chairman, Elbert Henry Gary. Good-paying jobs were a magnet for the Eastern European immigrants arriving in large numbers in the early twentieth century. "The Steel City" faces Lake Michigan just like its larger and more famous neighbor, Chicago.

The boy's future was forged in tragedy. His father was hit and killed by a drunk driver when Anthony was two years old. As a forty-year-old widow, Catherine was left destitute with six mouths to feed, and a seventh on the way.[1] Later Zale described his surroundings as a "slum."[2] Forced to assume the role of both parents, Catherine immersed her brood in the teachings of the Catholic Church. The Zaleskis were congregants at St. Hedwig Catholic Church where transplanted Poles worshiped. The family attended Mass every Sunday and said prayers before every meal. If her boys' moral compass nevertheless waivered when enticed by worldly temptations, Catherine reserved the right to mete out more earthly guidance. She beat her boys with sticks when they misbehaved. Zale later wrote that his mother "would have broken my neck if I had ever stolen anything from anybody."[3]

Young Anthony absorbed the teachings of the church and took them to heart. His faith was real. Years later, when facing potentially mortal challenges in the ring, Tony Zale would call on his faith to see him through.[4]

Zale's older brothers, Joseph and John, showed a talent for boxing. The Zaleski boys got caught up in the surge of interest for the sport in the

3. From the Open Hearth

1920s after the charismatic and hard-hitting Jack Dempsey seized the heavyweight title. Joseph and John eventually became all middle states champions, that era's version of the Golden Gloves.[5]

Their kid brother would outdo them by miles. Anthony watched and learned from his older siblings. When Joseph was once robbed of a decision, Anthony made a resolution: don't leave the issue to the discretion of judges.[6]

Tony Zale (*Sydney Morning Herald*/SMH).

The older Zaleski brothers' boxing exploits began receiving favorable press coverage. This led to a rebuke by the family's priest who, in a sermon before the entire congregation, sent an unmistakable message to the Zaleski brothers that boxing was not a fitting activity for Catholic youth. But they were unwilling to give up the sport. As a way of masking their continued participation, the brothers began boxing under the name Zale. This anglification also suited an American immigration system based on assimilation.[7] Anthony got the message and, even as an amateur, fought under the name Tony Zale.

Tony quickly grew into a boxing prodigy. Naturally strong, he enjoyed training and he liked to fight. A gym rat and a health nut, Zale felt at home in dank boxing gyms, which to him "smelled like Chanel No. 5."[8] Zale, who avoided alcohol and tobacco, created his own libations such as a mixture of parsley and spinach, boiled, cooled, and drank like iced tea. Others found his potables revolting.[9] In any event, as time went by, Zale's older brothers began begging off from sparring sessions with their kid brother.[10]

Zale was an outstanding amateur boxer. In 1932 he reached the Olympic finals for the middleweight class (maximum 160 pounds) to represent the United States in the games scheduled for Los Angeles. He lost the final as the result of a head butt that caused a serious cut over his eye.[11] Zale would go on to win the regional Golden Gloves middleweight title in 1934.

Zale was among thirty-two fighters selected from a field of fourteen thousand to represent the Midwest in an Intercity Golden Gloves Tournament held in Madison Square Garden. Photos of Zale taken during the trip show a stiff and awkward young man (nineteen years old at the time) in ill-fitting clothes with his fedora askance. He would never outgrow a painful shyness. Years later, he confessed that the only time he felt "free" was when fighting.[12] Bruce Springsteen observed that the real Elvis Presley was the person on stage; the rest of the time Elvis was acting. So it was with Zale in the ring. Most people would find frightful the experience of a competitive boxing match. For Zale it was his comfort zone. He found his means of expression within the confines of the squared circle, with the eyes of the world on him, in the brutal art of the sweet science.

The traits that would define his career—courage and toughness—were immediately apparent. When another member of the Chicago team—future heavyweight champion Joe Louis—injured his hand, Zale moved up a weight class to fight as a light heavyweight.[13] Zale's opponent was one of the best fighters on the New York/New Jersey team, future light heavyweight champion Melio Bettina. This Son of Rome looked the part of a primordial fighter, barrel chested and covered with a thick mat of black hair. Zale later recalled being "beaten to a pulp."[14] However, the portions of the fight available on YouTube show Zale giving a good account of himself, not budging an inch to the rugged Bettina. And Zale learned from the defeat. "He won by hitting me in the kidneys. I practiced jerking my elbow out at the right moment to crack my opponent on the wrist."[15]

Zale's bona fides as an athlete were confirmed when he received a football scholarship from the University of Wisconsin. A fast and powerful running back, Zale passed on the Badgers' offer and instead decided to become a professional prize fighter. The dutiful Zale was motivated to help the family's finances.[16] Zale later came to regret forgoing further education as he struggled to find a second career when his boxing days were done.

Prior to turning pro, Zale, concerned about a potential repeat of the eyebrow cut that cost him a shot at an Olympic gold medal, underwent a grisly medical procedure. He had the bone on his forehead shaved down. Remarkably, the primitive operation was carried off successfully. Zale never again lost a fight due to a cut.[17]

3. From the Open Hearth

Zale's professional career got off to an inauspicious start. Fighting in small clubs to merely "survive,"[18] Zale lost nine of his first twenty-nine fights, a huge letdown to an amateur of Zale's pedigree. Zale was stopped by Frank "Roughhouse" Glover on March 27, 1935, in Cincinnati, and that loss was quickly followed by two more, including a knockout defeat at the hands of Johnny Phagen. His managers lost interest in him. Zale's disappointment was such that he quit the ring. Tony, who had started working in the mills as a boy after school hours,[19] joined his older brothers full-time at the Gary Works.[20]

But alas, Anthony Zaleski was not cut out to punch a time clock. He also hated the infernal regions of the plant. "It seemed like I worked in the steel mills since I was weaned, breathing the burnt air, catching the hot rivets that could burn a hole right through you."[21] When Tony complained to his older brother, he was met with a stern, Depression-era rebuke: "Stop bitching. Be thankful you got a job."[22]

After two and a half years before the open hearth, Tony decided to follow his instincts and give boxing another try. "I knew this was the way out for me," he later reflected.[23] This time things would be different and Zale would find his destiny in the ring. He would give the sport his sweat and blood, and the sport would give him his name and renown. Zale, with his brothers' help, found solid management in Art Winch and Sam Pian. Management, in turn, hooked Zale up with some outstanding trainers, eventually including the legendary Ray Arcel. Notable is that Arcel, who worked with some of the very greatest of all time, men such as Ezzard Charles and Roberto Duran, always held Zale in the highest esteem. Zale's determination and total commitment set him apart. Training Zale, Arcel said, "was an education in itself."[24]

Zale, a grinder blessed with the virtue of patience, worked at developing his crowd-pleasing style. He could box, but he preferred to slug. He utilized his immense strength and excellent conditioning to pressure his opponents. His left jab was formidable as a punch, but was also used to blind his opponents as Zale stepped inside, where he preferred to work. When his opponents were hurt, Zale used his straight left as a battering ram to breach his victim's last defenses.

Zale's trademark was body punching. Recipients found the sensation unpleasant in the extreme: "like getting hit in the stomach with a hot poker and having it just left there. It hurt all the way to your toes."[25] The results were often ghastly, with Zale's opponents conscious but rendered virtually helpless. Zale would then apply the coup de grace with his favorite combination: a right to the heart, the solar plexus, or the kidney (dropping the opponent's defenses), followed by a left hook to the head.

He could dish it out and he could take it. Zale could be knocked down, but he always got up. He excelled at the ultimate test for a championship-caliber boxer: gamely fighting back after being hurt. If body punching was Zale's trademark, his fighting heart was his brand.

Zale's professional career advanced, in more of an upward slope than flashy leaps forward. Later he admitted it took him "ten long years to really make it work."[26] Zale rarely had an easy fight, at least not against top-flight competition. He was even knocked out in the first round by Jimmy Clark, a former Olympian. Clark, an African American, was robbed of the Olympic gold at the 1936 Berlin Olympics (immortalized by Jesses Owens) by a terrible decision. Zale's response to the crushing defeat (Zale's record stood at a pedestrian 25–12–1 after the loss) was to practice for hours on blocking the punch that did him in: a right cross. Four months later Zale fought Clark again and this time stopped his opponent in the eighth round. A rubber match resulted in Clark kissing the canvas eleven times inside of two rounds, finally being carried out of the ring.

Defense was not the priority for Zale. He was willing to "take two to land one."[27] But still Zale's defense was better than his image as a wade-in slugger might suggest. Opponents (including Billy Conn and Graziano) noted that Zale was more difficult to hit than they had assumed.

The middleweight division has long been considered boxing's most prestigious. The division's greatest champions, and even some contenders, are generally considered the best ever to step into the ring. The names are boxing royalty: Stanley Ketchel ("The Michigan Assassin"); Sam Langford ("The Boston Bonecrusher"); Harry Greb ("The Pittsburgh Windmill"); Charley Burley (considered the best of the "Black Murderers' Row"); Carlos Monzon ("Escopeta," i.e., Shotgun); Marvelous Marvin Hagler; Roy Jones, Jr.; and the greatest of them all "pound for pound," five-time middleweight champion Sugar Ray Robinson. In the late 1930s, however, the middleweight division was unsettled, referred to as the "the muddleweights" by Nat Fleischer of the *Ring* magazine, "the bible of boxing." Foreshadowing the decline of the sport toward the end of the twentieth century, multiple champions were recognized by differing sanctioning bodies. Zale set out to impose order on the chaos.

As Zale racked up victories, he earned a reputation as the best

3. From the Open Hearth

middleweight in the Midwest. But he was still largely unknown outside of the region. That was about to change.

Al Hostak, who owned a piece of the middleweight crown, observed Zale sparring while traveling through Chicago. Not impressed by Zale's gym work, Hostak decided to offer the young upstart a nontitle bout at Chicago Stadium. Hostak was tall for a middleweight and used his jab to good effect. The "Savage Slav" had a reputation as a fearsome puncher and boasted a record at the time of fifty-one victories against only two defeats. Elected to the World Boxing Hall of Fame in 1997, in 2003 Hostak was rated as one of the greatest one hundred punchers of all time by the *Ring* magazine. Bottom line: Hostak was the real deal and for Zale represented a major step up in the level of competition. Zale considered Hostak the greatest fighter he ever faced.[28]

The champ thought fighting Zale would mean an easy paycheck. This was a dangerous delusion. Hostak decked Zale in the first round, but Zale got up fighting. The match turned in the sixth round with a Zale right to Hostak's heart, followed by a left to the ear. Hostak's head was sent spinning, and he remained on the defensive for the remainder of the fight. Zale took the unanimous decision.[29] "I figure it took me ten years to throw that one punch," Zale later reflected.

Hostak's pride was stung. He felt Zale benefited from hometown scoring. Hostak offered Zale a rematch, but this time with the title on the line—and with the site moved to Hostak's hometown of Seattle. The judges were not required in the rematch as Zale battered Hostak senseless, winning on a technical knockout in the thirteenth round. Zale forced the action and opened a cut over Hostak's eye in the eighth. Then he went to work on his opponent's eyes, first closing one and then the other. Hostak was down for a nine count in the twelfth and then floored and finished. Zale's attack was "one of the finest seen in the Pacific Northwest."[30] Zale's manager was quoted as saying they knew Zale could not win a decision in the hostile venue, so they strategized for a knockout, "and that was just what [Zale] did."[31]

Now owning a piece of the title, Zale risked it against Steve Mamakos, the "Golden Greek." This championship fight would further cement Zale's growing reputation for bad-ass toughness. Mamakos was a real talent and considered by some to be the best fighter to come out of Washington, D.C., before Sugar Ray Leonard. And this Greek was tougher than a $2 steak at a roadside diner in Rahway. Zale considered Mamakos the toughest man he ever fought.[32]

Zale first outpointed Mamakos in a nontitle bout, but the fight was competitive enough to earn Mamakos a shot at the title. One month later, on February 21, 1941, the two squared off before fourteen thousand in Chicago Stadium. Mamakos went on the attack and badly cut Zale's mouth in the first round. In the fifth, Mamakos floored Zale, who bounced up quickly but then absorbed a terrible beating. Some observers felt the champion was saved by the bell, "within seconds of losing his title."[33] The Greek closed Zale's left eye in the eighth. Mamakos built up an edge on points as the bout moved into the championship rounds—those rounds never fought unless the championship is on the line, when both fighters are in pain, frequently bleeding, and tired. Needing a knockout to retain his title, Zale launched a furious comeback and tore into Mamakos.

In the thirteenth round, Zale finally floored Mamakos toward the end of the stanza. Saved by the bell at the count of six, the still groggy Mamakos was dragged back to his stool. His cornermen sent out the glassy-eyed Greek for the fourteenth. This was a mistake. Zale later said he was "amazed" Mamakos was sent out. Amazed, but pitiless. Like a predator sensing vulnerable prey, he shot across the ring and smashed Mamakos to the canvas. The challenger crumpled into the resin, not moving a muscle as he was counted out. The boxing scribes thought it was best fight seen in Chicago for years.

Mamakos never fully recovered from the savage beating. His career went into a tailspin. The Golden Greek won only three of his next fifteen fights. His wife forced Mamakos to retire, and he took a less dangerous job in the mailroom of a newspaper.[34]

Growing in confidence and strength, Zale then offered Hostak a chance to reclaim his title. By this point, Zale was in Hostak's head. On May 28, 1941, in Chicago, Zale destroyed Hostak with a vicious right to the kidneys in the second round. Hostak groaned audibly, folding in pain. Hostak was down eight times before the referee mercifully stopped the fight.[35] The United Press wire report referred to Zale as "the man of steel from Gary, Ind."[36]

Zale was now a respected champion. He was tough as nails and his fights were exciting. Always in top condition, Zale invariably gave fight fans a good show. He forswore alcohol, not only for its deleterious effect on his conditioning, but also for the associated loss of control. Even in the guttural fight world he inhabited, Zale never used profanity because he felt it set a bad example.[37] Zale seemed to have an intuitive sense of the behavior the public expected of a champion, or at least what 1940s America expected. He never bragged or threatened. Prefight theatrics

3. From the Open Hearth

were kept to a minimum. But he didn't lack for confidence. When asked about his upcoming opponents, his normally inscrutable visage, covered with scar tissue from hundreds of fights, tended to reflect a thin but ominous smile. To paraphrase Norman Mailer, Zale's face "could give a Marine sergeant pause in a bar fight." A testament to Zale's popularity was the crowd of 135,132 drawn to Zale's fight with Billy Pryor in 1941, still the U.S. record (albeit a "no charge" promotional event put on by the Milwaukee brewer Pabst).

Zale was the strong, silent type taken to an extreme. The boxing writer for the *Newark Evening News* Willie Ratner noted that "Tony seldom speaks above a whisper—when he speaks at all."[38] "Miserly" with his words,[39] according to sportswriter Jimmy Cannon, Zale was unassuming outside the ring and tended to blend into the background. He had no entourage. The idea of paying someone to serve as his bodyguard would have amused Zale. When traveling he would simply show up at a gym and start working out. The locals were astonished to learn they were in the presence of the middleweight champion of the world.[40] Most considered Zale "decent" and a "nice guy." Totally down to earth, Zale would talk to anyone who approached him. But he preferred to keep quiet as he rarely saw any reason to speak.[41] His nephew recounted difficulty reconciling how his kindly uncle was the same person as the man-killer observed inside the ring.[42] To others, even while acknowledging his dignified demeanor, Zale exuded an undercurrent of menace. Cannon admitted to being frightened by Zale.[43]

Zale's self-denial extended to sins of the flesh. He declined to partake of the carnal pleasures afforded by mid–twentieth-century celebrity. At a restaurant in New York City, Zale was once bracketed by two dolled-up blondes in a corner booth. Titillated by the prospect of bagging the champ, the blondes both started rubbing Zale's thighs. He bolted from the joint.[44]

The ladies must have been bemused by Zale's reticence. But following the dictates of his religion, Zale sought to satisfy his needs within the confines of a traditional marriage. Perhaps because of the loss of his own father, or the brutal way he made his living, Zale yearned for a warm and tranquil family life. It was not to be.

Zale met a vivacious Polish American girl named Adeline Richwalski. He was smitten. Adeline was from a wealthy family and cultured. She was a trained classical musician.[45]

There were warning signs that the romance might be ill fated. The Zaleskis thought it was an odd match but, knowing the ways of the heart, trusted in God. More troubling was the reaction of Adeline's father when Zale asked for her hand: he tried to talk Zale out of marrying his own daughter. She was erratic and irrational—"not quite right," Adeline's father warned. Zale went ahead anyway.[46]

Zale's next professional milestone was equally challenging. He was offered the chance to unify the middleweight crown against the tough Georgie Abrams at Madison Square Garden in 1941. Abrams was the leading contender of the New York State Athletic Commission following the decision of Billy Soose to relinquish his slice of the title to move up in weight class. Abrams was confident and in great shape. "Zale only knows how to fight one way. He always bulls his way towards you, looking to catch you with that left hook to the gut."[47]

This was a time when white fighters branded themselves with their ethnicity. Abrams, a Jewish fighter who wore the Star of David on his boxing trunks, was the betting (nine-to-five) and crowd favorite.[48] This matured version of Zale had not been seen in New York, and regional prejudices of the day may have influenced the betting odds. Before the advent of television, even the boxing scribes had little to go on other than reputations built on out-of-town press reports.

What the boxing writers saw impressed them but also gave some qualms. Despite his upright character, Zale was willing to bend the Marquis of Queensbury Rules when necessary. In the fourth round Zale headbutted and inadvertently thumbed Abrams's right eye. Abrams's eye closed, and his face became a curtain of blood.[49] The sixth round was awarded to Abrams when Zale hit him with a low blow.[50] Arthur Daley of the *New York Times*, while admiring Zale's fighting qualities, was taken aback by his roughhouse tactics. He described Zale's fighting style as "cruel and relentless."[51] This was not the only time the adjective "cruel" showed up in stories describing Zale's ring performances.

Zale took a clear-cut decision.[52] Zale buckled Abrams's knees on several occasions and was the more busy fighter. The fight may have been stopped if not for the fact that the championship was on the line.[53] Abrams suffered a hemorrhage of the right eye after the fight and was rushed to the hospital.[54] His head ballooned to twice its normal size. Abrams was hospitalized for months and almost lost his eye.[55] The manly Abrams offered no excuses and refused to blame Zale's tactics for his defeat. Instead, he attributed his loss to Zale's body punching. Abrams even expressed relief that he came into the fight in the best shape of his life. Otherwise, things could have been much worse. Zale became the first undisputed middleweight champion since Jersey's Mickey Walker, the Toy Bulldog.

Most of the boxing writers were impressed. Willie Ratner of the *Newark Evening News* found that "[t]here is nothing of the fancy Dan stuff about Zale. All he knows about fighting is to walk in and keep punching all the time. True, he does get hit rather often, and it's possible to knock him down ... [but Zale] does get off the canvas, and that's what makes you like him."[56] Jimmy Powers of the *Daily News* noted that "Zale ... can give and take, is a worthy tenant of the throne once occupied by Walker and I think he'll be a fighting champion."[57] Stanley Weston of the *Ring* thought Zale "a sandy-haired assassin with piercing blue eyes and fists capable of chopping bone."[58]

Despite his hard edge in the ring, no one considered Zale to be a brute or a sadist. Legendary sportswriter Jimmy Cannon first met Zale at the well-known boxing training camp in Pompton Lakes, New Jersey. Cannon sized up Zale as a man with an obvious talent for violence balanced by extraordinary self-control. He only used violence to make his living.[59] Zale, according to Cannon, was admirable because he did not allow the moral squalor of boxing, or the accolades that came through his expert application of force, to debase him. Although quiet, Zale was completely transparent. He accepted without complaint the cruel reality of a sport that demanded he go as far as his talent and conditioning could take him every time he stepped into the ring.[60]

Just as Zale achieved recognition as the undisputed middleweight champion of the world, World War II intervened. In that America, celebrities were expected to don the uniform and serve. Athletes were no different. Zale signed up and thereby lost his prime fighting years to the war effort. He willingly exchanged meager paychecks from Uncle Sam ($60 a week) in place of the millions he would have made if allowed to cash in on the championship. Zale was a man who loved his country and would do anything to protect it. He never once griped about what his service cost his finances. Zale's title would be frozen for his four years of service. But he had one more fight before shipping out.

Slick boxers could give Zale trouble. Pittsburgh's Billy Conn was a light heavyweight (maximum 175 pounds) best known for his near-upset of the great Joe Louis. Conn, known as "Prince William" for his matinee idol looks and cocky Irish charm, even slipped into one of the most famous moments in film history: the "I coulda been somebody" cab scene in *On the Waterfront* (1954). Filmed in Hoboken, New Jersey, Rod Steiger's character tells Marlon Brando, "You could have been another Billy Conn."

The bout was not competitive, at least on the score card. Conn easily outpointed Zale in Madison Square Garden. But Conn, the larger man who outweighed Zale by twelve pounds, was forced to admit that he couldn't make Zale back up. He expressed frustration and surprise at how often Zale made him miss. Willie Ratner noted that Conn "failed to muss Tony's hair."[61] After digesting one of Zale's body shots, Conn decided discretion was the better part of valor ("I said the hell with this"[62]) and fought Zale at long range.[63] Later Conn said he could not eat for a week as a result of Zale's depth charges.[64] Zale, who liked to fight, was not impressed. "He fought like I was the big guy. I had to come to him. He didn't make the fight. That's no way for a fighter to be," Zale commented in disgust.[65] Zale's reputation, especially for courage and toughness, grew in the defeat. Years later Nat Fleischer of the *Ring* would write: "No man who saw that Zale-Conn fight will ever forget how Tony stood up to the bigger man."[66] But fighting Conn only yielded a $10,000 purse to Zale.[67]

As befitting his style, Zale's registration for the Navy was low key. "Name," demanded an officer. "Anthony Zaleski." "Profession." "Professional boxer, middleweight." The officer responded: "I'd hate to be in your shoes, Zaleski. Tony Zale's due here this week."[68]

Zale spent most of the war in Puerto Rico serving as a physical fitness and boxing instructor.[69] Not surprisingly, Zale proved to be an excellent instructor in hand-to-hand combat. He was a natural at breaking down and communicating the elements in a clear and concise manner. And he made a difference. Decades later, Zale's nephew was approached by an elderly veteran. The man credited Tony Zale with saving his life. The GI's unit was overrun by the Nazis in the Ardennes forest in what would become known as the Battle of the Bulge. Out of ammunition, the man was charged by a German with a bayonet. Recalling Zale's training, the American parried the thrust and planted a right cross on the German's jaw. The one-punch knockout was followed by a more permanent dispatch with cold American steel.

Zale planned on keeping his title when he got out and he kept in top shape. "His mental discipline paid off," said Ray Arcel. "Nothing tempted him."[70] Upon the end of the war and Zale's honorable discharge, his title was unfrozen, and boxing's sanctioning bodies pressured Zale to either retire or defend.

3. From the Open Hearth

During Zale's war-related absence, a new crop of young middleweights arose. Two of the best were New York products: Jake LaMotta of *Raging Bull* (1980) fame, and a young knockout artist named Rocky Graziano. Zale was presented with the choice of which of these two he would fight. "I'll take Graziano," said Zale.[71]

4.

Black Sheep

Tony Zale lost his father at age two. Thomas Rocco Barbella, a.k.a. Rocky Graziano, may have been better off if he'd never known Nicola Barbella, his father.

Rocky's dad had been a professional boxer, a bad one who went by the name "Fighting Nick Bob." Once he finally accepted reality and gave up a career in the ring, Fighting Nick Bob found his only comfort in the bottle. And a foul and nasty drunk he was.[1] Not the type to suffer in silence, Fighting Nick Bob took out his frustrations on those closest to him. Through verbal and physical abuse, and his selfish laziness, he drove his wife, Ida, to an insane asylum. To his son Tommy Rocco, he ingrained resentment, defiance, and violence.

Rocco was born on New Year's Day 1919 in the family's railroad flat on the Lower East Side of Manhattan. A midwife helped bring Rocco into the world, while his father got cockeyed with his unemployed buddies in the front room.[2]

Fighting Nick Bob, too drunk to work, filled the black hole in his soul by pitting his boys against one another. The only toys he gifted were boxing gloves. Nick staged boxing matches between the three-year-old Rocco and his six-year-old brother Joey.[3] After being used as a punching bag by his brother, more physical abuse, typically a sharp slap to Rocco's head or even a leather strap, was imparted by the father. When not being beaten or tortured, Rocco was turned loose to run wild on the congested city streets, where he twice was hit by passing cars. He once fell off a roof, but his descent was fortunately disrupted by the web of clotheslines common to the era.[4]

Rocco's mother, Ida, who lost twin baby girls to pneumonia contracted in their cold-water flat, was unable to cope with the family's dismal existence. She sought comfort in secret drinking and eventually was diagnosed with a nervous breakdown.[5] Rocky loved his mother, and it tore him apart watching his father beat her, but he felt

4. Black Sheep

powerless to do anything about it. Even words of comfort escaped him.[6]

The inverse Dr. Spock approach to child rearing yielded predictable results. The black sheep of the family, Rocky barely knew his siblings.[7] Rocco grew into an angry and rebellious young man, with a chip on his shoulder the size of boulder. He was a serial truant from school, as he saw no value in education. Rocky dropped out in sixth grade when he was twelve years old. Barely literate, Rocco took offense to minor slights, or none at all. Quick to anger, he resorted to violence to settle disputes, real and imagined.

Rocco became Rocky to his gang. His approach to street fights was no holds barred. Thumbs in the eyes and knees to the groin were fair game. The Rock considered himself the best street fighter in the history of the Lower East Side.[8] Petty theft, including stealing coal for the family's potbelly stove—the only source of heat in their flat—became a way of life.[9]

Rocky joined a gang of hoodlums. They lived on the streets, swiping low-end consumer goods. Some of his gang eventually drew long prison terms at Sing Sing Prison in Ossining, New York. One was fried in the electric chair. Another was shot dead at an after-hours club.[10]

Rocky's life was on a bad trajectory. He was arrested and sent to a Catholic reformatory.* "The door went shut and I heard the click of the big lock and it was like all the sunlight went out of the world forever."[11] Discipline, in the form of draconian and even sadistic punishments, was prioritized over "reform."[12] While the Church claimed ignorance of sexual abuse well into the twenty-first century, Rocky claimed to learn of it at a reformatory in the 1930s.[13] Rocky's reform stint established a pattern of his approach to dealing with incarceration: (i) defiance of his jail keepers, and (ii) assaulting other prisoners to establish his dominance and robbing them of their measly possessions (e.g., cookies, toothpaste, and cigarettes).[14]

Tribalism ruled on the Lower East Side. Rocky defied and cussed his nemesis Casey the Cop. It was only when an Italian talked that he listened.[15] After Rocky and his gang stole from and harassed Jewish

---

*Rocky occasionally palled around with Jake LaMotta of *Raging Bull* (1980) fame, who he had met in the reformatory. As much of a nightmare as Rocky was as a boy, LaMotta was worse. Rocky quipped that his gang would play hide-and-seek, and no one would look for LaMotta. Jake's retort was a drinking story—after a night of hard partying, LaMotta asked the Rock whether "dhat is da sun or da moon?" Rocky supposedly replied, "I don't know, I'm not from this neighborhood."

merchants, they brawled with a gang from "Jew Town." Rocky hurled bricks at the Jews who carried galvanized garbage can lids as shields.[16] He broke up with his first girlfriend because he learned she was Jewish—an astonishing revelation to Rocky because he thought all Jews had beards.

Sexual initiation came early and often. Rocky lost his virginity at the age of fourteen at a whorehouse in Chinatown.[17] The local communist club (not uncommon in pre–Cold War urban America) offered additional opportunities. Although the Rock thought the Reds were "creeps" who spouted off incomprehensible nonsense, he was intrigued by their nontraditional attitudes toward sex. So Rocky and his gang chose to endure the unendurable: tedious lectures on Marxist economic theory. The reward was access to the "free love" philosophy of the Bolshevik women. "We didn't like to pay for anything either," Rocky observed.[18]

Rocky's crimes grew more serious. His first real jail time was spent at the notorious Tombs Jail in Lower Manhattan.[19] It was a hellish place. "They threw me in a cell where there was a drunk with puke all over him."[20] The guy in the cell next door had an invitation: "Hey kid—want a little loving? I can get the guard to put you in with me."[21] The drug addicts would scream and cry all night. "In the black and the stink of the night, you begin to think you are in jail with a bunch of monsters—all zombies, queers and junkies."[22] Rocky's mother scraped together enough money to bail him out of the Tombs, but he quickly ran into trouble again and was sentenced to the State Vocational School at Coxackie in Greene County, New York.[23]

"Vocational school" was a misnomer. Coxackie was a prison for the worst juvenile delinquents, too young to be given the chair. When the warden's attempt at intimidation failed, he tried bribing Rocky with candy and cigarettes. Rocky threw them back in the warden's face.[24] Unable to break Rocky, they shipped him back to the city, where he ended up back at the Tombs. Rocky must have been deficient in vitamin D because he went five months without seeing the sun.[25]

The Rock's next stop was at the New York City Reformatory, a.k.a. the "Farms," located in Goshen in Orange County. Rocky hooked up with a clique of other Lower East Siders and earned their respect when he flattened three guys in a single confrontation. His fellow Lower East Siders assumed the Rock must have used a weapon. "All I need is these," replied Rocky, holding up his fists.[26]

Jailhouse Rocky was undeniably brutal, but he was not a bully. He

4. Black Sheep

challenged only the strongest competition for the purpose of establishing himself as top dog, the toughest in the joint. The Rock even extended protection to the young and the weak from sexual predators.[27] Rocky got released from the Farms on parole in 1939.[28]

Up to this time, a career in boxing was something Rocky never seriously considered. His father's failed career as a boxer was one consideration. Another was that Rocky liked how he looked and did not want his face smashed in. Moreover, and incredibly, the Rock considered boxing with gloves to be for sissies because, in his view, real men fought with bare fists, the better to draw blood.[29] But a friend, Terry Young, himself a tough guy and aspiring boxer, convinced Rocky to give the sport a try. In his first fight at the local Boys Club, Rocky knocked his opponent senseless with a flurry of wild lefts and rights. Although totally unrefined, Rocky's talent—especially his power punching with his right hand—was obvious to everyone.[30] The sport suited his personality: he liked to beat up people and had plenty of experience. Boxing was also legal, and it provided, to Rocky's way of thinking, an easy way to make money. Rocky won an Amateur Athletic Union title as a welterweight and began making a name for himself in the ring.[31]

Trouble kept finding Rocky. Still on parole, he was accused of statutory rape. Graziano was hauled before the parole officer—none other than baseball's Iron Horse. After his diagnosis with the terrible disease that would bear his name, Lou Gehrig took the job of commissioner on the parole board.[32] By all accounts, Gehrig took his job seriously and worked hard to assess each case before him, especially with troubled young men. Gehrig would ask himself whether the individual before him was a victim of circumstance or just a plain hardened criminal. In Rocky's case, Gehrig saw an irredeemable loser and came down hard. He sentenced Rocky to six months at the Farms, the "reform school." Pissed off, Rocky told Gehrig to "go to hell."[33] "I felt like killing him," Rocky confided in a later interview.[34]

The warden at the Farms was familiar with Rocky from his first stint. He did not appreciate the Rock's attitude. A prison race riot, triggered by the warden's foolish decision to show the mixed-race prisoner population a movie about slavery, was the warden's excuse to ship out the Rock. He was sent off to Rikers Island.[35]

Even Rocky had to admit Rikers was a tough place. At nineteen he should not have been placed in the general prison population, but he could not help himself and copped an attitude with the Rikers warden. The head screw retaliated by assigning the Rock to a job in the

Brick City Grudge Match

prison laundry, domain of the sexual predators. One, the "Countess," was a giant of a man who persisted in his attempts to seduce Rocky. The Countess was predictably knocked cold by a Graziano right cross. But the lecher remained undeterred. When the Countess came to his senses, he praised the Rock: "Lover. You're strong!"[36]

Rocky served out his five months and was released. This was the first time since the Rock was eleven years old that he was not "in the system."[37] But the system was not done with him. Two months after his release, he received a draft notice from the U.S. Army.[38]

Graziano did not adjust well to military service. He could care less about geopolitics and disliked being told what to do. "F*ck you" was a typical response to orders from superiors. Rocky would sleep in, defying reveille. He eventually went AWOL from basic training at Fort Dix in the Jersey Pine Barrens (according to Rocky, "the loneliest, lousiest place in the world"). The fugitive was captured and dragged back before an Army captain who, in the process of dressing down the urban wild man, was met with Rocky's right fist planted on his jaw. The officer was knocked cold.[39]

Rocky ran away. Somehow he made his way out of the Pine Barrens and back to the Lower East Side. In need of money, he went to the famous Stillman's Gym on Eighth Avenue in Manhattan and immediately impressed onlookers with his punching power. But, foolishly, Rocky followed a buddy to a police station house and was recognized and dimed out to the Army. Two military police officers slapped cuffs on the Rock and took him to a guardhouse on Governors Island named Castle William, or Castle Bill.[40] His guard there was the aptly named Sergeant Prude. The sadistic guard set out to break the Rock. "Eat my shit and like it," Prude cursed at Rocky, all while disparaging Rocky's mother and sisters. He made Rocky clean the blockhouse with a toothbrush while on his hands and knees. But Prude was no more able to crack the Rock than anyone else. Rocky told Prude to "blow it out your ass."[41]

The Army finally released Rocky with orders to report to Fort Dix. To Rocky's shock, he was released without supervision. Suspicious that the Army was setting him up, the Rock went home and failed to report as ordered to Fort Dix.[42] Fate smiled on Rocky again when a kind and honest boxing manager (an oxymoron if there ever was one), Irving Cohen, took Rocky under his wing.[43] Rocky lied to Cohen, telling him he had been honorably discharged from the Army. Rocky also told Cohen that his surname was Graziano, the name of a guy who ran

4. Black Sheep

with Rocky's street gang. Rocky began boxing professionally under that name.[44]

In hindsight, Rocky came to see the name change as a milestone in his self-transformation into a new and better man. As he said in his acclaimed (and brutally honest) autobiography, *Somebody Up There Likes Me* (1955), the name change, like Don Draper in *Mad Men*, gave him his job and the rest of his life. A cleaner break from his father is difficult to imagine. If Anthony Zaleski changed his name to conform and assimilate, the Rock altered his handle to escape his past.

After he racked up a few knockout victories, the long arm of the law reached out and grabbed Rocky. Two cops pinched the Rock while at a weigh-in for a fight. Rocky had been charged with desertion by the Army, yet actually caught a huge break when the officer he slugged did not press charges. He was court-martialed, dishonorably discharged, and sentenced to a year of hard labor at Fort Leavenworth in Kansas.[45] There would be no running away this time.

"A military correctional facility," Fort Leavenworth was a hellhole filled with an assortment of Army rejects, ranging from the mentally ill, to perverts and hardened criminals. Rocky joined the Fort's boxing squad. He dismantled his overmatched competition. Rocky quickly went from an Army pariah to the beneficiary of special perks. He came to see boxing as his ticket to material success and resolved to pursue a professional ring career after his release.[46]

Rocky's perceptive manager, Irving Cohen, understood Rocky had championship-level talent. But Cohen also recognized Rocky's hatred of regimentation and distain for training as serious impediments. Cohen's coping strategy was essentially twofold: find the right trainer and motivate Rocky with carrots rather than sticks. Cohen found the ideal trainer in Morris "Whitey" Bimstein, a veteran of seventy professional fights himself and a free spirit similar to Rocky in his resistance to conformity, formal schooling, and training. For his carrot, Cohen picked up on Rocky's very serious attitude toward money and used that as the motivator.[47]

With his career path coming into focus, Rocky's personal life underwent a dramatic change. Indeed, Rocky's transformation from a hardened street criminal and Army washout, to a respected professional, and then on to champion, would not have been possible without his having met and fallen in love with Norma Unger.

Norma was a beautiful Jewish girl from a different world than Rocky. Norma saw something in the Rock that others missed: a

Brick City Grudge Match

generous heart and a hunger for redemption. Norma pursued Rocky, using Rocky's sister as matchmaker. Rocky, emotionally still in the troughs of adolescent male self-centeredness, was initially oblivious to Norma's charms. But Norma was persistent, and finally Rocky succumbed. The couple was married on August 10, 1943, at City Hall in Manhattan. Rocky, whose purses early in his boxing career were very small, could not afford the fee for the marriage license. Norma pawned her gold Star of David gifted by her mother. Rocky was embarrassed and promised to buy it back when he won his next fight. Rocky was good to his word, both in regard to the medallion and also with his wedding vows.[48] Rocky and Norma would go on to enjoy forty-seven years of marital bliss, a true love story.[49]

Like many New York fighters before him, Graziano worked his way up by fighting on undercards in Jersey. His first fight in Newark was in Laurel Garden in December 1943. The Rock's opponent was a Romanian, Milo Theodorescu. Graziano knocked Theodorescu cold in the first round. The still groggy Romanian got to his feet and staggered toward Rocky with the intention of kissing his conqueror on the forehead, European-style. Unfamiliar with the custom, Theodorescu's manner seemed strange to Graziano. Rocky became alarmed and sought to evade the smooch. The confused foreigner persisted and finally knocked heads with the Rock, who suffered more damage than from the fight.[50]

Rocky's first big-name foe was William "Billy" Arnold, a classy African American fighter from Philadelphia. Arnold was a rising star who had beaten better fighters than Rocky. Arnold was a slick boxer, who sported highly developed defensive skills students of the game appreciated—he was hard to hit. Rocky's "defense," by contrast, consisted of a crude imitation of the prototype crowding slugger, Jack Dempsey, a.k.a. the Manassa Mauler. Rocky would tuck in his chin behind his left shoulder and occasionally bob his head as he sought to corner his opponents, then unleash his powerful overhand right—"like a thunderbolt." Attempts to refine Graziano's technique met with limited success, largely because Rocky understood his limitations ("I could be a boxer if I wanted, but I wasn't a good boxer and I knew it."). The bookies made Arnold a five-to-one favorite.[51]

The fight unfolded as the bookies—and Arnold—expected. Like many of Graziano's opponents, Arnold assumed he could easily evade Rocky's wild punches and win a decision on points. And, as expected, Arnold opened the fight by peppering Rocky's face with sharp jabs and well-timed crosses. Arnold easily took the first two rounds on points.

4. Black Sheep

Then, in the third round—out of the blue—Rocky connected with a thunderous overhand right and put out the lights.[52]

Rocky's powerful right-hand punch earned its own nickname for putting his opponents to sleep: "rock-a-bye." Graziano the fighter was blessed with rip-cord muscles and cannonball shoulders. He had power to spare and killer instinct to use it. And, essential for a fighter with the crowding style, the Rock had the ability—and the guts—to absorb the punishment dished out by his opponents as he waited to land his haymaker. Like Dempsey before him, and Smokin' Joe Frazier afterward, Rocky's aggressiveness, toughness, and explosive power excited fight fans.

As he embarked on one of the most spectacular knockout streaks in boxing history, Graziano's celebrity took off like a rocket. The New York sportswriters loved Rocky. He made good copy. The writers were the first of many creative types, including actors, comedians, and photographers, who found Rocky fascinating. They examined the Rock like he was some exotic primitive. The sportswriters intentionally misspelled words to capture phonetically Graziano's extreme New York accent.

His appearance was unusual. At the time, people tended to wear their Sunday best when attending most events, even something as mundane as a ballgame. Rocky, in contrast, did not seem to own a tie and his clothes never seemed to have met an iron. He was restless and always on the move. The need for constant activity was ingrained from his time growing up on the streets: standing around might get you pinched, or at least harassed, by the man. The thick mop of jet-black hair protruding from his scalp was rarely combed.

Rocky was now considered a contender. But more was required to earn a shot at Tony Zale's coveted crown. Graziano was determined to blast his way past the other contenders who stood in his way. His victories in his run up to his first title shot were impressive—sensational really—and testify to his ability as a boxer. The fates of the men he defeated—some of the most prominent athletes of their time—speak to the incredibly harsh and precarious existence of the fighters who laced up the gloves for a living.

Rocky knocked out Al "Bummy" Davis at Madison Square Garden—an overhand right put Bummy in queersville. Bummy was eventually killed when he intervened to stop a robbery at a bar where he was dining. Although unarmed and shot in the neck, Bummy—pressing a napkin to the bullet hole to stem the flow of blood—nevertheless chased four armed gunmen down a dark alley where he met his demise.[53]

Brick City Grudge Match

Next up for Rocky was the reigning welterweight (140 to 147 pounds) champion, Freddie "Red" Cochrane, who won the title from Fritzie Zivic in 1941 under questionable circumstances at Ruppert Stadium in Newark. The nontitle bout would go on to be recognized as the 1945 "Fight of the Year" by the *Ring* magazine. Graziano's match with Cochrane unfolded like Rocky's other fights against top competition. Cochrane easily outpointed the Rock over the first eight rounds. Then the pattern repeated itself: at the end of the ninth round, Rocky connected with an overhand right. Cochrane was saved by the bell but in bad shape. He was counted out in the tenth.[54] A rematch two months later ended in Cochrane absorbing another "fearsome battering" by the "glowering East Side bomber," as put by the *Newark Star Ledger*'s Anthony Marenghi.[55] The end came in the tenth round with the seventh knockdown of Cochrane.[56] Red would go on to contract Alzheimer's disease and passed away at a veterans' hospital in East Orange, New Jersey.[57]

Rocky then sought revenge for two lost decisions to the tough and experienced boxer Harold Green. Green, who had turned professional at age fourteen in order to feed his hungry Bronx-based family, schooled the raw Rocky in the finer points of his new profession. But Rocky learned from his losses. He got his revenge in his third fight with Green, poleaxing his opponent with an overhand right in the third round.[58] The knockout, in the greatest arena of them all—Madison Square Garden—caused a sensation. The fight drew 18,592 who paid $103,370 to watch the "pugilistic death-slinger from the East Side."[59] Rocky's reputation as a knockout artist and reliable draw—a promoter's dream—was made. Rocky Graziano would go down as one of the greatest draws ever at the Garden.

Rocky had his knockout streak broken when he outpointed the highly regarded George "Sonny" Horne. Some holdout skeptics noted that Horne, unlike most of Graziano's welterweight (147 pounds) victims, was a true middleweight (160 pounds). Rocky himself was a tweener, weighing in at approximately 153 pounds. The thinking was that the Rock's power might not be as sleep-inducing to the larger men. But most reporters put aside such speculation, in large part due to how Graziano battered Horne. As stated by Willie Ratner of the *Newark Evening News*, "[W]hat does he have to do, kill the man?"[60]

At that point, only one fighter stood between Rocky and the Man of Steel: Marty Servo, a.k.a. Mario Severino. A Golden Gloves champion, Servo's amateur credentials were as impressive as Zale's, checking

4. Black Sheep

in with a record of ninety-one wins against only four losses. Servo's professional career was distinguished by an outstanding record, including two close losses by points to the greatest "pound-for-pound" fighter ever to grace the ring, Sugar Ray Robinson. Even counting the two losses to Robinson, Servo's professional record still stood at forty-two wins against only four losses when he entered the ring for his fight with Graziano.[61]

Rocky was charged up by the prospect of getting a crack at the title—and the money that came with it. He was not about to let Servo stand in his way. Rocky tuned up Servo from the opening bell. He broke Servo's nose (he would breathe through his mouth for the rest of his life) in route to a second-round TKO victory.[62] Graziano's performance "left the jammed Garden stunned," staring "unbelievingly as Servo, the welterweight champion of the world, fell easy prey ... to the most murderous puncher in the middleweight division."[63] Marty Servo eventually developed lung cancer and would die at age forty-nine, destitute and living off the handouts of strangers.[64]

Graziano had done his job and earned his shot. His fight with Servo drew a gate of $170,000, the third highest in indoor history, and most ever for fighters under 175 pounds.[65] Zale agreed to put his title on the line against the young knockout artist. The suits went to work, arranged the details, and put the agreement down on paper.

The stage was now set for the first of three legendary encounters. These two midcentury Americans would meet in a squared circle constructed on the infield of America's ultimate cathedral to the national pastime: Yankee Stadium. Two years later, in their final encounter, these same men would meet across the Hudson River in a minor league ballpark carved out of the streets of Newark. When it was over, the names of Zale and Graziano would be linked forever.[66]

As Rocky approached his first confrontation with the thirty-three-year-old Zale, his confidence was cresting. He assured all who would listen that the result was a foregone conclusion. Perhaps Graziano was influenced by those pundits who felt Zale's four-year layoff, coupled with his age and nearly two hundred fights (amateur and professional), would combine to serve as Zale's kryptonite. Some thought it was an outright mismatch: "[A] lot of the folks were around saying what a terrible thing it was to feed a nice fellow like Zale to a guy like Rocky."[67] To be sure, Zale was a respected champion but considered "colorless" and hardly unbeatable. Willie Ratner of the *Newark Evening News* summed up the conventional wisdom: that Zale was "a very tough fellow," with

Brick City Grudge Match

a decent record but nothing extraordinary.[68] Rocky was younger of (twenty-seven), in his prime, and riding a string of spectacular knock-out wins. On fight day, the *Daily News* headline blared, "GRAZIANO ODDS SOARING." All the late action came in on Rocky, including a flood of last-minute cash into Brooklyn-based bookies.[69] They installed Rocky as a nine-to-five favorite.[70]

Rocky figured Zale would be like all the others. He would cave—or quit—when hit with the Rock's thunderbolt of a right hand. But Tony Zale was not like the others. Indeed, the champion would test the young challenger in ways he never imagined.

5

A Fighting Champion
(Zale Graziano I—Yankee Stadium, September 27, 1946)

The excitement generated by anticipation of a big fight is like nothing else. That strange mix of heightened senses, passionate advocacy (sometimes boiling over into tribal hatred and violence), and anxiety is only released when the bell rings and fight begins. Often the fight itself is a big letdown. But in those rare instances when the fight lives up to the buzz of a match capturing the public's imagination, the stuff of legend is made. And so it was with Zale Graziano I.

Sportswriter W. C. Heinz's "The Day of the Fight" is considered a classic and is still read in journalism schools.[1] In the article, Heinz reports on Graziano's routine from the time he awoke through the conclusion of the fight. As Rocky went about his business, crowds surged toward and surrounded the hometown hero. Some shook their fists at Rocky while yelling encouragement ("Flatten him for me, Rocky"). Kids ran by his side. One woman told the Rock she would be attending the fight with an undertaker, "so you don't have to worry and you can hit [Zale] as hard as you like." Other fans sought to inspire Graziano with spirituality ("I prayed for you last night").

The first official business that day was the weigh-in. The State Building where the weigh-in was held was ringed with a raucous, surging mob, only held at bay by a police cordon. Graziano and his team shoved their way through to the elevator, which brought them to a large room filled with men, some standing on chairs. Graziano stripped in front of them, took off his wristwatch and ring, and put on a pair of boxing trunks. Rocky got on the scale and his weight of 154 pounds was announced to the spectators, who then buzzed with banter while photographers' flash bulbs sent out blinding outbursts of light.

Brick City Grudge Match

An official called out for Tony Zale. A door to the left opened, and the champion, who had not been seen in New York for four years, walked out into the grand room. Zale was naked except for his boxing trunks and a pair of street shoes. A hush enveloped the room that had been buzzing a moment earlier. The crowd instinctively parted as Zale walked to the scale. He did not look at Graziano. Zale weighed in at exactly 160 pounds, the middleweight limit. His manager quickly ushered Zale off the scale. The photographers then shouted at the fighters to assume fighting poses. Rocky quickly accommodated, then followed by Zale. Face to face and eye to eye for the first time, Graziano smiled at Zale, who responded with his own less pronounced grin.

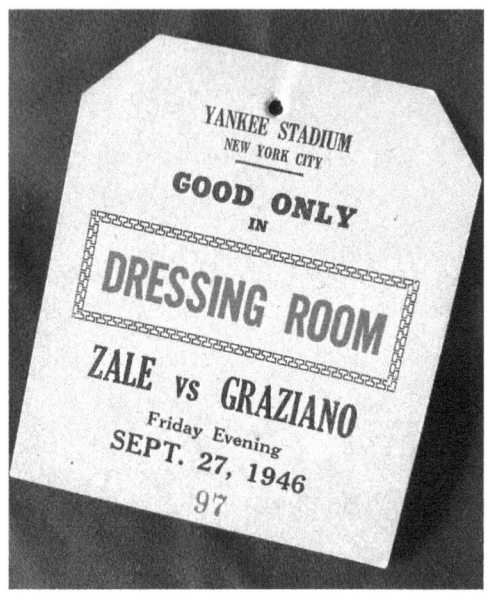

Locker room pass for Zale Graziano I, Yankee Stadium, September 27, 1946 (courtesy of Ted Zale Family).

The official work done, both men were then forced to endure the anxious hours before they would begin tearing each other apart. When it finally came time, Rocky was driven to the stadium by an entourage. His fellow New Yorkers shouted at him from the sidewalks. More shaken fists. His car stopped at a light, and one fellow thrust a wad of bills in Rocky's face. He was betting his life savings on the Rock so he could win his bride. The shouting, from contorted faces "mouths open, eyes wide," followed Graziano all the way until he climbed into the ring in the House that Ruth Built.

Zale Graziano I was not filmed. The fight was televised on NBC, but there is no video from that primitive era of TV.[2] We are left with photos and written accounts of what happened in the ring that night in the Bronx over seventy-five years ago. The fight has been described in writing many times, but most of the accounts were years afterward. The extraordinary reputation of the fight—thrilling ebbs and flows

5. A Fighting Champion

overlaying extreme and primitive violence—is such that in researching this book I wondered whether, with the passage of time, hyperbole had distorted the reality.

Contemporary observers were in universal agreement that the fight was extraordinarily violent. The next day's edition of the normally staid *New York Times* blared "SAVAGE BATTLE IS WAGED" beneath the headline setting forth the result. The fight was "vicious, from start to finish," wrote Willie Ratner of the *Newark Evening News*.[3] "[A] brawl ... from the first round," wrote Anthony Marenghi of the *Newark Star Ledger*.[4] The *Ring*'s Nat Fleischer described "a savage brawl" that was "a throwback to the bare-knuckle era."[5] James Dawson of the *New York Times* wrote the contest "was savagely and furiously fought" from the "start to finish."[6] Within one week of the bout, the *Times* described the fight as "one of the great fights in fistic history."[7]

The details reported prove the thrilling drama. The first round was Zale's, who, after absorbing some of Rocky's best blows, floored Graziano flat on his back with a left hook. The specter of a quick Zale knockout loomed but then dissipated with Zale's imprecision.[8] Rocky, who had never observed Zale in the ring and only barely met him, had been told Zale was a mechanical fighter. This was true, to a degree. Rocky made the mistake of assuming "mechanical" meant "slow." One round was enough to prove to Graziano that Zale was the quickest man he ever fought.[9]

By the second, Rocky had fully recovered and began battering Zale around the ring. At the end of the round, Graziano "crashed the champion to the corner with two rights coming as a crescendo to a furious attack."[10] The picture of Zale on the canvas is the image of a beaten fighter—his left leg jackknifed at the knee and crumpled beneath his hind quarters; his mouth smeared with blood; his eyes in a thousand-yard stare—with the young challenger hovering and waiting to pounce. The bell ending the second round saved Zale and deprived the Rock of a surefire knockout. Carried back to his corner, Zale told his cornermen—to their astonishment—that his right hand hurt.[11] Turned out Zale had broken his thumb. His brain trust told Zale to use his left.[12]

As Rocky tore out of his corner at the start of the third, he was met by a deafening roar as the crowd screamed for him to finish Zale. Adding to the cacophony was a low-flying prop plane circling above the stadium.[13] Rocky could taste it and unleashed a frightening barrage. Willie Ratner thought Zale was finished as Graziano used him "as a punching

Brick City Grudge Match

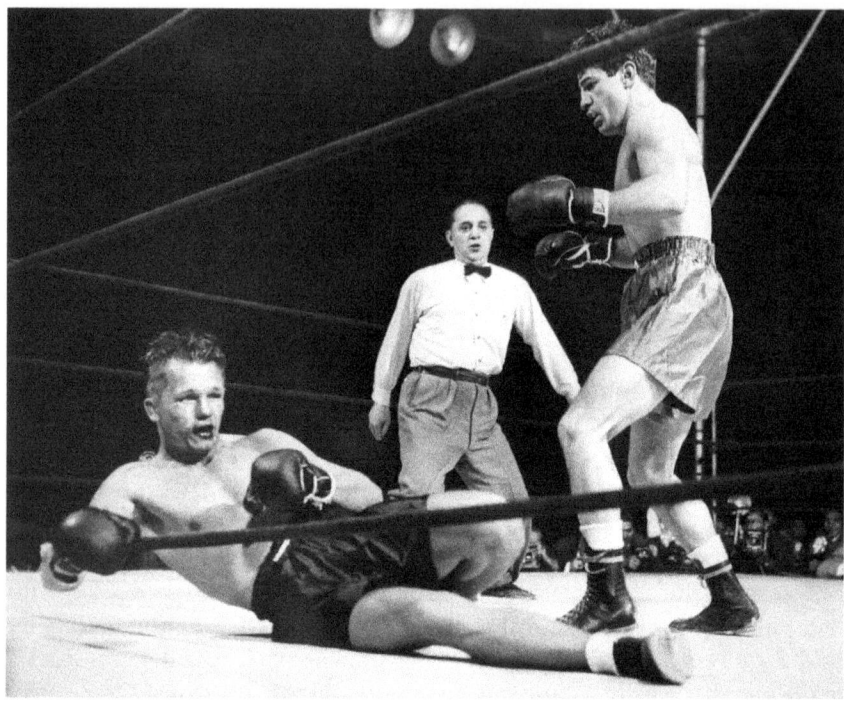

A dazed and bloodied Zale on the canvas near the end of the second round with a glowering Graziano eyeing his prey (Gamma-Keystone, via Getty Images).

bag," further bloodying Zale's mouth and nose.[14] To Al Marenghi, the Rock "heaved up punches like boulders," and "it did not seem humanly possible the champion could last much longer."[15] Zale's senses were dulled and his orientation confused. At the end of the round Zale strolled to Rocky's corner and "when directed to his own stool, acted as if a mistake had been made, and not by him."[16] Later, Rocky would write that Zale frustrated his quest for the KO by the use of subtle ring generalship ("It's like every split second I start my long swing somebody invisible pulls him back just half a step, and the punch whistles off his skin."[17]).

In the fourth round Zale, "displaying a preserve of mind that startled spectators,"[18] began "one of the most incredible rallies in recent prizefight history."[19] A Zale body shot took Graziano's wind away and put the Rock on the defensive.[20] The crowd, previously partisan to the hometown challenger, began shouting encouragement to the game, but

5. A Fighting Champion

apparently outgunned, champion. In his novel *The Professional*, W. C. Heinz described the two men standing toe to toe, each trying to destroy the other, with the crowd "sitting out there in the darkness screaming for more." The fighters reminded Heinz of "two pre-historic monsters ... ready to fight to the death and with the jungle all around them echoing to the noise and the horror of it."[21]

Momentum swung back to Graziano in the fifth with a series of left hooks that had Zale tottering. Rocky—"with the fury of a demon, lashing out with paralyzing fists"[22]—unleashed another astonishing cannonading, which had Zale staggering around the ring and close to being finished.[23] Zale's nose and mouth were bleeding heavily, and his left cheek was crimsoned. Spectators wondered what was holding up Zale. Sportswriter Jimmy Cannon observed that Zale had trouble even setting "his arms in the fighting pose."[24] He scarcely made it back to his corner at the round's end.[25] Graziano "looked flabbergasted" that Zale had survived.[26] Rocky said to himself: "This is a fighter, this Tony Zale. Anybody else I ever fought would be dead now."[27] The spectators were in an uproar, "with cheers thundering from the stands, the crowd boiling over in emotional frenzy."[28]

Between the fifth and sixth rounds, Zale's cornermen worked furiously to revive the champion, massaging his legs, applying ice to his back, and slapping his face.[29] Some at ringside were yelling at referee Ruby Goldstein to stop the fight. The *Ring*'s Nat Fleischer turned to the man sitting next to him and remarked: "Too bad, it'll all be over next round. Zale can't stand that punishment much longer."[30] Goldstein went to Zale's corner, looked him over, and asked Zale how he felt. "I'm all right, Ruby," was Zale's response. Goldstein gained further assurance from Zale's cornermen. He decided to let the fight continue.[31] Zale's trainer Ray Arcel told Zale, "[D]on't let this guy take your title away from you," encouraging him to load up with one last big shot.[32]

The bell rang for the start of the sixth frame and Graziano continued to carry the action. Blood from Zale's mouth and nose flowed. About halfway through the round, out of the blue and "like a shot from a gun,"[33] Zale uncorked a right to the body quickly followed by a left, which landed high on Rocky's jaw, near the temple. Rocky next recalled admiring the prop plane above the stadium. He then saw the referee counting over him, except he could not hear anything. Finally, as Graziano's senses returned, he realized where he was and jumped to his feet—a split second too late as he had been counted out.[34] Rocky

Brick City Grudge Match

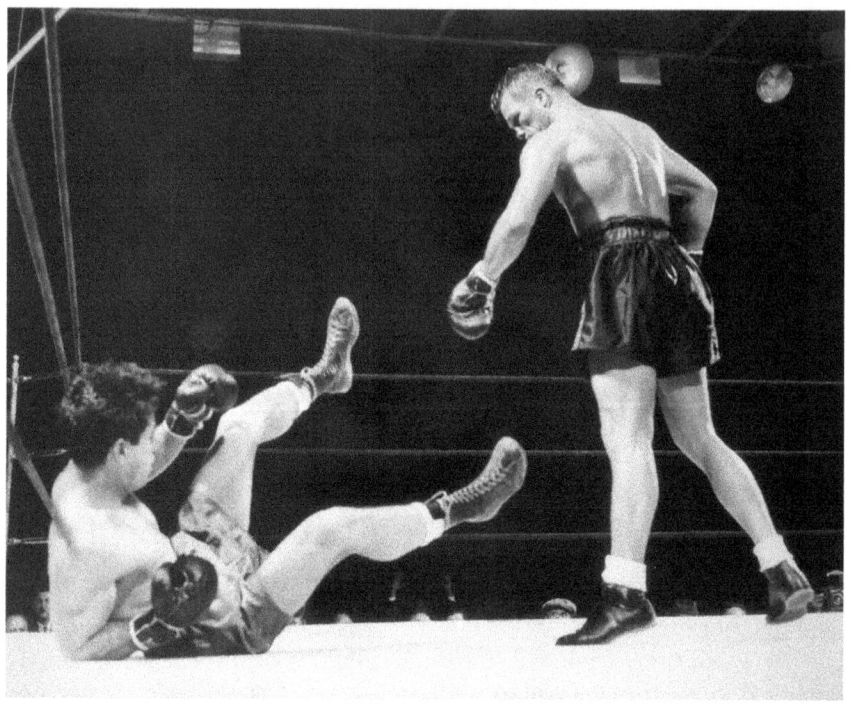

Zale stuns onlookers by knocking out Graziano in the sixth round (Gamma-Keystone, via Getty Images).

went at Zale and, when restrained by the referee, protested but to no avail.

Ringside observers were stunned as there "was no indication Zale was about to uncork the haymaker."[35] Arcel admitted it was a hundred-to-one shot.[36] Some thought the count was fast, but Nat Fleischer confirmed that his own stopwatch had Rocky down for over ten seconds. The crowd was still in an uproar as the fighters left the ring to walk to the locker room. Rocky, who was unmarked except for a bloody nose, took a swing at one fan who accused him of taking a dive.[37]

Reporters found a battered Zale in his locker room, icing his broken right hand in a galvanized bucket (he would wear a cast for three weeks and undergo another month of physical therapy).[38] His face looked like raw hamburger, with red welts over both eyes.[39] Mentally, Zale was not all there, repeating the same answer ("clean living") to every question. His trainers chased the reporters away and went to work reviving Zale. He required assistance to make it to the shower.[40] After his head cleared,

5. A Fighting Champion

trainer Ray Arcel asked Zale how he did it. "You know, Ray, I said many prayers and God heard me."[41]

The fight was immediately branded a classic. Longtime boxing announcer Don Dunphy considered the fight the most thrilling he ever witnessed.[42] The *Ring* named it fight of the year for 1946.[43] In less than one year, the *Newark Evening News* deemed the fight "historic."[44] The praise for Zale was even greater. Former heavyweight champion Gene Tunney said Zale's performance was the greatest display of heart he had ever witnessed.[45] Zale was named the *Ring*'s Fighter of the Year for 1946, and he won another award as the man who did the most for boxing.[46]

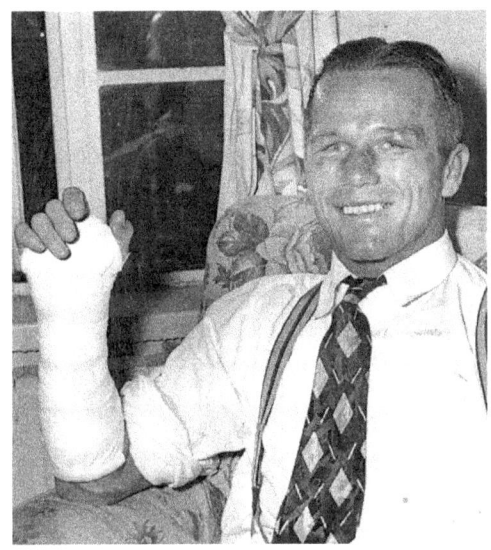

The Victor: Zale in a cast after his first clash with Rocky (courtesy of Ted Zale family).

The astounding victory defined Zale's career, shaped his legacy, and made his reputation. Other fighters had more talent, but none better exemplified the traits boxing fans held in the highest esteem. To Zale—a man of the past even in his own time—midcentury America gave "the old respect men once had for champions in this country,"[47] wrote Jimmy Cannon. Cannon was not referring to the modern uses of the word "champion," meaning the winner of a contest or an advocate for a cause. Cannon meant the ancient meaning, from Late Latin and dating back to the time of the Roman centurions: "campionem"—"gladiator, fighter, combatant in the field."

One of Zale's biggest fans was his young challenger. For the remainder of Graziano's life he always paid Zale the highest respect— "the toughest man I ever fought." But by tasting defeat in such an agonizing fashion, Rocky faced the harsh reality of all losers. Reporters questioned his guts. In a typical review, Willie Ratner wrote that Graziano was "found wanting" at the time of maximum testing.[48] Worse, Rocky's own people from his neighborhood shunned him. Some had taken Rocky's prefight boasts as meaning the fix was in, and they lost

Brick City Grudge Match

money betting on him. Like the poor slob who lost his life savings and maybe his bride. This was money these working people could not afford to lose.[49] Rocky's former pals along Second Avenue began crossing the street at his approach.[50]

And things were about to get worse for the Rock.

6

Never Lay Down for Any Man

"I had one hundred and eleven fights and I never took a dive for anybody.... I'm very proud of that." Mountain McClintock, Requiem for a Heavyweight

In addition to immediately being recognized as a classic on its sporting merits, the first Zale Graziano fight was also a smashing financial success. The crowd at Yankee Stadium clocked in at 39,827, producing a gate of $342,497, the second highest amount for a nonheavyweight fight.[1] Each fighter received 30 percent of the gross, or $80,000 each, $878,543 in 2020 dollars.

A rematch was a no-brainer. The contract for the first fight didn't require Zale to give Rocky a rematch. Typically, it was the champion who was guaranteed a rematch in the event he lost. The contract for Zale Graziano I was an anomaly in that Zale did not receive the standard rematch option—a concession to Graziano's strong bargaining position based on his superior drawing power.[2] As the *Ring* noted, "Zale is a fine fighter and grand champion but there is no record that New Yorkers ever knocked down doors to see him in years gone by."[3]

Zale was motivated to sock away as much money as possible. The war had deprived Zale of the opportunity to cash in on his title. At the press conference for the first fight, Zale forthrightly conceded that he selected Graziano over the other contenders because of Rocky's drawing power.[4] A rematch with "Golden Boy" Rocky was the obvious move from a business perspective. Anthony Marenghi of the *Newark Star Ledger* noted in his story the day after the fight that "a cry for a second match" started "a minute after the bout ended."[5] But not everyone was on board. The middleweight division Zale reigned over was loaded with talent— probably one of the deepest and most talented divisions in the history of boxing. The younger men who made up the contenders had grown impatient for their shots at the title. They hungered for the prestige and financial rewards that only came with the championship. As succinctly put by light heavyweight champ "Slapsie" Maxie Rosenbloom ("Slapsie" because Rosenbloom tended to hit with an open hand rather than a fist and accordingly KO'd few opponents), "It's a hellava feeling to be called champ. It makes you feel proud all over. It's better than the dough and damn near as good as the broads."[6]

Graziano was ranked third in the division after his first fight with Zale.[7] Some in the boxing press pushed for Zale to fight the number one contender, Jake LaMotta, the "Bronx Bull." LaMotta certainly had the credentials. He was declared the number one contender by the *Ring* and also by the National Boxing Association (NBA). This organization represented thirteen states and was seen as counterbalancing the New York State Athletic Commission as the dominant regulatory body. For New Yorker LaMotta to receive recognition as the top contender by the NBA stamped him with nationwide approval. LaMotta's résumé included a win over Sugar Ray Robinson, to that point the only loss suffered by the greatest ever "pound-for-pound" fighter. Other close (and even disputed) losses to Robinson only enhanced LaMotta's standing. To his credit, LaMotta ducked no one, including members of the famed "Murderers' Row," a group of African American fighters so talented they were avoided.*

But LaMotta came with baggage. A lot of baggage. Some considered LaMotta a psychopath. As an old man, LaMotta admitted that on some level he felt he did not deserve to live, and fought accordingly.[8] Most who knew him, even within the boxing community, hated the man. "[A] reprehensible, obnoxious, despicable sonnuvabitch" was not an uncommon opinion.[9]

Passionate in its promotion of LaMotta for a title shot, the *Ring* attempted to humanize the Bull. The effort strained credulity. LaMotta, who beat his first two (of seven) wives, was described by the magazine as "one of the nicest chaps you'd ever want to meet." The Bull, who would go on to throw a fight, was also pegged as "a man of his word."[10] Jake, who would serve six months hard time for inducing a minor to prostitution, was depicted as a nascent scholar who "spends a good deal of time

---

*Long neglected, the stories of these gladiators were finally unearthed and brought to light by author Harry Otty in his book *Charley Burley and the Black Murderers' Row* (self-published, Tora Book Publishing, 2010). Boxing historian Springs Toledo followed in 2017 with his fabulous *Murderers' Row: In Search of Boxing's Greatest Outcasts* (self-published, 2017).

6. Never Lay Down for Any Man

reading scientific subjects ... preferably the atom bomb."[11] Even the *Ring*, however, had to concede that Graziano had earned a return engagement with Zale. The *Ring*'s Nat Fleischer suggested that Zale and Graziano should agree to meet LaMotta within ninety days of their rematch.[12] "LaMotta must be given an opportunity to fight for the crown," thundered the bible of boxing.[13]

The number two ranked contender was Pittsburgh African American Charley Burley, considered the best of the Black Murderers' Row.[14] A legend to students of the fight game, many of Burley's contemporaries considered him to be the finest middleweight out there—the "uncrowned champion." Others, including light heavyweight champion Archie Moore, considered Burley the greatest boxer ever.[15] The *Ring* conceded that Burley "was too good for his own good" and considered him to be the equal of LaMotta.[16] But Burley's prospects were hurt not only by his ability, which led other fighters to duck him, but also by a lack of visibility. By the time of the first Zale Graziano fight, Burley had only fought once in New York.[17]

Coming in behind Rocky as the number four contender was Europe's great hope, Frenchman Marcel Cerdan. American observers who questioned the quality of Cerdan's opponents were mollified when Cerdan took a decision over African American veteran Holman Williams (another member of the Murderers' Row). Any doubts about the Frenchman's ability were blown away by Cerdan's impressive victory in his stateside debut over Georgie Abrams, the man Zale had defeated to unify the middleweight title.[18]

Regardless of arguments for other combatants to a title shot, the boxing public wanted Zale Graziano again. Fighting LaMotta or Robinson may have yielded as little as one-tenth the purse for Zale.[19] James P. Dawson offered the opinion that a Zale Graziano rematch was "undeniably the most attractive match available in the sport."[20] Zale set about to give the public what they wanted. He agreed to fight Rocky at Madison Square Garden on March 21, 1947.[21] The rematch was expected to score a gate of over $500,000, which would eclipse the record for an indoor fight by more than $300,000.[22] The Madison Square Garden bout would never happen, and the rematch was almost lost as well.

Rumors were circulating that Graziano was rattled by his loss to Zale. His spirit, they said, had been wrecked and his confidence faltered. It was also reported that the Rock's management was struggling to get him back in the ring. Nat Fleischer of the *Ring* was troubled by this talk, recognizing that Rocky did more than any other fighter to keep the sport in the spotlight. "He is an aggressive, colorful battler, one the public enjoys seeing."[23]

The Rock finally signed up for a tune-up match with a journeyman named Reuben "Cowboy" Shank, but then wrenched his back in training. His management called off the fight and Rocky forgot about it.[24] A couple of weeks later Graziano was pulled over by the cops. The Rock figured he was speeding or ran a red light. Although no longer a real criminal, he remained a chronic violator of rules of the road. He became concerned when the "bulls" told him that the New York district attorney wanted a word with him.

A series of assistant DAs grilled Graziano for fifteen straight hours.[25] They asked Rocky about his cancellation of the Cowboy Shank fight. Evidently a syndicate of New York gamblers had bet $135,000 on Shank, a boxer not in Rocky's league. Graziano eventually admitted receiving an offer of $100,000 to take a dive against Shank, but the briber—who Rocky claimed he could not identify—was joking. More to the point from Rocky's perspective, he had not taken the bribe or taken a dive ("There wasn't even no fight. So what you got your balls in an uproar for?").[26] The problem for Graziano was that Rule 64 of the New York State Athletic Commission required boxers to report any offers of bribes.[27] Moreover, the DA was convinced that Rocky knew the identity of the man offering the bribe. The DA also had suspicions that Rocky faked his back injury and pulled out of the Shank fight because he feared retaliation for his failure to go through with the fix.[28]

Rocky thought the whole thing was bullshit. Just the latest effort by "the man" to frustrate his attempt to go straight. Boxing attracted many weirdos, grifters, and petty frauds—along with truly dangerous hoods. "Underworld characters have always dallied on the outskirts of the fight game and dabbled in its workings," noted Jack Kearns, the manager of Dempsey and Mickey Walker. It gave these shady operators a "certain exalted standing" in their shadow world.[29] Characters of this type frequently offered bribes and proposed get-rich-quick schemes. Rocky undoubtedly knew the identity of the man who offered the bribe, but he was no rat.[30] The district attorney could pound salt.

Graziano had support among influential sportswriters. W. C. Heinz, the columnist for the *New York Sun*, thought the charge against Rocky was contrived to distract attention away from the authorities' failure to solve an entirely unrelated case concerning the murder of a policeman.[31] Heinz's unvarnished support for Rocky earned him the rebuke of his supervisors at his conservative paper.[32]

6. Never Lay Down for Any Man

On January 31, 1947, Rocky appeared before the State Athletic Commission. The case received unprecedented coverage for a boxing-related legal proceeding.[33] Jake LaMotta, who stood to gain from the Rock's misfortune, attended the hearing.[34] The new county district attorney, Frank Hogan, conducted the hearing. Rocky testified and admitted not only to receiving and not reporting the Cowboy Shank bribe offer, but also another bribe offer in a prior fight against Bummy Davis.[35]

On February 7, 1947, the commission issued its decision. Rocky's New York boxing license was revoked indefinitely.[36] The *Ring*, in the minority of the boxing press, took the view that the commission had no choice. Recent revelations about corruption in the sport ("under-cover managers and thugs who are the real 'owners' of many of our best fighters") required a hard line be taken.[37] Red Smith and W. C. Heinz, on the other hand, blasted the commission for a decision that in their view reeked of hypocrisy and political expediency.[38]

With Rocky unlicensed to fight in New York the question became whether other licensing bodies would follow suit. Zale, for obvious financial reasons, wanted the rematch. He stood to be the "principal victim" of Graziano's suspension as he would lose out on a $100,000 purse ($1,075,107 in 2020 dollars) if the rematch was cancelled.[39] Graziano's technical violation of the rules of the New York State Athletic Commission did not trouble Zale. To Zale, the important point

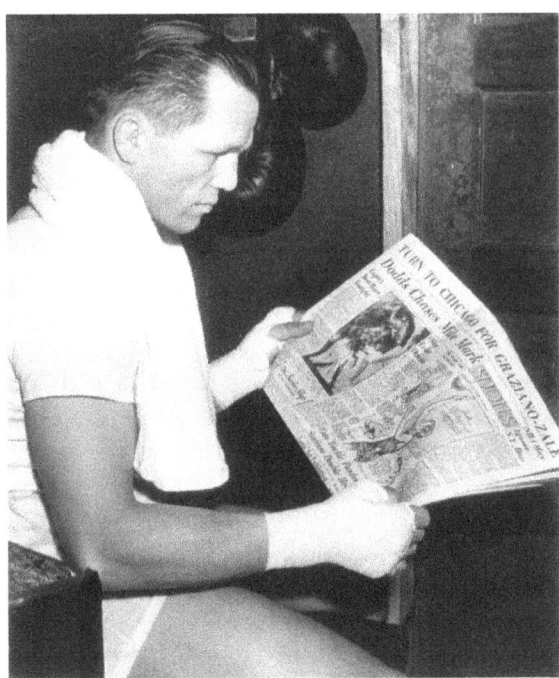

Zale reading about Rocky's troubles (AP Wire photo; author's collection).

Brick City Grudge Match

was that Rocky did not accept the bribe or throw the fight—unforgivable sins in the eyes of Zale and other real boxing people.[40] In the memorable phrase of Springs Toledo, throwing a match generated "a stench that could never be overcome" by a fighter.

On February 19, 1947, the National Boxing Association let it be known that it would not block the rematch in states outside of New York.[41] The Newark Armory was identified as a possible site for the rematch, but was quickly ruled out because of New Jersey's reciprocal agreement with the New York State Athletic Commission—it was initially thought Graziano was also barred from fighting in New Jersey.[42] The rematch was quickly rescheduled in Zale's adopted hometown of Chicago. Plans to hold the bout outdoors at Wrigley Field or Comiskey Park were scrapped when it was determined that a postwar lumber shortage made it too costly to build infield stands.[43] The fight was moved indoors at Chicago Stadium.

With his victory in the first match, Zale's bargaining position improved. This time around the fighters would not receive equal pay; rather Zale would take 40 percent of the gate to Rocky's 20 percent.[44] And this time Zale had the option of demanding a rematch in the event he lost his title.[45]

The Rocky Graziano that Zale would meet in Chicago was different from the man he had faced off against in Yankee Stadium. Shocked at being KO'd for the first time in his career, any delusions the Rock had about Zale's speed, power, and most of all his toughness and determination, had been disabused. Accusations that he was a quitter in the ring enflamed Rocky's passions and stoked his anger. What's more, Graziano knew he was finished as a fighter if he lost the rematch.[46]

Ordinarily, Rocky's free spirit and restlessness made him unwilling to endure the drudgery of training. This time Graziano's trainers had a fighter who was more than willing to pound the heavy bag, blitz the speedbag, and jump rope for hours. To toughen Rocky's midsection for Zale's incapacitating body punches, the Rock's trainers repeatedly threw a one-hundred-pound medicine ball at Graziano's stomach.[47] Rocky's treatment of sparring partners was downright abusive as twice he ran out of them and was forced to increase the pay to get anyone to take the job.[48]

Graziano also knew he had to prepare his mind for the coming struggle. He had to match Zale's extraordinary determination to pry loose the coveted crown from Tony's tenacious grasp. The night before the fight, W. C. Heinz was with Graziano. Heinz, who had grown close to Rocky, admitted he lost his objectivity and was rooting for Graziano to whip Zale. Heinz impressed on Rocky how essential it was for him to win the fight. "If you lose tomorrow night you're done, not only in New York, but everywhere. You have to win, Rock," Heinz told Rocky.[49] This was not news to the Rock—he knew the score. Graziano had already come to the terrible realization that he might have to kill Zale in the ring to realize his own ambitions.[50] He would crush Zale or die trying.

On the way back to his hotel, Heinz felt pangs of guilt. He was urging Rocky to risk all in a desperate bid for victory while Heinz sat comfortably at ringside "looking up into the brutality."[51] Heinz had seen what Tony Zale could do to a man in the ring. Like the time Zale almost ruined Georgie Abrams's right eye and beat Abrams's head into twice its normal size. Heinz knew Zale would be ready to do his best—he always was, every time he climbed through the ropes.

Zale, shaking off the rust of his war-imposed inactivity, had looked impressive in scoring knockouts in all five of his nontitle, tune-up fights. He seemed to be defying father time. The champion was training for the rematch in Wisconsin, chopping down trees and logging hours of roadwork.[52] A photo from the time shows Zale sparring with Jackie Darthard, an upcoming black middleweight. Darthard would rise to number six in the rankings before he died less than a year later following a knockout loss to Bert Lytell. This time around, the bookies made Zale a seven-to-five favorite.[53]

The stage was set for the second chapter of the Zale Graziano epic. Like their first bout, the rematch would go down as one of the most brutal and memorable fights in boxing history. As Rocky would write years later, "This was no boxing match. It was a war and if there wasn't a referee, one of the two guys would have ended up dead."[54]

7

Blood and Thunder
(Zale Graziano II—
Chicago Stadium, July 16, 1947)

The second Zale Graziano fight took place indoors. Chicago Stadium opened in 1929 and was the largest indoor arena in the world at the time. It was also the first with an air conditioning system, but it was rudimentary and largely ineffective. The day of the fight saw temperatures climb to over eighty degrees.

The packed arena was steaming hot, described as "sweltering"[1] and a "Turkish Bath."[2] A reporter at ringside had a thermometer and recorded the temperature at one hundred degrees. The heat, sweaty crowd, and smoke from burning cigars made a pungent combination. Columnist Jimmy Cannon reported that the stench "was enough to turn your stomach."[3] The miasma would remind observers of a Chicago slaughterhouse once blood started flowing in the ring.

No film exists of the second Zale Graziano contest, other than disjointed fragments apparently taken by a handheld 8mm camera shot some distance from the ring. The home movie reveals little more than two blurry figures standing toe to toe, throwing plenty of leather with bad intentions. For any meaningful understanding, we are left once again with photographs and written reports. Like the first fight, the second bout is considered one of the greatest and most memorable in boxing history. And the second was boxing's biggest event that year, selling out and more than doubling the gate of the previous record for an indoor match.[4]

The crowd came expecting another brawl. They knew neither Zale nor Graziano were looking to "fool around with any 15-rounds-to-a-decision panty waist stuff."[5] These two just weren't cut out that way. The crowd got what they paid for—the fight "lived up to its billing like a government bond."[6] Spectators were "half hysterical most of the way."[7]

7. Blood and Thunder

Zale opened the first round with confidence. He had a way of exhibiting disdain for opponents once inside his squared world. Cannon noted the sadistic utterances of the crowd as Zale contemptuously opened the bout by showing Rocky zero respect. Zale caught the Rock with a heavy blow on the left eye—Rocky said it felt as if Zale had crashed the butt of a gun into his face[8]—opening a cut. Zale then dug a shot to Graziano's gut. Rocky reacted by doing a sideways crabwalk, his mouth slowly opening as if preparing to vomit.[9]

At the beginning of round two, Zale, following the cruel logic of boxing, began peppering the Rock's left eye, ruining the work of Graziano's cut man who had closed the wound between rounds. Rocky's blood would flow for the rest of the fight. He repeatedly wiped his glove over his eye in an effort to clear his vision. Just when it appeared Zale might be on the brink of a lopsided win, Rocky set Zale back on his heels with a right to the chin and finished the round strongly. Graziano won the closely contested round.[10]

Zale put Graziano through a living nightmare in the third round. Rocky described it as "the worst round I ever lived through in the ring."[11] Zale quickly floored Graziano with a right to the jaw. Rocky jumped up without a count, with a contemptuous grin on his face.[12] He fought back the best he could, but he had trouble finding Zale, who methodically circled toward Graziano's blinded left eye. Zale appeared as nothing but a red blur to Graziano. When Rocky tried to cover up, Zale rudely smashed Graziano's hands back into his face.[13] Graziano's left eye cut was now wide open (Zale "played a tattoo on it"[14]), covering both men in gore. Toward the end of the round, Zale hammered a right to the Rock's right optic and it immediately began to close.[15] Graziano was now virtually blinded.

Referee Johnny Behr visited Graziano's corner between rounds. Rocky's trainer had to beg to let the fight continue. Behr agreed to give Rocky one more round, mordantly observing, "They give you the chair for murder in this state."[16] Zale then carried the fourth, the slowest of the fight, but Rocky landed a big right toward the end.[17] Between rounds Rocky's cornerman used the hard edge of a quarter to break the skin over Graziano's right eye to bring down the swelling.*

The fight turned in the fifth frame. Rocky got a second wind[18] and seized the momentum with an aggressive two-fisted attack, only briefly

---

*This incident may have been the inspiration for the "cut me, Mick" scene in Sylvester Stallone's *Rocky*.

Brick City Grudge Match

halted by a Zale left hook to the body, which doubled up the Rock. Zale seemed to lose energy and the Rock started to tee off ("terrific time bombs were right on target"[19]). After the fight, Graziano reported that he realized Zale could no longer hurt him. Whether that occurred because Zale became fatigued or because Rocky had a surge of adrenaline—or a combination of the two—was beside the point. A booming Graziano right to Zale's head toward the end of the round (drawing a loud "oooh" from the crowd[20]), and Zale's "wandering aimlessly into a neutral corner" after the bell rang, set the stage for the fateful sixth.[21]

Rocky used his pent-up rage—rage at Zale for knocking him out at Yankee Stadium and turning his own kind against him, rage against the various authority figures who had tormented him for years, and just rage—as motivation. He wanted to kill Zale, although Graziano was in such a fury it could have been anyone who stood in his way ("I don't even know any more who I am killing, whether it's a cop or a guard or somebody who ratted on me or Tony Zale or who."[22]).

A right to Zale's chin at the start of the sixth initiated a shocking Graziano fusillade. Jimmy Cannon counted thirty-six times that Rocky hit Zale. Zale, who gave up ground grudgingly, began walking backward, initially in a slow retreat but then like a staggering drunk. Zale's arms dropped, his eyes went dead, and he took on a deathlike pallor. Graziano's punches altered Zale's angular face into a bloody mess.[23] Rocky, "wild eyed, sneering [and] snarling,"[24] drove Zale "from rope-to-rope" and "corner-to-corner."[25] A *Life* magazine photograph captured the ferocity of Graziano's attack—Rocky, with his right eye closed, shouting with exertion as he lands one of his full-armed rights, with Zale's head snapping back. This time, the Rock would close the deal. No more Zale rallies. No more being saved by the bell. Graziano beat Zale senseless. Out on his feet, Zale turned his back on the Rock and collapsed over the middle rope. Zale hung there for a moment while Graziano continued to swing from odd angles, as if he were trying to drive a spike into Zale's back. To Cannon it appeared as if Zale's bones had melted. His bloody face drooped into the battery of photographers at ringside. Referee Behr mercifully stepped in and pulled the frantic Rocky off the helpless Zale. The fight was over. Rocky Graziano was the middleweight champion of the world. Behr noted that Zale's eyes had ceased to focus,[26] and he "wanted no murder on his hands."[27]

Graziano could hardly believe it. When handed the ring microphone for a comment, the Rock thought back to the years of struggle for himself and his family: "Hey, Ma—your bad boy done it."[28] Later, in

7. Blood and Thunder

Referee Behr pulls Graziano off the helpless Zale, draped over the ropes "like a ragdoll." Rocky Graziano is the middleweight champion of the world (AP Photo).

his dressing room packed with well-wishers, hangers-on, and the press, the Rock's "face, one eye cut and the other closed, was twisted into a grotesque grin ... the perfect picture of the abysmal brute."[29] The raucous scene was only interrupted when Zale pushed his way through the crowd to offer his congratulations to the new champ.

Rocky earned the title with a remarkable performance, including an incredible display of fighting heart. The same press that questioned his guts after Yankee Stadium now had to eat crow (although each press member suggested it was someone other than themselves who implied Rocky was yellow). "The kid *they said* was not game enough to take the kind of punishment Tony Zale handed out, won the title by doing just that" (emphasis added).[30] To Nat Fleischer of the *Ring*, Graziano "proved that he possessed the fighting qualities of a title holder—the spirit and the courage that makes champions."[31] Rocky had taken Zale's "best wallops and stood his ground."[32] Rocky had turned the tables on Zale in a "blood and thunder brawl," a "raw, brutal, bloody affair, much like their first encounter."[33]

With the immortal Joe Louis in a postwar fade (as confirmed later that year when Louis took a controversial decision over Jersey Joe Walcott), Graziano was now the biggest star in boxing.[34] The Rock received

Brick City Grudge Match

a hero's welcome when he returned to Gotham: a "riotous homecoming welcome given him at New York Grand Central Station, [the] most genuine and wholehearted ever accorded a fighter in the city's history."[35] According to the calendar, Graziano was just entering his prime. Jack Dempsey opined that winning the title would improve the Rock, and predicted that Graziano would whip Zale if they ever met again.[36]

The morning after the fight, Jimmy Cannon was packing for his trip back to New York. The phone rang. On the other end was an angry Tony Zale. Zale argued the referee should not have stopped the fight. Cannon felt obliged to set Zale straight. The columnist reminded Zale that he was sitting at ringside and had observed the entire hellacious beating Rocky had just laid on him. Cannon bluntly told Zale that he could have been killed if not for the referee's intervention. Zale's response stunned Cannon: "I had a right to get killed for my own championship."[37] That is why Zale was great, Cannon thought. But the exchange also troubled Cannon, who hoped Zale would retire and save his health.

Zale had other ideas. He was ornery and in no mood to exit gracefully and leave the stage to younger men. Zale would exercise his option for a rematch with Graziano and seek to reclaim the title he had owned for six long years and come to wear like his own skin. But he faced seemingly insurmountable obstacles. Zale's advancing age and the horrible beating he had taken from the Rock raised obvious questions. Rocky's fists had ruined and effectively ended the careers of other top-notch fighters. And those men were contemporaries of Graziano, not geezers like Zale. Moreover, history itself stood in Zale's way. One of oldest maxims in boxing is: "They never come back." No middleweight had reclaimed the championship for over half a century.

The old lion would have to find the lost trail.

8

Born Dead with a Black Eye
(Jersey Pugilistica)

The sport of boxing in the United States is traced to England, although its origins date back to before the time of Christ. Considered the national sport of Britain, boxing was introduced in the American colonies in the 1700s and took hold in urban areas around 1800. The sport initially justified itself as a nonlethal option of settling disputes (in contrast to, for example, dueling), and as way for men to demonstrate their fighting skill. These more elevated rationales were undermined by full-on freakshows in the roughhewn backwaters of the new republic (e.g., the pitting of human vs. animal and even mentally disabled contestants).

The response of early American authorities to the sport was more restrictive than in the United Kingdom. Puritan values, fears of lawlessness, and distaste for the lower classes sparked significant legislative and judicial action.[1] New Jersey was one of the first states to outlaw prizefighting. In 1847, the New Jersey legislature amended the penal code:

> Prize fighting: *And it be enacted* that every person who shall be engaged in any fight or combat, with fists, commonly denominated prizefighting, whether such fight or combat be for money or any other valuable thing, or merely to test the skill or bodily powers of the pugilists or combatants, and every person who shall be aiding, assisting, or abetting, in any such fight or combat, shall be deemed guilty of a high misdemeanor, and on conviction thereof, shall be punished by imprisonment at hard labor, not exceeding two years, or by fine, not exceeding one thousand dollars, or both.
> N.J. Rev. Stat. 257 §88 (1847).

New Jersey's criminalization of boxing was primarily motivated by a desire to stamp out gambling associated with the sport (hence the reference to "prize fighting"). Other states worried that boxing attracted the wrong kind of people. Many considered boxing fundamentally immoral and degrading, yet relatively little concern about the well-being of the boxers themselves was observed.[2]

An 1842 trial in New York captured the mindset of public officials. Boxer Thomas McCoy died after a bare-knuckle brawl lasting 120 rounds and 2 hours in duration. Eighteen individuals, including the seconds, ring keepers, and the "attending physician," were indicted for manslaughter. Justice Charles R. Ruggles read the jury their instructions:

> A prizefight brings together a vast concourse of people; and I believe it is not speaking improperly of such assemblages, to say that the gamblers, and the bullies, and the swearers, and the blacklegs, and the pickpockets, and the thieves, and the burglars are there. It brings together a large assemblage of the idle, disorderly, vicious, dissolute people—people who live by violence—people who live by crime—their tastes run that way, and though some respectable people probably were there ... you can readily perceive the influence which such assemblages are likely to exercise on the public peace, and morals, and taste; and you can estimate correctly the propriety and necessity of that law which forbids their existence. Upon that spot, then, no one can hesitate to say—even had no fatal result ensued—there were collected a body ferocious and demoralized. The assemblage was in itself indictable as an unlawful one.[3]

After receiving these hardly dispassionate instructions, the jury returned guilty verdicts after three hours of deliberation.[4]

Nonetheless, some prominent public officials supported the sport. While serving as the police commissioner of New York City in 1896, Theodore Roosevelt resisted pressure to shut down boxing matches. TR, who credited boxing training for his own transformation from a sickly youth to an adult of robust health, explained his reasons for refusing to stop a fight at Madison Square Garden: "I see nothing wrong with boxing so long as the law is followed. Boxing is a great sport. Too bad our schools don't take it up. If they did, we would have more courageous young men and less corner bullies to contend with.... I love a good scrap and I admire the fighting spirit in any man."[5]

In New Jersey the sport remained a polarizing political issue in the early twentieth century. Some, like Roosevelt, considered boxing a sport requiring a high level of skill and a good way to encourage fitness. While boxing remained illegal in New Jersey until 1918,[6] bouts nevertheless were held in secret locations such as on barges where police were unlikely to intervene.

In truth, boxing's prohibitionists faced an uphill battle due to the

8. Born Dead with a Black Eye

sport's popularity and associated money-making potential. Newspapers would lambast the sport for its brutality in their editorial pages, while simultaneously offering extravagant coverage of matches on the sports pages. Editors faced conflicting pressures and tended to come down on the side of giving the public what it wanted ("[Y]our paper is insupportably dull, and [I] can't read it unless it contains an account of all the prize fights").[7]

Assemblyman Joseph Hurley introduced a bill in 1917, after the United States became engaged in World War I, to legalize boxing in New Jersey. The Hurley Boxing Law was signed in 1918. Supporters of the bill declared that "boxing could not be considered a brutal sport in these days of war, but that on the contrary it was useful to young men."[8] One of the conditions of passage was that decisions could not be entered (as a half-hearted way to discourage gambling). This rule led to many so-called newspaper decisions in New Jersey, where sportswriters covering the bout would declare a consensus winner.

Boxing fully emerged from the shadows with arrival of a man from the West. William Harrison "Jack" Dempsey, the Manassa Mauler, was a character and national icon like no other. Rising from an impoverished background, he went from the mining camps in his native Colorado, to a life as a hobo riding the rails, to a saloon brawler. A human melting pot—part Scot, part Irish, part Cherokee, part Jewish—he won the heavyweight championship on the nation's birthday in 1919, in a brutal dethronement of the giant Jess Willard. Just as Babe Ruth's home runs revolutionized baseball, Dempsey's weaving, crowding, and slugging style changed boxing forever. His thrilling fights, coupled with his amiable personality and the arrival of mass media, made Dempsey one of the most famous men in the world. This "flame of pure fire" in the ring connected with the public in a manner difficult to fully understand.[9] Dempsey's popularity, joined with a sense that the veterans who risked life and limb during World War I should not be deprived of entertainment, resulted in widespread legalization of boxing in the early 1920s.

Just three years after boxing's legalization in New Jersey, Dempsey generated the first "million dollar gate" ($1,789,238; $23 million in 2021 dollars) from his bout with Georges Carpentier at Boyle's Thirty Acres in Jersey City. A crowd of eighty thousand packed into a stadium built from plywood just for the occasion. The fight claimed significant "firsts," including the first world title fight broadcast over radio and first attended by a large number of women. The contest was a mismatch as

Brick City Grudge Match

Dempsey and Carpentier mix it up at Boyle's Thirty Acres in Jersey City (Library of Congress).

Dempsey easily flattened his French opponent in four rounds. Despite the fight's spectacular commercial success, the do-gooders refused to throw in the towel in their opposition to the sport and sought to have Dempsey arrested after the fight.[10] Dr. Wilbur F. Crafts, superintendent of the International Reform Bureau, pompously proclaimed that a test case would be brought to determine whether the bout was legal. Crafts also promised to impeach Governor Edward Edwards and other state officials who attended the fight.[11] The threats went nowhere.

Although the sport had cleared the low bar of legality and took on immense popularity, its image remained ambiguous. For as long as boxing has existed, it has both fascinated and revolted in equal measure. The brutality, corruption, and weird hangers-on prompted sportswriter Jimmy Cannon's memorable observation that "boxing is the red light district of sports." Cannon, who owed a large part of his considerable reputation to his writings about boxing, conceded reformers had a point when they argued boxing should be "made as illegal as the selling of cocaine."[12] This ambivalence persisted throughout the twentieth century. In 1984, the American Medical Association called for the abolition of the sport, citing "the dangerous effects of boxing on the health of participants."

Despite the danger, or perhaps because of it, boxing became embedded in America's cultural landscape. Top-notch writers and filmmakers were fascinated by and drew creative inspiration from the sport. The post–World War II era saw the flowering of a highly literary style of sportswriting heavily influenced by Ernest Hemingway. Cannon, Red Smith, and W. C. Heinz had the talent to elevate their columns into miniature works of art. These three men—all legends in the business—did some of their finest writing covering the Zale Graziano fights. Hemingway, who had notable failures in his attempts to capture boxing's essence, instead directed readers to Heinz's *The Professional* as the finest novel about boxing.

Boxing's association with the movies goes back to the dawn of the film business. And that connection was birthed in New Jersey. Thomas Edison, who led the film industry into the 1910s, captured two fights at his studio in East Orange, New Jersey, in 1894. *The Corbett-Courtney Fight* was the top-grossing film in the early days of the motion picture industry.[13]

Hollywood has made more films about boxing than any other sport.[14] Some of Hollywood's biggest box office draws of all time have portrayed boxers, including James Cagney, Errol Flynn, Kirk Douglas, John Wayne, James Earl Jones, Robert DeNiro, Denzel Washington, and Will Smith. The spectacle of two men waging real battle in a brightly lit ring surrounded by darkness—potentially a matter of life and death—is inherently dramatic.

In an interesting footnote illustrating the connection between movies and boxing, an indoor boxing area in Newark, Laurel Garden, was the setting for legendary director Stanley Kubrick's first film. The short documentary, *Day of the Fight*, followed the same format as Kubrick's 1949 photo spread for *Look* magazine where he followed Rocky Graziano from the time he woke up, through his preparation, and finally to the fight in the evening. In the film, middleweight contender Walter Cartier and his manager (his identical twin brother) are followed by Kubrick's intrusive camera from breakfast to church to the anxious moments in the dressing room prior to the fight, through Cartier's knockout victory. The film, available on YouTube, has an eerie quality. Students still analyze *Day of the Fight* for themes that would appear later in Kubrick's work.[15]

The plotlines of early boxing films tended to conform to the ideal of the American Dream, with lower-class boys fighting their way to the top and triumphing over long odds. A different type of boxing film emerged with the film noir movement in the postwar era—when Zale and Graziano met in their three classic bouts.

Film noir emerged from Hollywood and reached its creative peak in the late 1940s. The war changed attitudes. Americans were looking for more mature content, including a forthright acknowledgment that playing by the rules did not always pay off. European film directors fleeing the war brought along a visual style and sensibility that matched the darker subject matter.[16]

The greatest works of noir fiction take place in Los Angeles in the 1930s and 1940s.[17] Noir fiction set in New Jersey has come much more recently, somewhat surprisingly given the state's history of corruption, organized crime, and sensational crimes (e.g., the Lindbergh kidnapping and trial). While late to the genre, New Jersey–inspired noir ranks with the very best (e.g., *The Sopranos*).

Three of the best regarded noir films have boxing as their focus: *Body and Soul* (1947), *The Set-Up* (1949), and *Champion* (1949). They bracketed the third Zale Graziano bout. All three of these films, in different ways, used noir style to criticize the exploitation of fighters.[18]

In *Body and Soul*, John Garfield's protagonist is a common man corrupted by the lure of success. Some view the film as a socialist morality tale about the ruthless capitalistic system. Others interpret the movie as a denunciation of corruption and violence.

In *The Set-Up*, Robert Ryan plays one of the few noble characters in his long and distinguished Hollywood career. Ryan's "Stoker" Thompson, an over-the-hill fighter, tries to hang on in the hope of catching some one-punch magic. Fight fans are portrayed as sadistic deplorables bellowing for blood in a sweaty, smoke-filled, and claustrophobic arena. The "set-up" of the title refers to the sell-out of the protagonist by his manager, who accepts a bribe on the understanding that Ryan's character would take a dive. Unwilling to split the ill-gotten gains and confident his fighter will lose even without taking a plunge, the manager's best laid plans are thrown asunder when Stoker shocks by knocking out his young and upcoming opponent. The manager flees, leaving his fighter to bear the wrath of the mobster who lost money on the frustrated fix.

In *Champion*, Kirk Douglas is a man from a poor and dysfunctional family. He fights his demons while climbing the rankings, using, abusing, and discarding relationships along the way. He finally wins

8. Born Dead with a Black Eye

the middleweight title, only to find a black hole where his soul once resided.

While Jersey led in popularizing the sport, it was also one of the world's most prolific producers of boxing talent. Perhaps the greatest pound-for-pound fighter ever from Jersey was Tony Zale's predecessor as undisputed middleweight champion. "I was born dead, with a black eye," said Edward Patrick Walker, a.k.a. Mickey Walker. The black eye came from the physician's instruments used to extract the baby from his mother's womb.[19] Walker—a brawler from birth—grew up in the largely Irish Keighry Head section of Elizabeth. He had an independent streak a mile wide and a love for the ladies and drink.

Mickey's father tried to tame the rambunctious boy with thrashings, to no avail. The stick having failed, the family tried the carrot. His uncle placed the boy in a cushy job at an architect's office. A duck out of water in the plodding, buttoned-down corporate environment, Mickey was fired when he slugged a coworker.[20]

Mickey Walker preferred the fast lane. As a teen, he trained his fists on roughnecks and freight yard hobos. Walker learned early on he could handle big men just as well as the small ones. Although he topped out at 5'7", he feared no man and cemented his reputation by taking on the giants of the heavyweight division.

Walker turned pro at the age of seventeen. Fighting primarily in his hometown and in Newark, Mickey burned a hole through the welterweight division. He won the crown from wily veteran Jack Britton at Madison Square Garden in 1922. His "Jersey Bulldog" nickname eventually morphed into his better-known moniker as the "Toy Bulldog." He moved up to the middleweight division and won that title in 1926. In between he fought and lost to Harry Greb in possibly the matchup of the highest-rated pound-for-pound fighters in boxing history. After the official match, Walker and Greb allegedly engaged in a drunken brawl later that night at a saloon. "Sober or stiff, I belted the guts out of the best of them," said Walker.[21]

Walker lived an equally colorful life outside the ring. Once he earned some jack, he bought a mansion in Rumson. During prohibition he teamed up with Al Capone to run illegal booze up the Jersey coast.[22] He managed to get married seven times—to four different women. One Cadillac escaped the grasp of a rapacious divorce lawyer when Mickey rolled it down a river embankment.[23] Binges, parties, and Hollywood starlets filled the gaps between fights.

Yet somehow he remained a top-notch fighter for over a decade.

Walker is still the only welterweight champion to ever rank as a serious contender for heavyweight honors. His decision to move up and campaign among the heavies seemed insane at the time. But he gave a good account of himself, scoring a win over Johnny Risko (a man who beat seven Hall of Famers) and, most famously, earning a draw with former heavyweight champion Jack Sharkey.

Walker's run with the big men came to a crashing halt on the wrong end of Max Schmeling's powerful right fist. It was Schmeling who best captured what it was like to see the stout-hearted Irishman in the ring. Years before he faced off with Walker, Schmeling saw him defend his middleweight crown in London against Scot Tommy Milligan. Watching Mickey Walker fight was a revelation for the German: "[I] grasped for the first time how much concentration, mercilessness, and toughness American boxers brought to their profession. The way Walker hammered down his challenger ... remained an unforgettable lesson for me. Here it was demonstrated to me for the first time how unconditionally the boxer puts his existence on the line."[24]

Walker remained in the public eye after his fighting days ended. He bought into several taverns, including the Wagon Wheel in Keansburg where he employed a kid named Frank Sinatra. Walker also owned a piece of the Blue Moon in Newark where Jackie Gleason tended bar and entertained.[25] He even became an accomplished artist (Walker's painting style was described as "a true American primitive"[26]).

An anecdote from the Bulldog's postboxing career exemplifies not only his enduring popularity but also the connection Depression–era Americans felt for its champions. Walker was making his way to a Joe Louis fight at Yankee Stadium when he was approached by a hobbled old woman. "I want to shake a great Irishman's hand," she said. The champ took the old lady's hand into his fighter's paw. His other hand dug into his pocket, which produced three wrinkled dollar bills. Walker placed the modest jackpot into the woman's hand, who replied: "God bless you, Mickey."[27]

Walker's susceptibility to excessive drinking did not mix well with working in bars. All of his forays into the alehouse business eventually failed. The Bulldog never claimed, unlike some boxers, to have been ripped off by his managers. He knew damn well where the money went. Estimated to have earned $3 million in the ring, the money was spent faster than it came in. He made ritual out of burning in his fireplace canceled checks from the millions he spent on his fast living.[28]

Walker eventually slipped out of the news. His memory started

8. Born Dead with a Black Eye

to fail. In 1974, at age seventy-two, Walker was found unconscious on a street corner in Flatbush, Brooklyn. The cops thought Mickey had passed out drunk. He was diagnosed with amnesia, acute anemia, and advanced Parkinson's disease. While in the hospital, money came from an unexpected source: Max Schmeling. The German never forgot Walker and sent him $500 a month.[29] The Bulldog would pass nine years later in Bruce Springsteen's hometown of Freehold, New Jersey.[30]

Great Jersey-bred champions followed the path trod by the Bulldog. The list of contemporaries of Zale and Graziano is impressive: Cliffside Park's Gus Lesnevitch (light heavyweight); Union's Freddie "Red" Cochrane (welterweight); and Garfield's Tippy Larkin (light welterweight). This was a time when being a contender mattered, and Jersey produced such top-ranked men as Irvington's Charley Fusari and Newark's Freddie Archer. Other Newark natives who made their mark at this time included Allie Stoltz (lightweight), Abie Bain (middleweight), and Lou Halper (middleweight).

At the time of the Zale Graziano fights, New Jersey was considered to have produced more quality boxers than any state except for New York and California.[31] The *Ring*'s June 1947 issue carried an article on a crop of rising Jersey-based contenders, highlighting fighters such as Cliffside Park's Tommy Baker (featherweight), Hoboken's Joe Lucignano (welterweight), and Montclair's Willie "Red" Applegate (heavyweight). Applegate, who pitched briefly for the Newark Eagles in 1947, would go on to lose a decision to Rocky Marciano.

Two contemporaries of Zale and Graziano deserve special attention. Jersey's second heavyweight champion was Jersey Joe Walcott (the first being North Bergen's James J. Braddock, "The Cinderella Man"). Arnold Cream was born in 1914 in South Jersey's Merchantville Township. His parents came from the Virgin Islands. The fifth of twelve children, Arnold quit school and went to work at age fifteen after his father died. It was the depths of the Depression and money was in short supply. He found his way to a local gym where his punching power attracted attention. Cream turned pro at age sixteen (then weighing 135 pounds) and changed his name to Joe Walcott, in honor of his fistic hero, a welterweight champion from Barbados—"The Barbados Demon" Joe Walcott. Jersey Joe Walcott's first fight yielded a purse of $7.50 (KO of Cowboy Wallace in the first round).

Walcott's power and ring savvy scared away opponents, and he struggled to make a living boxing. He drove trucks and washed dishes

Brick City Grudge Match

between fights to make ends meet. His boxing career was up and down, and in 1940 Walcott "retired" after being knocked out by the huge Abe Simon in Newark. Boxing history was changed when promoter Felix Bocchicchio convinced Joe to give the sport another chance. Incredibly, after over four years of inactivity, Walcott shot up the heavyweight rankings. The great Joe Louis eventually agreed to fight him for the heavyweight title. Jersey Joe shocked the boxing world by flooring Louis twice. Only a controversial decision deprived Walcott of the championship. Three other failed bids for the most prized possession in all of sports followed. Then, in his fifth try, Joe finally climbed the mountain when his perfect left hook separated Ezzard Charles from his sense and his title. At thirty-seven, the "Camden Methuselah" became the oldest man to win the heavyweight title, a record that stood for forty-three years until George Foreman won the crown from Michael Moorer at age forty-five. Jersey Joe, fearless and willing to step in with the most powerful punchers in boxing history, lost the championship in a furious battle with Rocky Marciano a year later. Yet he remained immensely popular. As Arnold Cream, he was elected sheriff of Camden County in 1971, the first African American to hold the job. Walcott died at age eighty in 1994.

The other elite Jersey-bred midcentury boxer was one of the greatest lightweight champions ever. Ike Williams turned pro at the tender age of fifteen. By his eighth match he was fighting eight-rounders. Ike fought often, against stiff competition, frequently against larger men. By 1947 he had secured his title by knocking out Bob Montgomery. Williams's trilogy with Kid Gavilan should rank among the greatest. The man is something to behold in the old fight films: a natural who hit hard with either hand and could box or slug with anyone. Williams' destruction of former champion Beau Jack in 1948, available on YouTube, demonstrates like no words can Ike's speed and power. Ike's big wins read like a who's who of the lightweight and welterweight divisions of the era. In 1948, the *Ring* named Williams Fighter of the Year, and he received the Edward J. Neil Memorial Award for contributing the most to boxing. Unfortunately for Ike, by this time he had drifted under the control of Frank "Blinky" Palmiero, a lieutenant of Frankie Carbo, a.k.a. "Mr. Gray." Blinky, who was said to have murdered at least six men, got his nickname because he could never look anyone in the eye. Ike ended up with Palmiero because he had attempted to manage himself but learned the hard way no one would fight him without a manager. Williams later claimed that he saw no money during his banner year, including the $32,000 he earned for destroying Jack. "Blinky stole everything from me but my eyes," Ike later recalled.[32] But no one could steal the fact of Ike's greatness in the ring. Williams died in 1994 at the age of seventy-one.

Hard times were the fertile soil for the bumper crop of boxing talent emerging in mid–twentieth-century America. The Great Depression buffeted millions of Americans, especially those at the bottom of the socioeconomic ladder. Second-generation immigrants and black men, in particular, were carried by circumstances into the ring. "It was very hard to get jobs before the war, and if you did, you were lucky to make six dollars a week. You could make a lot more fighting, especially if you were any good," said Danny Kapilow, a welterweight who once fought Graziano to a draw.[33] Zale agreed and made the point in an even more elemental manner: "You fight to keep away from being hungry."[34]

Ethnic pride also drove men to learn how to fight. "As a kid growing up in an Italian and Irish neighborhood in West New York, New Jersey, right across the Hudson River from Manhattan, I got into a lot of fights being called a Jew bastard or worse,"[35] said Charley Gellman, who fought under the name Chuck Halper. Gellman, who went on to graduate from Columbia and became a high-ranking union official, won sixty out of sixty-five bouts and is a member of the New Jersey Boxing Hall of Fame.

In this Golden Age of boxing, Newark remained an active venue but had lost some of the luster it once held as a boxing center. In the old days, many famous champions fought in Newark, including Greb, Schmeling, and Tony Canzaneri. Rocky Graziano fought in Newark on his way up, in addition to fighting in several other Jersey venues, including Highland Park, New Brunswick, Elizabeth, and Paterson. However, with the passage of the Walker Law, which legalized boxing in New York, the big fights tended to take place on the east side of the Hudson. Jersey and Newark were the places where up-and-coming fighters earned their way to fights on the big stage at Madison Square Garden. Newark native and Jersey sportswriting legend Jerry Izenberg wrote, "[I]f you hadn't won a main event in Newark, then you hadn't earned the right to even see Madison Square Garden."[36]

In the era of Zale and Graziano, most boxing events in Newark were held at Laurel Garden. This was an indoor arena located at 457 Springfield Avenue in Newark's Central Ward. Initially a beer hall, it was converted to a boxing arena in the 1920s and continued to host

Brick City Grudge Match

boxing matches until 1953 when the wrecking ball hit.[37] Laurel Garden had no air conditioning and lacked proper ventilation. Famous Newark novelist Philip Roth wrote, "You could be asphyxiated by merely one gulp of what passed for air" in the place. The unsentimental Roth considered half the fighters at Laurel Garden to be "bums." Yet as a boy Roth still found the experience a perverse thrill, with crude men yelling abuse and encouragement at the fighters in a "course Newark libretto."[38] In the steaming summer months boxing matches were moved to a small outdoor area known as the Meadowbrook Bowl on South Orange Avenue.[39] Bigger events were hosted at Ruppert Stadium, home of the baseball Bears and Eagles.

Ruppert Stadium was built on the footprint of Newark's first significant baseball stadium, Wiedenmayer's Park. That wooden structure was destroyed by fire in May 1925. Located in the East Ward Ironbound Section (because the area was bounded by railroad tracks), also known as "Down Neck" (because of a bend in the Passaic River resembling a neck), the area was then a working-class neighborhood. The property was purchased by Charles L. Davids who needed a place for his minor

Ruppert Stadium, Newark, 1949 (Newark Public Library).

8. Born Dead with a Black Eye

league baseball team to play. Davids constructed a twelve-thousand-seat steel-reinforced baseball stadium. In 1927, Davids was forced to sell his creation, originally named Davids Stadium, to Paul Block, publisher of the *Newark Star Eagle*. Block fared no better than Davids and sold the stadium and the team to the owner of the New York Yankees, Jacob Ruppert. In 1932, Ruppert expanded the facility to nineteen thousand seats and did away with false modesty by rechristening the park Ruppert Stadium.[40]

In 1941, Elizabeth's Red Cochrane won the welterweight title from Fritzie Zivic at Ruppert Stadium. The circumstances were questionable. Cochrane, while a gutsy mixer, was a club fighter who generally fought locally and had not shown championship-level talent. Cochrane is considered by some to be among the most pedestrian of boxers ever to win a "lineal" title (i.e., "the man who beat the man" who previously held the championship in that particular weight class). In any event, no one thought Red was in Zivic's class. Fritzie is a Hall of Famer who bested legends like Charley Burley, "Homicide" Henry Armstrong, and Jake LaMotta. No less an authority than Sugar Ray Robinson said he learned more about boxing from fighting Zivic than any other opponent. Cochrane was a four-to-one underdog.

So how did Zivic lose to Cochrane? Some have suggested the fight was fixed. Elizabeth had a reputation as a mob town. Others suggested the referee was on the take. In New Jersey at the time the referee was the sole arbiter (i.e., he not only refereed the fight but also served as the only judge in the event the bout went to a decision).[41] However, contemporaneous reports of the fight made Cochrane the clear winner on points.[42] A more plausible rumor has it that Cochrane's shrewd manager arranged to get the colorful Zivic fixed up with a hooker on the eve of the fight. The scuttlebutt goes that the lady wore out Fritzie leaving him in poor shape to face Cochrane. The *New York Times* report on the fight noted that Zivic was uncharacteristically "lethargic."[43] Zivic easily outpointed Red in a nontitle rematch.

In the United States, the sport of boxing, while remaining morally ambiguous, reached the peak of its popularity in the mid–twentieth century. The sport has experienced a long decline in the ensuing years. Yet this ancient sport is unlikely to ever disappear completely, for the roots of boxing, and the intersection between the sport and the arts, stretch back to antiquity. In 1978, Jacques Cousteau's divers searched a wreck of a Roman ship at the bottom of the Aegean Sea. Amid the debris field they found something worth retrieving. The *Calypso*'s divers ascended

Brick City Grudge Match

to the surface and scraped away the accumulated sediment. They were stunned to discover a perfectly preserved two-thousand-year-old bronze statue of a boxer. The unknown pugilist assumed much the same pose as Zale and Graziano when they took their publicity shots before their famous bouts.[44]

9

Landing the Big Fight

Rocky thought his spectacular victory over Zale in Chicago and ascent to the middleweight throne completed his journey to redemption. He had played by the rules and made it the top of the toughest racket out there. His troubled youth was in the rearview mirror of his powder blue Cadillac. He sparkled as the toast of the town and the brightest star in boxing's firmament. Surely the New York State Athletic Commission would restore Graziano's license and allow the Rock to defend his title in his home state.

Seeking to capitalize on the new champ's celebrity, the *Ring*'s October 1947 issue featured a lengthy story on Graziano titled "Rocky Road to Ring Royalty," followed in November by a gushing cover story comparing Rocky to the legendary middleweight champ Stanley "The Michigan Assassin" Ketchel. Perhaps even more colorful than Graziano, Stanislaw Kiecal, a.k.a. Stanley Ketchel, ran away from home at the age of twelve and became a child hobo. A job as bouncer in Butte, Montana, led to his boxing career. Ketchel turned pro at sixteen and relocated to California where he built his reputation and eventually earned the middleweight title. An aggressive, fearless, and violent man, Ketchel the fighter was an unpolished brawler with a huge punch, just like Rocky. He scored forty-eight knockouts in his fifty-one wins. He fought all comers, up to and including heavyweights.

But unlike Graziano, who ultimately was tamed (at least outside the ring), Ketchel never tried to control his less savory appetites. He was rumored to have hit brothels with his friend, heavyweight champion Jack Johnson. Ketchel and Johnson's friendship was such that they planned a "fight" with each other in what actually was a scripted farce. The plan went awry when Ketchel double-crossed Johnson and floored the "Galveston Giant" with a surprise right to Johnson's head. Embarrassed and irritated, Johnson quickly got to his feet and attacked Ketchel. A Johnson uppercut removed a row of Ketchel's chompers and knocked him cold. In the film of the fight, Johnson can be seen methodically removing Ketchel's teeth from his boxing glove.

Perhaps if he had lived longer Ketchel would have eventually sought domestic tranquility. But the rabble-rouser was destined to die young and leave a good-looking corpse. He left this world in 1910 at the tender age of twenty-four while still the champion. Under murky circumstances, Ketchel was shot to death at a remote ranch in Missouri. Some said he had run afoul of a jealous common-law husband. Another story had it that Ketchel had angered a ranch hand by upbraiding him for mistreating a horse. A third theory posited that a Bonnie and Clyde–type duo of drifters had targeted the flush champ (known to carry wads of cash) for robbery. The truth seemed to be part of all of the above.

Ketchel was shot while eating breakfast. Perhaps expecting trouble, he was armed with his own Colt 45. As the Michigan Assassin lay prostrate, the shooter smashed Ketchel in the face with his own gun. Ketchel was also relieved of his diamond ring (rumors that the thief also severed Ketchel's ring finger and kept it as a macabre trophy proved unfounded). Ketchel's death threw the middleweight division into chaos. A new champion was not crowned until Frank Klaus was officially recognized in 2013.

In the *Ring*'s 1947 article, Graziano offered his assessment of the contenders for his middleweight crown. Rocky proved to be a better fighter than boxing analyst. Of Sugar Ray Robinson, the dominant welterweight king who was moving up to the middleweight division, Graziano suggested Robinson was washed up ("not as good as he used to be"). At the time Sugar Ray was in the midst of a ninety-one-fight unbeaten streak and would go on to win the middleweight championship a record five times. Robinson remained a ranked contender well into the mid–1960s. Graziano was equally dismissive of Europe's champ, Frenchman Marcel Cerdan ("busy, but no kid"), and tough Steve Belloise ("ain't so young"). Rocky also commented on his old running mate and perpetual number one contender Jake LaMotta ("tough" but "not a real puncher"). The article mentioned two members of the Black Murderers' Row, Bert Lytell and Charley Burley, but the Rock passed on offering an assessment of these men (just like he took a pass on fighting them). Oddly absent from the contender review was the man the Rock had dethroned and who had a contractual right to a rematch.[1] Zale was still ranked as the number two contender, behind LaMotta.[2] The *Ring* and Graziano probably figured Zale's time was finally up and he would fade away.

9. Landing the Big Fight

Unknown to the Rock, the ghosts of his past were trailing him and gaining ground. Someone at the war department leaked Graziano's service record to the press. At a time when memories of the war were fresh, and the loss and sacrifice still painfully raw, much of the public was disinclined to celebrate the exploits of a man who had gone AWOL, was imprisoned by the Army, and dishonorably discharged. Self-serving politicians saw an opportunity. In October 1947 it was announced that the Illinois Athletic Commission banned from boxing any man dishonorably discharged by the armed forces. Other states fell in line. Graziano was now prevented from fighting in his home state of New York and the other most important boxing states. Caught off guard, Rocky was confused and uncertain of how to find his way out of what was essentially a public relations nightmare. "I was belted right out of the day back into the night I came out of, and I couldn't hit back because there was nobody to hit."[3]

Graziano's travails played out against a background of seismic changes in the fight game. Since the 1920s New York had dominated the sport. The New York State Athletic Commission was the regulatory body established in 1920 to oversee the enforcement of the Walker Law, which legalized boxing in the state. In the mid–1930s, a visionary Manhattan-based promoter moved into a position of dominance.

Michael Strauss Jacobs was one of eleven children born to a Jewish family from Dublin, Ireland. He "grew up as a cultural oddity in the Hibernian ghettos of the Lower West Side."[4] A born hustler, Jacobs started scalping tickets outside the second Madison Square Garden in the 1890s. Tough, ruthless, and with a head for numbers, he was alternately described as an avuncular presence ("Uncle Mike"), a cunning genius (the "Machiavelli on 8th Avenue"[5]), and less charitably as an epic cheapskate (the "stingiest man in the world"[6]). Jacobs methodically worked his way up and ultimately cornered the Gotham boxing market.

Jacobs's big move came when he locked in exclusive promotional rights to rising superstar heavyweight Joe Louis, the immortal Brown Bomber. At the time, Jacobs's signing of Louis was seen as a bold move because many in the industry didn't believe a black heavyweight champion could be successfully marketed to white audiences. Jack Johnson, the first black heavyweight champion and the man who had punched out Stanley Ketchel's teeth was, how to say, controversial. Some were rubbed the wrong way by Johnson's dating habits (i.e., he liked white women). As the *Ring* tried to put it tactfully, Johnson's "braggadocio, his pettier peccadillos," would have been overlooked, but his very public romances were a bridge too far; "unconventional that they were."[7]

Johnson's most well-known bout took on major racial overtones. None of the white contenders at the time were in Johnson's class. Some white people, including *Call of the Wild* author Jack London, were determined to wipe the defiant grin off Johnson's face. They started a movement to pressure former undefeated heavyweight champion Jim Jeffries to fight Johnson. Big Jeff had not fought in six years and had ballooned to over three hundred pounds while enjoying retirement on his alfalfa ranch in Burbank, California. Jeffries, dubbed the "Great White Hope," finally succumbed and agreed to fight Johnson. The ex-champ's decision was ill advised. Johnson was a great fighter in his prime and easily whipped Jeffries in the roasting heat of Reno, Nevada. Race riots erupted in several American cities after Johnson's win, and a film of the fight was banned. No black man had been given a shot at the heavyweight crown after Johnson's dethronement by Jess Willard in 1915 under questionable circumstances in Havana, Cuba.

With the memory of Johnson's reign still fresh, getting any black fighter a crack at the crown was no easy task. Jacobs handled this challenge with guile, portraying Louis as a sort of anti–Johnson, dignified and respectful. It helped that Louis really was dignified and respectful. Even after a shocking knockout loss to former heavyweight champion Max Schmeling, Jacobs still maneuvered Louis to a title shot against North Bergen's "Cinderella Man" James J. Braddock. Louis relieved the stouthearted Irishman of the title with an eighth-round knockout in 1937. The *Ring* would go on to celebrate Louis's unprecedented (and still unsurpassed) reign as heavyweight champ for its positive effect on race relations ("banishing the bigots").[8]

The Brown Bomber was Jacobs's meal ticket for the next decade plus. Jacobs's most successful promotion was the Joe Louis vs. Billy Conn rematch at Yankee Stadium on June 19, 1946. Although the fight was a flop ("a real stinkeroo," admitted Conn; Louis was war rusty and Conn bloated and lethargic), the gate was a titanic $1,925,504. Jacobs purchased a "baronial estate" in Rumson.[9] Like most fighters, Joe Louis did not do as well financially as his promoter.

The second Louis Conn fight had another distinction with greater long-term ramifications: it was the first heavyweight title fight ever broadcast on television. Although the basic technology for television dates back to the 1880s,[10] practical application of the medium took decades. Television of sports, in particular, was slowed by

9. Landing the Big Fight

primitive telephoto lenses, which could not bring the viewers close to the action.[11]

Mike Jacobs saw the potential in a marriage between television and boxing. The sport was immensely popular, and boxing's contribution to the early history of moviemaking was a documented fact. Perhaps more important, boxing was ideally suited to being televised. The bouts took place in a contained, well-lit ring. There were only two combatants. All of the action could be captured by one camera. In short, boxing was "something that television's early engineers could navigate."[12]

Boxing matches had been televised prior to the war, but these were more experimental efforts designed to convince business interests of the technology's viability. A more serious commercial effort was made when *Friday Night Fights* debuted on NBC in September 1944 reaching seven thousand sets in the East.[13] The Louis Conn rematch presented the perfect opportunity for a more ambitious effort. Material released from war storage enabled RCA to construct a picture one hundred times more sensitive than the prewar models.[14] Televisions placed inside taverns and bars drew overflow crowds and enabled the patrons to view the match from the same vantage point as an in-person spectator thirty feet from the ring. Customers were transfixed but also confused and enflamed as they thought the bartender controlled the telecast. They heaped abuse on the barkeep whenever the picture became fuzzy.[15] In the end, the experiment was a success. "By 1946, [boxing] accounted for nearly 40 percent of all television programming and was the driving force in TV sets booming sales."[16] The first Zale Graziano fight held on September 26, 1946, was televised on WNBT, NBC's television station.[17]

After his greatest promotional triumph, Mike Jacobs's reign as boxing's most powerful force appeared like it might go on forever. Then fate intervened: Jacobs suffered a stroke in December 1946. His right arm would hang limp for the rest of his life.[18] Jacobs's business associates lacked the acumen to maintain Jacobs's success and his power waned. By December 1947 Jacobs's financial backers began expressing serious concerns about the ongoing viability of the operation.[19] Blood was in the water and the sharks started to circle. The convergence of Jacobs's incapacity and the rise of television eventually led to Newark landing Zale Graziano III.

The Tournament of Champions, Inc. (TOC), formed as a New Jersey corporation in May 1947, was the first serious effort to challenge Jacobs and his Twentieth Century Sporting Club. Although unknown at the time, TOC was a promotional subsidiary of the Columbia

Broadcasting System (CBS).[20] The corporation was put together not by boxing men but rather entrepreneurs who saw opportunity in the application of television to boxing. TOC began televising fights on CBS. TOC offered larger purses to lure away talent from the atrophying Twentieth Century Sporting Club. Veteran boxing manager Al Weill was retained as TOC's front man. Weill would go on to manage legendary heavyweight champion Rocky Marciano.

The quest for control over the other Rocky—Graziano—brought TOC into direct conflict with Jacobs's flailing Twentieth Century Sporting Club. The Rock was the hottest property in boxing at the time in spite of the fact that he was unlicensed and unable to fight in the most important boxing states. He was even unrecognized as middleweight champion in his home state of New York. It stood to reason that the promoter who could get the Rock reinstated would win the battle for control over the middleweight crown.

Jacobs's successor was his cousin and legal counsel, Sol Strauss. Considered inept by most observers, Strauss at least had the sense to see the potential in Graziano. On January 22, 1948, at a New York Boxing Writers' Association dinner, Strauss took the opportunity to challenge Rocky's suspension. Strauss, his voice cracking with contrived emotion, pointed his finger at the New York State Athletic Commissioner Frank Eagan and, in courtroom style, said: "Why was Rocky Graziano suspended? Why can he not fight in New York State? He's just a political football. The public wants him to fight and nobody has the right to say no."[21]

While Graziano focused on his licensing problem, Zale kept active. The day after the Writers' Association dinner in New York, Zale met Al Turner in Grand Rapids, Michigan. It was Zale's first fight since his loss to Graziano in Chicago. Zale took control from the outset and, in a stunning display of hitting power, "catapulted his opponent out of the ring." Zale was declared the winner by knockout when his opponent's "feeble, but futile" attempt to get back in the ring failed.[22]

Despite Zale's power surge, the scribes were skeptical of his ability to beat Graziano. Associated Press reporter Whitney Martin noted that Zale had given it his all in Chicago, but it still was not enough. Martin doubted "the well-battered veteran" had enough left in the tank to beat a fighter of Graziano's caliber.[23]

On January 28, 1948, it was reported that Al Weill, acting on behalf of TOC, offered Graziano a guaranty of $120,000 to fight Zale at Convention Hall in Atlantic City. At the time, Convention Hall was the

9. Landing the Big Fight

largest indoor arena in the world and could comfortably seat forty-five thousand spectators.[24] Weill met with the managers of both fighters in New York, but no deal was struck.[25] "Too many obstacles came up. Right now, we're so far away from a fight, it isn't even funny ... much less news," said Weill.[26] Left unaddressed in the news reports was how Graziano could fight in New Jersey, which reportedly had a reciprocal agreement with New York to honor licenses and suspensions.

On February 6, 1948, it was reported that Graziano's manager, Irving Cohen, along with two associates were dragged before the New York State Grand Jury. Although the "trend of the questions" was unknown,[27] mobster Frankie Carbo, a.k.a. "Mr. Gray," had been seen at Rocky's postfight victory celebration in Chicago. Carbo, among other lines of work, was a button man for Murder, Inc. and was accused of ordering the hit on Bugsy Siegal.[28] Suave but vicious, Carbo had his claws deep into boxing and at the time was in the midst of expanding his malign influence over the fight game.[29] The same grand jury apparently heard testimony from "bookies and underworld characters."[30]

A week later Zale's manager said the Atlantic City fight was on again. Atlantic City's mayor, Joseph Altman, expressed his enthusiasm about his city hosting the fight.[31] Again, Graziano's licensing was not addressed.

At this time, Newark's two leading daily newspapers were the *Newark Star Ledger* and *Newark Evening News*—New Jersey's "paper of record." Testifying to the popularity of the sport, each paper had writers devoted exclusively to boxing. The boxing writers for both papers, Anthony Marenghi for the *Ledger* and Willie Ratner for the *News*, were well-known and highly respected. Both men picked up on the Jersey-focused rumors.

On March 4, 1948, Marenghi reported on a plan to work around Rocky's licensing problems. The idea was for Graziano to fight Sonny Horne in a nontitle matchup in Washington, D.C. The top D.C. boxing official was Heine Miller, a decorated Marine combat veteran. Miller would bless the bout on the condition that Rocky donated his entire $15,000 purse, less $1, to charity. The thinking was that Miller's approval, plus the donation to charity, would generate enough good publicity to get the Rock back in the ring.[32]

The plan worked to perfection and would ultimately pave the way for Zale Graziano III to take place in New Jersey. Heine Miller, in addition to being the boxing boss in D.C., was also secretary of the National Boxing Association (NBA). And the presiding president of the NBA was

Brick City Grudge Match

Abe Greene, the former head of the New Jersey State Athletic Commission. Greene, a newspaperman known as a true friend of fighters, made Graziano's reinstatement his personal crusade. It was reported that Greene actively worked with TOC to break New York's hammer lock to the benefit of Jersey.[33] TOC's designs on the heavyweight division rested with Jersey Joe Walcott who was scheduled for a rematch with Joe Louis in June 1948. TOC also signed up light heavyweight champion, Cliffside Park native Gus Lesnevich.[34] The idea was to bring New Jersey boxing back to the lucrative days of Dempsey Carpentier. Offering the Rock a haven in Jersey was a key part of the effort.

But the situation remained fluid. Zale, despite his contractual right to the rematch, felt compelled to lobby in the press for another crack at Graziano. "I hope I am not deprived of the chance. I think it is coming to me."[35] The ex-champ was keeping himself sharp by completing his own version of the bum of the week club. Zale TKO'd Bobby Claus in Little Rock on March 8, 1948, and just eleven days later tuned up Lou Woods in Toledo.

The other contenders were not sitting on their hands. On March 12, 1948, Frenchman Marcel Cerdan knocked out American up-and-comer Lavern Roach in the eighth round in Madison Square Garden. The Texan Roach was a handsome ex-Marine and earned the *Ring*'s Rookie of the Year award in 1947. He had the raw material to be a huge star. American observers were not impressed by Cerdan's win, chalking up the result to a Roach blunder in dropping his guard at an inopportune moment. Some predicted Roach would win a rematch.[36] But Roach would never fight Cerdan again. Instead, he became the first boxer killed on live television while engaged in a tune-up fight before a scheduled match with Sugar Ray Robinson. Roach was twenty-four years old.[37]

Graziano was not the only middleweight with licensing problems. Jake LaMotta was suspended for his behavior associated with his notorious fight with Billy Fox on November 14, 1947. This match, given extensive treatment in Martin Scorsese's *Raging Bull* (1980), aroused suspicions when LaMotta was seen cavorting with Frankie Carbo and Frank "Blinky" Palermo three days before the fight.[38] When the betting odds swung dramatically in Fox's favor shortly before the fight, officials felt compelled to warn the fighters about not throwing the fight. LaMotta's performance was a joke, barely raising his hands before the fight was stopped by the referee after four rounds. LaMotta attributed his poor performance to a spleen injury.[39] He had his license suspended for not reporting the phantom injury to the doctor in charge of the weigh-in

9. Landing the Big Fight

examination.[40] Later, LaMotta said that only a hammered drunk would not have realized he threw the fight. Boxing writer Dan Parker of the *New York Daily Mirror* expressed surprise that the actors union had not picketed the Garden given the weakness of LaMotta's performance. In 1960, LaMotta confessed he threw the Fox fight—in exchange, he claimed, for getting a crack at the title.[41]

With LaMotta at least temporarily out the picture, momentum for a Zale Graziano fight in Jersey continued to build. On March 22, 1948, it was reported that Rocky Graziano was under contract with TOC. On the same date, reports appeared that the rubber match would be signed and take place in either Jersey City or Newark.[42] A week later Anthony Marenghi reported an "organized effort" to land the big fight to take place at Roosevelt Stadium in Jersey City or Ruppert Stadium in Newark.[43] A few days later TOC's new front man, promoter Andy Niederreiter, was quoted as saying he expected the fight to be signed within a few days.[44] The next day Niederreiter announced TOC had posted a $10,000 bond to secure use of Ruppert Stadium for the fight to take place on June 9, 1948.[45]

One contingency remained: Rocky had to win his comeback fight against Sonny Horne scheduled for April 5, 1948. Horne was no pushover. A slick boxer, Horne lost only 10 bouts in 121 professional fights. He had fought Graziano two years prior and lost a controversial split decision. And Rocky had not fought since he won the title nine months prior ("If they don't ban me out of the ring, they'll rust me out," said a frustrated Rock[46]). Rumors circulated that the Rock was enjoying the championship a bit too much and was eighteen pounds over his fighting weight.[47] In his autobiography, Rocky acknowledged gaining "the wrong kind of weight," but attributed it to his licensing problems and the stress associated with his public humiliation from disclosure of his military record.[48]

By the time Graziano got into the ring, he did indeed look rusty. He missed the clever Horne with a lot of punches, sometimes by up to six inches. But the Rock's power advantage provided the edge he needed to take the ten-round decision. Horne was busted up and exhausted at the end.[49] Graziano wrote later that Horne, who had never been stopped but was in trouble during the sixth round, asked not to be knocked out. Rocky honored the request by carrying Horne until the end.[50]

Three days later Zale Graziano III was signed to take place on June 9, 1948, at Ruppert Stadium in Newark. The promoter TOC rented out Toots Shor's Restaurant at 52 West 51st Street in Manhattan for

Brick City Grudge Match

an elaborate signing ceremony reminiscent of boxing promotions before the austerity brought on by the war.[51] Toots Shor was a former door-to-door underwear salesman and bouncer. His niche was catering to celebrities. Yogi Berra supposedly said about Toots' joint: "Nobody goes there anymore. It's too crowded."[52] Jackie Gleason was a frequent patron. Gleason got his start in Newark and liked to tell a story about his days performing his comedy routine at Club Miami located in Newark's red-light district. A rough joint, Gleason said that "the rats went next door to eat." One night a rude member of the audience heckled The Great One to the point where Gleason asked him to step outside. The loudmouth proved to be heavyweight contender "Two Ton" Tony Galento, who proceeded to knock Gleason cold.[53]

Toots Shor also catered to those with less savory reputations: the FBI had an eye on Toots for his "association" with Newark mob kingpin Longie Zwillman.[54] The "most spendthrift barkeep in New York,"[55] Shor never let his high-profile customers pay for anything. Toots was best buddies with Joe DiMaggio, who loved being comped. Toots was close enough to openly call DiMaggio "Crum Bum," a risky move for most associates as Joe tended to surround himself with sycophants.[56] Shor's star started to fade when, his tongue loosened with liquor, he insulted Marilyn Monroe in front of the Clipper.[57] But in 1948 Toots was riding high.

TOC was sending a message by staging the signing ceremony at Shor's restaurant. Public relations people call it "preparing the battlefield." By offering a generous spread of chow and an open bar to the denizens of the boxing press, TOC virtually guaranteed favorable coverage. One unidentified writer was quoted as saying: "If this is the way the new outfit is going to promote, I am for them. They serve plenty of food and drink."[58]

The hucksterism was a shot across the bow of Mike Jacobs's Twentieth Century Boxing Club, already teetering as a result of Jacobs's stroke. Sympathy for the great man was in short supply. Someone blurted out, "[W]here's Mike Jacobs?" to the guffaws of the quickly inebriated crowd.[59] Oddly two of Jacobs's matchmakers were in attendance. They "gulped hard and shifted uneasily in their chairs," when it was announced that TOC had a contract for the winner of the third Zale Graziano fight to take on an opponent, speculated to be Marcel Cerdan.[60]

Blarney was on the menu. TOC's spokesman said the guiding principle of the new organization was to "promote the love of sports" and

9. Landing the Big Fight

"not to make money." Cynical reporters rolled their eyes. The theretofore mysterious "Wall Street millionaires" behind the TOC were identified as eight industrialists.⁶¹ Not identified were the media tycoons and real power behind the new organization, Lawrence Lowman of CBS and Charles Miller of the Music Corporation of America, who sought to exploit boxing's potential on television.⁶²

Tony Zale showed up first. A waitress offered the opinion that Zale was "ugly, in a handsome sort of way."⁶³ Zale noted he was lucky to get there on time because he got hung up at a church affair in Chicago. Flanked by his manager Sam Pian and his legendary trainer Ray Arcel, the challenger looked "at ease and confident." Zale said he was pleased "everything got straightened out" with Rocky's licensing so the fight could go forward. "I believe that titles are won and lost in the ring and that's the way I want to win it from Graziano," said Zale.⁶⁴ Once the Rock appeared, the press abandoned Zale, who was relegated to a quiet table in the corner of the room.⁶⁵

Rocky and Zale sign up for their third clash on the back of Toots Shor (AP Photo).

Brick City Grudge Match

Graziano had the "it" factor. He brought energy to a room. The press stampeded toward him, back-slapping and flashbulbs popping.[66] Rocky had to pry himself away by insisting on a need to shake Zale's hand.[67] Although the Newark fight would be billed as an epic grudge match, the truth was the two men liked and respected each other. Maybe even needed one another.

Rocky had to convince a skeptical American public to overlook his war record. Associating himself with the respected veteran Zale undoubtedly helped. And Zale, bland by nature outside the ring, needed Graziano's attention-grabbing energy and firepower to make the fight marketable. Beyond the obvious mutual benefits derived from a business perspective, the men shared a bond only truly understood by those who enter the ring. Athletes in other sports tend to shake hands in a perfunctory matter at the end of a game or match, but boxers tend to embrace or even hug one another, especially if the fight has been particularly brutal. Sometimes the embrace is mere ritual, "but more often than not it appears to be sincere and deeply meaningful, a tribute to each other's courage."[68]

The National Boxing Association's Abe Greene, sensitive to the public's attitude toward draft dodgers, gave a speech, long on platitudes but short on logical consistency, justifying restoring the Rock's license. Greene noted recent comments by FBI Director J. Edgar Hoover, who had attended the Chicago fight, to the effect that Graziano had paid his penance and deserved a break. Greene questioned the source and timing of the leak of the Rock's war record. But Greene also condemned Rocky in equal measure.[69]

Graziano had no choice but to grovel and sheepishly participate in the charade. It was torture. Without a tie and disheveled as usual, Rocky's discomfort was obvious: he "listened, fidgeted and seemed disquieted"; "alternately scowled and smiled"; "the bitterness of his heart frequently prompted angry stares." The champ was justifiably confused, humiliated, and angered by his circumstance. But he knew that Abe Greene, the NBA, and New Jersey were championing his cause—bringing the Rock out of "the ash-fraught depths of pugilism's crematorium."[70]

For New Jersey's boxing fans, the signing of the third Zale Graziano fight was a coup. No longer would New Jersey play second fiddle to New York ("the first resolute and positive step"[71] toward breaking New York's virtual monopoly over big fights). The largest gate in Newark boxing history was anticipated.[72] The appeal of Zale Graziano reached out

9. Landing the Big Fight

from Newark to "the state, the nation and the rest of the world."[73] Some even dared to dream of the big fight leading to construction of a mega outdoor stadium seating one hundred thousand and a Jersey version of Madison Square Garden, all built over "the dank moors of the Newark swamps."[74]

10

Racing Head-On into the Night

As Graziano and Zale readied to depart for their respective training camps, the boxing scribes set about framing the clash. Two dominant storylines emerged: Rocky's quest for redemption and Zale's capacity to overcome Graziano's edge in age.

Before he left for camp in upstate Ellenville, New York, the Rock told the *Newark Star Ledger*'s Frank Casale, "The faith Greene and some others have shown in me is not misplaced. I've made some mistakes but I've learned my lesson."[1] Graziano planned on three weeks of light training followed by three weeks of serious sparring.

On the eve of Zale's departure for Hot Springs, Arkansas, the ex-champ was forced to field questions about his risking *pugilistica dementia*. "I've seen lots of punch drunk fighters in my day. I don't intend to be one of them."[2] Paranoid at this point in his career about his legs failing at the crucial moment, Zale intended to focus his training on conditioning. Weeks of running, mountain climbing, ditch digging, wood chopping, swimming, and crossword puzzles were planned for the Ozarks. Only then would Zale shift to Chicago for gym work.[3]

On May 6, Zale left Hot Springs for his home in the steel city of Gary, Indiana. Each day he woke before the sun rose to pound the pavement before taking the thirty-two-mile train trip to Chicago. He then sparred five rounds at the Ringside Gym in the heart of the Loop in downtown Chicago. He was emphasizing his left hook.[4] After sparring, Zale would shower, get a rubdown, and then weigh himself. Unlike many fighters (e.g., Jake LaMotta), the ex-champ never had trouble making the 160-pound middleweight limit.[5]

Observers agreed that Zale looked to be in great shape, but he was getting hit by his sparring mates at an alarming rate.[6] Although Zale consistently expressed a calm confidence, veteran observers were wary. Willie Ratner of the *Newark Evening News* assessed Zale's third fight

10. Racing Head-On into the Night

with the "vicious punching" champion as "the most difficult assignment of [Zale's] career."[7]

Rocky displayed new tricks in his sparring sessions. Always known for his booming overhand right, Graziano was "startling spectators" by "displaying a sharp left hook."[8] But he pooh-poohed the idea that he was studying up on becoming a better boxer. "[W]hen I learn to box I will get my head knocked off."[9]

The champ was reported to be doing fifteen miles of roadwork daily in the Catskills.[10] This claim should be viewed with skepticism. The Rock was never fond of training. Although he later claimed he "trained hard" for the Newark bout,[11] Graziano also admitted that once outside the sight of his trainers he was prone to shutting down his runs in favor of mobile craps games with his entourage.

The restless urban dweller eventually had enough of country life. "You sit there and do nothing. Just fish and hunt and walk and play golf." Rocky had similar laments when forced to train at Pompton Lakes, New Jersey, where Joe Louis and other famous fighters trained for big fights. "There's nothing to do at night but listen to the lousy crickets."[12] In mid–May, suffering from "fresh air poisoning," the Rock abandoned the boonies and relocated to his natural habitat at Stillman's Gym in Manhattan.[13]

Some observers expressed concern over Rocky's condition. Stories appeared about Graziano keeping late nights at fancy New York City clubs and "sipping scotch with red wine as a chaser."[14] Graziano had his weight down to 162 pounds by May, but that was still heavier than he had ever fought. Nevertheless, it was thought the Rock's youth would render irrelevant "the abuses to which the Rock has subjected his physical machinery the last year or so."[15]

In a preview of the Rock's postboxing career as a pitchman, a haberdashery offered Graziano some fancy threads and "richly scented pomade" for his unruly hair. But Rocky was not yet willing to engage in puffery in exchange for cash and free stuff. "They'd throw rocks at me if I wore dem ties or coats or put that perfumed stuff in my hair."[16]

On May 3, 1948, tickets for the fight went on sale in Newark and New York.[17] On May 9, it was reported that the promoters had overlooked securing a necessary permit for the fight. Frantic phones calls and a $500 fee—and perhaps some greased palms—sorted out the snafu.[18] Director of Public Safety John B. Keenan was photographed handing over the permit to TOC's Andy Niederreiter at Newark's City Hall.[19]

On May 21, it was announced Zale, who had sparred forty rounds

Brick City Grudge Match

in Chicago, would be leaving the Windy City because he had run out of sparring partners. Zale had ruined several spar mates and demanded larger men who could absorb his heavy artillery. Zale's brain trust decided to decamp to Rocky's home away from home—Stillman's Gym in Manhattan. Zale demanded a hotel room close to Central Park for his predawn road work.[20] Zale arrived in New York on May 27.[21]

Sharing the same gym heightened tensions between the principals. Zale rebuffed a request for photos of both combatants in the Stillman ring. He explained such chummy pictures might suggest the fight was not on the level.[22] Some scribes doubted Zale's explanation. His reputation was such that no one believed any of his fights were fixed.[23] Indeed, after he retired Zale claimed no one had ever approached him about fixing a fight.[24] The hoods knew what the answer would be.

Zale, sensing Graziano was on edge, appeared to be messing with the Rock's mind. He irritated Rocky by insisting that the heat—not Graziano—beat him in Chicago. Although at the time he appeared to be at death's door, Zale now claimed he was "thoroughly fresh" when the fight was stopped by a panicked referee at the "first sign of blood." When questioned about Zale's fanciful account, Rocky replied incredulously: "Did you see the fight?" Zale prodded further by predicting he would KO Graziano in Newark within three rounds. This triggered Graziano: "Zale is trying to pull psychology stuff on me.... I had my head examined once and it's much thicker than the average one. A hammer could bounce off without making a hole ... no kind of psychology stuff is strong enough to give the business to my mind and help make my body a punching bag for anybody.... Zale better know this now. What he is trying to do won't work on me."[25] Zale graciously left Stillman's and moved his training sessions to a Catholic Youth Organization (CYO) gym located at 333 West 17th Street.* Zale would be associated with the CYO for the remainder of his life.

One week before the fight, Zale and Graziano made a trip across the Hudson River for their prefight physicals. Dr. Max E. Stern's office was on Milford Avenue in Newark. The doctor was an old timer and had been on the staff of the state boxing commission for over twenty years. Among the fighters examined by Dr. Stern was Louis "The Wild Bull of

---

*The Rock's insistence that he was too thick-headed to be psyched out reminds one of Bob Foster's prediction that Muhammad Ali could never psych Smokin' Joe Frazier because Joe supposedly did "not have enough sense to be psyched out." After Frazier crushed Foster with a vicious left hook (Foster's leg broke in his rapid fall to the canvas), Joe dryly observed that Foster "ain't so smart. He fought me didn't he?"

10. Racing Head-On into the Night

the Pampas" Firpo, the man who had driven Jack Dempsey through the ropes as immortalized in George Bellows' famous painting.[26]

To ensure order, Captain Gene O'Malley of the Sixth Precinct—who had earned the moniker "Smash" as a patrolman—was on hand with a battery of uniformed police officers. Rocky arrived first, driving up in his new Nile-green-colored car. Graziano parked close to a fire hydrant, but the captain gave him a pass with an authoritative nod.[27] A buzz started building and a crowd gathered, gaping at the Man of Steel when he made his appearance.[28] By the time they exited Dr. Stern's office, both fighters were met with cheers from a raucous mob.[29]

Dr. Stern found both men in excellent shape. He was particularly impressed with the Rock, who the physician proclaimed to be the finest specimen he had ever examined in his twenty-eight years as a doctor. "They're ready to go into the ring now."[30] The press in attendance noted Graziano's restless energy: "bounding in and out of seats," "conversational rambles," wisecracking, and "mischievous smiles." Zale was being Zale: "calm, but deadly serious."[31]

Boxing Commissioner Abe Greene used the occasion to set forth ground rules for the bout. Eight-ounce boxing gloves would be used, heavier than the two prior fights in New York (six ounces) and Chicago (five ounces). New Jersey was following many other states in increasing the cushioning as a result of a spate of ring deaths (described as "ring accidents"[32]). The most infamous ring fatality at the time was twenty-three-year-old Jimmy Doyle's death at the hands of Sugar Ray Robinson. That fight took place in Cleveland, Ohio, because Doyle had suffered severe knockout losses (including once being removed from the

A wary Rock is examined by Dr. Max Stern as Zale observes (AP Photo).

ring on a stretcher), prompting his native California to revoke Doyle's license for his own protection. Robinson was threatened with criminal prosecution. At an inquest, Robinson was asked if it had been his intention to get Doyle "in trouble." "Mister," Robinson replied, "it's my business to get him trouble." Robinson was not charged.

In the ensuing storm of negative publicity, the *Ring*, in the business of promoting the sport, bristled at criticism of boxing by "holier-than-thou" "do gooders." The *Ring* argued the number of deaths in boxing was "practically negligible" considering the number of bouts held annually.[33] Undeterred by the carnage, Rocky's camp objected to the extra padding and advocated for six-ounce gloves. Graziano's managers thought the two extra ounces might permit Zale to survive Graziano's headhunting, whereas the padding would make no difference to the impact of Zale's debilitating body shots. Greene ruled that the eight-ounce gloves would be used. Another recently implemented safety measure, the standing eight count, was waived by both fighters as the rule would only become mandatory in Jersey on July 1, 1948.[34]

New Jersey's unique scoring system generated much comment, especially because the referee was also the only judge. Scoring was on a round-by-round basis, not points. If the rounds were even (e.g., five rounds each in a ten-round fight), the referee could consider the margin within the rounds.[35] Given the extraordinary power of the referee, it was particularly important that the third man in the ring be highly competent and incorruptible. As a way of reducing the risk of bribery, Greene said he would select the referee from a slate of five candidates, but not name him until ten minutes before the fight.[36] Greene went into great detail about how the referee was to address cuts. The ref was required to consult with the attending physician before stopping the fight. The ref would also be directed to ignore the tradition of stopping the fight upon a cornerman throwing in the towel (gamblers were apt to throw in towels to sow chaos and salvage bets).

For his part, Rocky thought the detailed discussion about the procedure, especially the scoring system, was absurd. "You know Zale. And you know me. Heck, we go in there to bat each other's brains out and the quicker the better. One of us will be carried out of there fast." The Rock may not have agreed with the odds that made him a heavy betting favorite (trending at twelve-to-five), but he was in complete accord with the eight-to-one odds holding the fight would not go the championship distance of fifteen rounds.[37] Given the styles of the two fighters—reckless aggression with defense as an afterthought—and the

10. Racing Head-On into the Night

concentrated violence of the first two fights, no one thought the fight would go the limit. In view of Zale's age and his meltdown in Chicago, the conventional wisdom was that Zale had to take out Graziano early. Al Del Greco of Bergen County's paper the *Record* reported that Zale was training for nothing more than a three-round fight.[38] And indeed, Zale had privately told his trainer Ray Arcel that "I have to finish this early."[39]

The undercard would consist of six bouts of either four or six rounds. The names of these men are largely unrecognizable today, but the record reflects unmistakable quality. Bernie Dowd of Livingston was a lightweight who was to square off with Johnny "Red" DeFazio of Jersey City, a member of New Jersey's Boxing Hall of Fame. Ross Anzalone of New York was scheduled to face Andy De Paul, a Cliffside welterweight who closed his career with a 28–8 record. And welterweight Gene Salisbury of Jersey City (22–5 career record) was scheduled take on Newark's Cliff Stevens (14–3 career record). The semifinal matched Charley Zack of Scranton, Pennsylvania (33–2–1), against Navy vet and all-service middleweight champion Billy Kilroy, career record 33–8 with 21 KOs to his credit. The first preliminary bout would go off at 7:30 p.m., with Zale vs. Graziano scheduled to commence at 10:00 p.m.

But no one was buying tickets to see the undercard. The main event was the attraction. Everyone was familiar with what happened in their first two fights. Everyone knew both men came to scrap, not pussyfoot around. There would be no "feeling out," that early phase of most bouts where fighters take the measure of their opponent. Plus, both men had plenty of motivation. For Zale, victory would secure his place in Boxing's Hall of Fame and another lucrative payday. A loss would mean probable retirement and the end of the thing that occupied almost all of his time and mental energy. For Rocky, a win would, finally, complete his journey to redemption ("I realize that I'm like on trial in this fight"[40]), prove his superiority over the highly respected ex-champ, and probably be a springboard into a glorious championship run. A loss could very well mean a one-way ticket back to Palookaville.

The stakes were no mystery to the rivals. In the week leading up to the fight, both men offered a daily byline exclusive to the *Newark Star Ledger*. Rocky used his first article to note his extensive fight history in New Jersey. He expressed thanks for his early ring education in Newark, Jersey City, Elizabeth, and New Brunswick. With mordant humor, Graziano recalled those fights for their $50 purses, of which he would receive $5 after the "cuts" for the promoter, attending physician, management, etc. Despite the lack of scratch, Graziano noted with undisguised pride that he was undefeated in eight fights in Jersey.[41]

For his part, Zale directly addressed the elephant in the room: his age. "If they think I am too old, they will be surprised." He was no "old gaffer kidding himself. ... I have lived a clean life; I have never been wasteful with any of my physical resources."[42] Revealing, however, was Zale's white lie about his age: he claimed to be thirty-four years old when he was actually thirty-five. Zale's management and the promoter were undoubtedly pleased with the fiction. The Zale camp also kept mum on Zale's damaged left elbow. For years Zale had suffered from bone chips floating in the hinge of his left arm. His trainer Ray Arcel stayed up nights massaging and applying heat to Zale's elbow.[43]

In a further attempt to put the age issue behind him, Zale projected a cool confidence: "I'm in great shape. My legs, wind and speed are on a keen edge. It's just a matter now of keeping that edge."[44] Zale attributed his longevity to his clean living ("Smoking, drinking and night life never did any fighter any good."). The Man of Steel offered young fighters the same advice he would give decades later to his magnificent successor, Newark-born Marvin Hagler*: "Always keep in perfect condition."[45] On June 5, Zale conducted his last heavy workout, sparring three rounds with Rodger Whynott, shadowboxing, hitting the speed bag, and doing calisthenics. Zale planned on checking out Ruppert Stadium by attending the Newark Bears game the following day.[46]

The champ also claimed to be in peak condition. "I'm in the best shape of my career; was never better for any fight."[47] The Rock's estimate of his condition was based on feel, as he acknowledged not being a scientific fighter.[48] Graziano sensed he was over the rust from his enforced inactivity, and he was ready "to swap punches with Tony until I flatten him. I'm not going to start retreating at this rather late point in my career."[49] Rocky understood Zale's best chance was for any early knockout, but argued Zale "won't get that chance. I'll take the pace away from him; I'll do the early fighting, and if he slugs with me so much better. I'm younger and more rugged and I can last longer."[50] The champ had learned from Zale in their first fight to "never stop throwing rocks."[51] On June 4, Graziano held a spirited sparring session with Dick Wagner, a good light heavyweight. The Rock battered his mate relentlessly through three rounds and had the larger man bleeding profusely by the

---

*Zale, who tended to be miserly with praise of the boxers who came after his era, was a big Hagler fan. He must have sensed a kinship with "the Marvelous one," appreciating Hagler's monk-like conditioning regiment and seek-and-destroy mentality in the ring.

10. Racing Head-On into the Night

end of the session.[52] By June 6, three days before the fight, Rocky was done with serious training and engaging only in "light exercising."[53] That same day, Zale ran five miles in Central Park and then attended a Bears doubleheader at Ruppert where he was introduced to the crowd.[54]

On the eve of the fight, Zale disputed claims that Graziano was a dirty fighter. Anyway, he knew how to deal with cheap shots. Zale's real concern was about the referee stopping the fight "too soon." Of course, what Zale considered "too soon" was different than most. Zale, who refereed fights after he retired from fighting, felt some refs "are easily moved by a show of blood or a knockdown"[55] (one can only imagine how the boxers felt about Zale being responsible for their safety when he was the third man in the ring). Again, Zale argued he was not too old ("I've come to full maturity in my life."). He planned on winning the fight and continuing boxing for another three or four years.[56] Graziano, perhaps playing his own head game, chose this time to raise the age issue. The six years' difference in their ages, plus the two previous brawls, "would be a big handicap against Zale. How long can a guy go on?" asked the Rock. "I'm gonna win. I don't predict no round. I'm gonna try to knock him out early."[57] Even if Zale floored him early (as he had in the first two fights), the champ figured "I can outlast him."[58]

The logistics for the fight started coming together in earnest. The city installed traffic controls around Ruppert Stadium and set down strict rules on parking. Directional signs were set up on the Pulaski Skyway in anticipation of fans coming over from Jersey City and New York (on the Newark side, the Pulaski connected with Routes 1 and 9, which afforded easy access to the ballpark on Wilson Avenue). Bus companies arranged pickups at the Port Authority in New York. Newarkers were instructed to take buses from the Essex County Courthouse. Two hundred patrolmen were assigned to keep order.[59] Forty detectives were assigned, primarily to keep an eye out for pickpockets.[60] Newark Fire Chief Burnett had fifty of his men on call in the event that the maze of electric wires covering the stadium, or careless smokers, sparked a blaze.[61]

The ring was constructed over the pitcher's mound at Ruppert Stadium. The ring itself was from the Newark Armory, which hosted Golden Glove matches.[62] Once constructed, it was clear that the ring did not meet the regulation twenty feet square (ultimately measured at eighteen feet).[63] The smaller surface was thought to favor Zale as his aged legs were not suited to chasing. Both men probably would have preferred fighting in a phone booth.

Seating was expanded to more than double the usual capacity

of fourteen thousand.[64] Sixteen thousand chairs were set up on the field.[65] The record attendance at Ruppert was twenty-three thousand for a Bears game in 1938. That figure was expected to be surpassed. The record attendance for a fight in Newark was twenty thousand, drawn to Wiedenmayer's Park stadium in 1918 on the lot next to Ruppert to watch Benny "The Ghetto Wizard" Leonard take on Ted "Kid" Lewis.

Promoters reported an advance gate of $268,000, more than enough to cover their fixed expenses. They expected a final gate of between $350,000 and $400,000, which would triple the record for a Newark match (in 1920 the heavyweights Harry Wills and Fred Fulton pulled a gate of $103,000 at the Sussex Avenue Armory).[66] Concessions had one hundred thousand bottles of beer ready to slake the thirst of fans. The thirty thousand hot dogs were probably an afterthought.[67]

One big question about the fight promotion remained open: would the fight be televised? The promoter TOC claimed that it had been offered $75,000 for television rights but had turned it down.[68] Although the promoter attributed its decision to high-minded principle (televising the fight would "betray" the spectators who bought tickets[69]), the real reason for the blackout was concern that television might suppress the live gate.[70] TOC President Ben B. Bodne announced "no one will be able to sit in a bar room and view this fight."[71] Newspaper advertisements promoting the fight were unambiguous: "POSITIVELY NO TELEVISION."[72] The promoter was particularly concerned about New Yorkers not traveling across the Hudson if they could watch the fight in a neighborhood bar.[73]

But doubt lingered about the sincerity of TOC's representations. Boxing promoters were known to hedge their bets by denying fights would be broadcast only to then put the match out over the airwaves—in exchange for a fee, of course. Word got out that Dumont Television Studios had wired Ruppert to telecast the fight. Television equipment in that era weighed a ton, and no one would lug it around for no reason.[74] Newark taverns were advertising that the fight would be broadcast. Salesmen for Ballantine Ale, brewed in Newark, were going around assuring pub owners that Ballantine had offered $100,000 for television broadcast rights. Although Ballantine's public relations department denied any such thing, Dumont and New Jersey Bell Telephone Company, whose wires would be used to broadcast the fight, were sending conflicting messages.[75] Pub owners laid odds the fight would be televised, and many displayed posters advertising the fight with Ballantine

10. Racing Head-On into the Night

as the sponsor.[76] TOC did receive $25,000 for granting rights to RKO Productions to film the fight. A platform was constructed down the first base line to support seven motion picture cameras.[77] Proper lighting required installation of twenty-six diffractors, which made the ring a "blaze of illumination" when darkness fell, "like a Hollywood set."[78] Alas, Zale Graziano III would be the only match of the famous trilogy to be captured on film. To this day, you can find 8 and 16 mm prints of the fight on eBay.

In any event, in 1948 radio still ruled the broadcast world. The Mutual Network had broadcast rights. New York Yankee announcers Mel Allen and Russ Hodges would call the blow-by-blow action, which would be broadcast to 450 stations around the country. Western Union would have forty operators at ringside sending dispatches to newspapers around the world. Four hundred press passes had been issued to reporters from every state, plus Hawaii, Canada, England, France, and Australia.[79]

As the eyes of the sporting world turned to Newark, local newspapers continued to run stories about the sensational Powers/Rowe shooting. Other stories appeared—some of historic significance and others fleeting—that give a window into the times:

- The Soviets cut off access to Berlin in an effort to squeeze out the Western allies. This precipitated the first major showdown of the Cold War. President Truman reacted to the Reds' aggression by ordering the Berlin Airlift.
- On May 22, 1948, a charter fishing boat capsized two miles off the Manasquan Inlet at the Jersey Shore. Two men drowned while the survivors clung to the hull. The Coast Guard was investigating whether overcrowding was the cause.[80]
- On May 25, 1948, Harold Adamson, a member of the American Legion, was found dead—his skull crushed—in a hotel room in Long Branch. The door of his room was locked from the inside. The outspoken anti-communist had a history of heavy drinking and violence.
- On May 29, 1948, Warden Joseph W. Buckley of the Hudson County Penitentiary was indicted along with several subordinates for grift and harsh treatment of prisoners. Buckley was accused of, among other things, stealing food, gasoline, and building supplies, and forcing prisoners to paint his Belmar summer home.[81]

Brick City Grudge Match

- On May 30, 1948, famous baritone singer and former Rutgers gridiron star Paul Robson refused to disclose to a congressional committee whether he was a communist.[82] Two days later, Robson picketed outside the White House against the Mundt–Nixon bill (named for future president Richard M. Nixon, the bill sought to compel Communist Party members to register with the government).[83]
- On June 3, 1948, Newark Police censors banned the showing of the French film *Passionelle*, and its cofeature, *Torment*, for being "too risqué." Advertisements had promised exploration of "forbidden themes."[84]
- On June 4, 1948, President Truman kicked off his underdog campaign for the presidency in Tony Zale's hometown of Gary, Indiana.[85]
- On June 7, 1948, the U.S. Senate passed a law outlawing poll taxes for veterans (the poll tax had been deployed in the South since Reconstruction for the purpose of disenfranchising black voters). Thirty-four Republicans, plus three northern Democrats, broke the filibuster and overcame the opposition of the Dixiecrat wing of the Democratic Party to pass the law. The remaining slate of civil rights legislation went down to defeat.[86]
- On June 8, 1948, Dr. Neil S. McLeed of Highland Park blew his brains out with a .32-caliber revolver. The physician was scheduled to be sentenced on his conviction for providing abortions.[87]
- Union buster and alleged Murder, Inc. button man Albert "Mad Hatter" Anastasia, who had beaten a rap for assault and battery a year prior, pled guilty to tax evasion at the Federal Courthouse in Newark.
- Joyce Eigner, a Woodridge High School majorette, was barred from participating the Memorial Day parade for wearing shorts.[88]
- An article in the *Newark Star Ledger* bemoaned the failure of urban renewal in Hoboken where "broken down tenements" still lined the streets.[89]

While the boxing world was focusing on Newark, the other middleweight contenders jockeyed for position. Jake LaMotta, in his first fight after his suspension arising out of the Billy Fox fix, knocked out Ken Stribling in the fifth round at Griffith Stadium in Washington. The

10. Racing Head-On into the Night

Bronx Bull apparently still had some work left to regain the trust of fight fans: his Stribling fight drew a measly gate of $13,626.[90] From the other side of the Atlantic, European middleweight champion Marcel Cerdan was upset by lightly regarded Cyrille Delannoit in a controversial decision. The loss appeared to end Cerdan's prospects for getting a crack at the winner of the Graziano Zale fight. In Hamburg, Germany, a name from the past resurfaced: former heavyweight champion Max Schmeling, then forty-two years old, lost a decision to thirty-nine-year-old Walter Neusel—a man Schmeling had beaten thirteen years prior. Observers described the geriatric bout "listless" and "studded with clinches."[91] In his autobiography, Schmeling admitted to being washed up and the fight an embarrassment, but, in the timeless lament of many old fighters, he needed the money.[92]

Outside the boxing scene, the sports world hummed along. Most important to Newarkers, the Bears sat atop the International League standings. The Jersey City Giants trailed in fourth place. The Eagles, in what would turn out to be the final season of the Negro leagues, had regressed from their 1946 championship to a .500 ball club. In the majors, the Yanks trailed the Cleveland Indians, despite the Bombers having beaten Rapid Robert Feller before 78,431 fans in the front end of a Memorial Day doubleheader.[93] In a Senators-Athletics game in D.C., a riot erupted when an umpire inadvertently deflected a ball thrown in for the decisive ninth-inning play at the plate. Enraged Senators fans hurled bottles, beers cans, and a dismantled seat at the ump, who was escorted off the field by police.[94] In golf, Ben Hogan was picked as the favorite to win the U.S. Open at the Riviera Country Club in Los Angeles.[95] Rutgers football coach Harvey Harman predicted an improved squad for the 1948 fall season.[96]

When the sun rose on the day of the fight, Wednesday, June 9, the predetermined schedule provided for the fighters to appear at noon for the weigh-in at Newark's beautiful City Hall. The weigh-in would go on as scheduled, but the major variable for any outdoor boxing match—the weather—threatened to put a damper on the ceremonies. Heavy rain was predicted for the afternoon and evening.

Tony Zale was the first of the principals to show up at City Hall. The ex-champ, sharply dressed in a tan suit, briskly strode up the imposing steps. Rocky then appeared, like he had just rolled out of bed, dressed in a cream-colored jacket with no tie and uncombed hair.[97] Graziano announced that he was staying at the Robert Treat Hotel in Newark. Zale declined to reveal where he was staying because he did not want to

Brick City Grudge Match

be bothered.[98] Zale's lodgings were said to be "close" to where the Rock was crashing.[99]

Newark Mayor Vincent J. Murphy, Newark Director of Public Safety John B. Keenan, and New Jersey Boxing Commissioner Abe Greene greeted the fighters. Rocky, chomping gum, wisecracked with His Honor the Mayor. Like everyone else, Mayor Murphy was charmed by the champ.[100] The fighters were presented with their boxing shorts (Graziano, black with a red stripe; Zale, purple). Both men were then presented with a choice of several pair of eight-ounce boxing gloves. Graziano, who had been laughing and joking, suddenly turned sour. He was still upset about Jersey's newly adopted rule requiring the eight-ounce mitts, as the champ preferred the six ouncers stipulated in New York. The Rock finally settled on a pair ("the best of a bad lot"), but he griped about "too much stuffing in the knuckles, the part you hit with ... but what the heck, I'll flatten Zale anyway."[101] "I'll get it over quick. May be in the foist round."[102] It was announced that the *Ring*'s Nat Fleischer would serve as knockdown timekeeper at ringside.[103]

The weigh-in was scheduled to take place in the commission counsel chamber. The chamber was large enough to handle the throng of reporters and photographers on hand for the elaborate ceremony. It also seemed an apt forum given the verbal jousting and political back-and-forth that made the daily work product of the city government.[104]

When it came time

Graziano and Zale assume a fighting pose for photographers after weigh-in at Newark City Hall (AP Photo/John Rooney).

10. Racing Head-On into the Night

for the weigh-in, the fighters left the chamber to strip down. Director Keenan noted the number of women in the gallery of the commission chamber. He banged his gavel and pronounced that the fighters were about to be weighed. The ladies did not get the hint, so Keenan explicitly stated the fighters may have get totally nude to make the weight. The female contingent then filed out.[105]

As it turned out, neither man had to go buck naked to make the weight. Zale, the challenger, weighed in first and tipped the scales at 158.75 pounds, one and a quarter pound under the middleweight division limit. Rocky weighed in at 158.5 pounds, the heaviest of his career.[106] Otherwise, the tale of the tape reflected the two men were remarkably close in physical dimensions: height (identical, 5'8.5"); reach (Zale 69 inches; Rock 68.5 inches); and fists (identical circumference, 9 inches).[107] The big difference between the two could not be measured by a scale: their relative ages.

The boxing scribes offered their impressions of the fighters' condition as revealed by their stripped-down appearances. Frank Casale of the *Newark Star Ledger* thought Graziano "was pasty and his jowls had a flabby hang," with "ugly blemishes on his back." Zale, in contrast, appeared "physically superior, with eyes and skin clear." Casale's fellow *Ledger* writer, Anthony Marenghi, thought Graziano looked just fine but opined that Zale appeared "a trifle overdrawn and taut."[108] Willie Ratner of the *Newark Evening News* agreed with Marenghi and thought Zale's face appeared "grim and drawn."[109] Dr. Max Stern, who had examined both men a week prior, maintained his opinion that both men were "in perfect condition," but added that Zale was "phlegmatic," while the Rock was "sharper, friendlier."[110]

For his part, Zale was not buying Graziano's jocular façade. He sensed the champ was "nervous as a cat."[111]

The elaborate ceremony amounted to a taxing workout for the principals with endless small talk, glad-handing, and backslapping. The fighters were hounded by photographers. Graziano estimated he posed for over one hundred photographs.[112] Both men were seasoned professionals and understood their obligation to promote the fight, but they did not have to like it.

The weather was not cooperating. Rain started coming down in buckets, thunder boomed ominously, and lightning zigzagged across the sky. At 3:15 p.m., the fight was postponed until the following day, June 10. It was decided no second weigh-in would be required.[113] Mayor Murphy, who had a previous commitment he could not get out of (i.e., attending commencement exercises at the Newark College of Engineering [now NJIT]), was one of the few people pleased with the postponement.[114] Hotel owners in the Big Apple were also pleased as out-of-towners attending the fight would be forced to lodge for another night.[115]

The fighters approached the layover differently. Zale went to his undisclosed location and skipped rope and shadowboxed.[116] Then he played gin rummy with his manager. Rocky, strung out from the weigh-in hoopla, returned to the Robert Treat Hotel, ate a steak, and tried to rest. Unfortunately, he was being hounded by his neighborhood buddies and other acquaintances for tickets. "The phone has been ringing ever since I checked into this joint. I need rest and quiet and I can't get it here." Oddly, Graziano complained that his location was supposed to be secret even though he had told the press about his lodgings, had his picture taken outside the hotel entrance, and even invited reporters to his room. In any event, the champ had enough of the racket and decamped to an unnamed "flea-bag" motel, informing his managers he would see them at Ruppert Stadium the following night.[117]

Rocky examining rainy skies after the fight was postponed on June 9, 1948 (Acme Telephoto; author's collection).

The extra day meant another installment in the boxers' daily bylines.

10. Racing Head-On into the Night

Zale expressed his disagreement with those observers (like the *Ledger*'s Marenghi), who thought Zale should use the extra day, and the waiver of another weigh-in, to put on some pounds. The ex-champ considered that approach foolhardy. Adding weight might slow him down, and Zale expected "to use speed to win this fight and title—speed to duck his punches and get inside" of Graziano's punches. "A little thing like stepping inside a punch and hooking to the body can win or lose a fight." Ringside observers might miss it because it could "happen in the hundredth of a second."[118] One midwestern writer felt the delay favored Graziano because he was too stupid to be bothered by such things ("scarcely [having] any mentality at all").[119]

Rocky expressed bursting confidence. The champ said he was "keen as ever," and "strong as a bull." The Rock planned to "knock Zale bow-legged with my first punch ... flatten Zale in one of the early rounds."[120] The boxing press were virtually unanimous in their endorsement of the Rock's assessment. In addition to having the edge in youth, the scribes also gave the Rock an edge in the power of his punch and motivation: a "fierce desire for vindication and reinstatement." Zale was given the edge in "smartness" (i.e., ring savvy) and conditioning, but he was considered too old. The nation's sports editors were polled by the Associated Press, and the Rock got the nod from 221 of 262 scribes—a 5–1 edge.[121] Even Indiana reporters gave Zale little chance ("[E]verything is in Graziano's favor.").[122]

The Jersey sportswriters were in accord. Sid Dorfman, in his "Expert View" column, thought Zale was deluding himself by thinking he could compete with the champ: "clinging to the slender threads of passing time."[123] Worse, Dorfman suggested Zale was suffering from Low T. Graziano was part of a younger and more "virile crop."[124] Anthony Marenghi picked Graziano by knockout within eight rounds, doubting Zale had the durability to pull off the upset. Marenghi also noted that Zale was virtually the only fighter knocked out by Rocky whose career was not ruined by the experience.[125] Frank Casale chose not to believe his own eyes from the weigh-in where he perceived Zale to be the finer specimen and picked the champ by KO within ten rounds. Like the others, Casale cited the age difference as the decisive factor.[126] Willie Ratner of the *Newark Evening News* noted the age difference, Zale's meltdown in Chicago, and Graziano's incentive to win the fight— it would "re-establish" Graziano with a bright future before him. Ratner picked "da Rock."[127] Al Del Greco of the *Record* in Bergen County picked Graziano by a KO in four.[128] Not all of Greco's readers agreed: one man

Brick City Grudge Match

Pulaski Skyway, late 1940s (photograph by Marion Post Wolcott; Library of Congress).

called Greco and boldly predicted "[t]hat Polack is gonna knock that Wop right into your lap with a punch in the belly."[129] Jimmy Powers of the *Daily News* thought Zale had lost his ability to absorb punishment, and he predicted Graziano would "fell Zale in Newark."[130] The only local sportswriter of any prominence to pick Zale was Hy Goldberg of the *Newark Evening News*. Goldberg opined that in the second fight Zale was done in by the heat of Chicago Stadium. Ruppert Stadium, in contrast, was outdoors, and the temperature was projected to be moderate at fight time.[131] Still, the bookies set the odds at almost three-to-one (thirteen-to-five) that Graziano would vanquish the ex-champion.

By the afternoon of June 10, the dark clouds were clearing over the Jersey meadowlands. The promoter made the decision to go ahead with the fight. Word spread throughout Newark and across the Hudson River to Gotham. Ruppert Stadium opened its gate at 7:00 p.m.[132] Thousands of fight fans began making their way to the Bears' home park. A line of headlights from the massive automobiles of the time could be seen heading west over the Pulaski Skyway. Those big old dinosaurs were carrying muckety-mucks from the Big Apple. Scads of fans were being disgorged at Newark's Penn Station. Buses from Penn Station and Broad

10. Racing Head-On into the Night

and Market streets quickly became overloaded, and many fans choose to walk to Ruppert Stadium—a test of "pedestrian courage, stamina and patience."[133] They came for the "unexcelled magnitude of this Newark sporting event."[134]

Once again New Jersey would be center of the boxing universe.

11

Newark Grudge Match
(Zale Graziano III— Ruppert Stadium, June 10, 1948)

Paul Cavaliere sat in the dressing room that he shared with Rocky Graziano in the bowels of Ruppert Stadium. Cavaliere had read the newspaper reports indicating he was one of several candidates under consideration to referee Zale Graziano III. In Jersey the boxing referee was the sole arbiter: the only judge in the event the fight went the distance and required a decision. But Cavaliere was not anxious because he already knew he would receive the assignment. He was tight with Abe Greene, the former boxing commissioner for New Jersey and the man most responsible for resurrecting Graziano's career and bringing the big fight to the Garden State. Indeed, Cavaliere was the deputy boxing commissioner. Cavaliere's son, Paul Jr., called Greene "Uncle Abe."[1]

The modest pay Cavaliere would receive for the work was appreciated, but he probably would have performed the service for nothing. Zale Graziano III would be the biggest fight Cavaliere would ever work as a referee. The whole sporting world was watching.

Serving as a boxing referee was one of three careers for Cavaliere. He started out as a professional prizefighter himself, and a damn good one at that. For most of his boxing career Cavaliere campaigned as a heavyweight. He fought from 1922 to 1936 with a slate of 111 wins in 115 bouts.[2] He defeated Jimmy Braddock, "The Cinderella Man," who would go on to win the world heavyweight title in a stunning upset over Max Bear. Braddock was undefeated when beaten by Cavaliere, working on a string of twenty-one consecutive knockout victories. Cavaliere would go on to take a decision over "Two Ton" Tony Galento to win the New Jersey state heavyweight title—at the time a big deal.* Cavaliere

---

*Years later, Two Ton admitted to Cavaliere's son that his father's defensive prowess was such that Galento "could not hit him in the ass." Interview with Paul Cavaliere, Jr., 8/27/21.

11. Newark Grudge Match

was never knocked out and was only floored twice in his career. He got off the floor to win both of those bouts.[3] He was inducted into the New Jersey Boxing Hall of Fame in 1971.

The truth is that Cavaliere was one of those fighters who was too good for his own good. Other boxers avoided him be because he was a master boxer and defensive specialist. Gene Tunney was quoted as describing Cavaliere as the "cleverest heavyweight in the world."[4] Potential opponents saw little reason to get their ears boxed off by Cavaliere and get paid peanuts for the privilege.

With few fights available and in the depths of the Great Depression, Cavaliere secured work as a sparring partner. He trained seven world champions, including heavyweight champs Gene Tunney, Jack Sharkey, and Max Bear; and light heavyweight champ Jack Delaney. After Max Schmeling, in a shocking upset, cut down a young Joe Louis, the Brown Bomber's management brought in Cavaliere to teach Joe how to block Schmeling's devastating straight right-hand punch ("der schläger"). He sparred over one hundred rounds with Louis while the champ was in his prime. Louis never floored Cavaliere, despite Louis's reputation for not holding back on his sparring partners.* Cavaliere lost his gig with Louis after he had the temerity to approach Mike Jacobs and ask for the opportunity to challenge Louis in a real bout for the title.[5]

Cavaliere secured a job as a truancy officer for the Paterson Board of Education. But he missed the ring. Cavaliere told his friend New Jersey Boxing Commissioner Abe Greene about his desire to become a referee. Greene loved the idea. Cavaliere would go on to become Jersey's top "third man in the ring." He refereed hundreds of main events. Cavaliere developed a reputation for competence and incorruptibility that earned respect. His integrity also generated hatred from the more undesirable elements in the game. An imposing man with a scared and pockmarked face, Cavaliere told the hoods where to go when they tried to bribe him. An example of his integrity was when he awarded a decision to an opponent of a fighter managed by Jack Dempsey. The Manassa Mauler was in attendance at Newark's Laurel Garden when Cavaliere handed down the unpopular verdict. Dempsey accepted the call and offered nary a word a criticism. Another tough decision had Cavaliere

---

*Interestingly, Cavaliere's son, Paul Jr., recounts that his father thought Max Bear had a bigger punch than Louis. He also considered Jack Sharkey a more clever fighter than Gene Tunney. Tunney, however, had the mentally fragile Sharkey by a mile on the virtues of focus and discipline. Interview with Paul Cavaliere, Jr., 8/27/21.

threatened by the manager of a mobbed-up fighter. Cavaliere subsequently received a call from the fighter's Jersey-based Godfather who profusely apologized to Cavaliere ("I want you to know you are a fair guy. We are very glad when you referee our fights."). On another occasion, Cavaliere selected as the victor the opponent of a fighter controlled by the notorious Frankie Carbo, a.k.a. "Mr. Gray." Carbo, in a sign of respect, told Cavaliere after the fight, "That was a good call, Paul."[6]

As Cavaliere waited in the dressing room, spectators settled into their seats. Boxing royalty was well represented at ringside. Jack Dempsey was seated next to Abe Greene. Dempsey's great rival Gene Tunney, who spent much time after his boxing career serving on corporate boards, was seated next to retail magnate Bernard Gimbel, president of Gimbels Department Store in New York.[7] Top contenders Jake LaMotta, Sugar Ray Robinson, and Charley Fusari were in attendance. Other champions and contenders were there, including future heavyweight champ Ezzard Charles, light heavyweight champs Gus Lesnevitch and Melio Bettina (the man who pummeled Zale as an amateur), and former champs Barney Ross and Billy Soose. Mike Jacobs, although in ill health, made his way up from his Rumson mansion. When Joe DiMaggio appeared at ringside he was rushed by autograph seekers.[8] Political and industrial leaders crowded in. New York City Mayor Bill O'Dwyer made the trip across the Hudson. Another ringside spectator was Paul Cavaliere, Jr., the referee's son, an eighteen year old who graduated from St. Peter's Prep in Jersey City the previous day.[9]

Not for the first or last time, visitors from the Big Apple and the rest of the country were not shy about showing their disdain for New Jersey. The *Ring* derisively referred to the Garden State as the "Skeeter State." Newark was said to be "soot-stained."[10] While some considered Ruppert the finest minor league stadium in the country, the grandees at the *New York Times* labeled the place "a dull, dump and discouraging setting." It was "bewildering," sniffed *Times* writer Arthur Daley, "that this most attractive brawl which should have been staged in a New York ball park, is shunted off to the wilds of Newark."[11] Jim Ward from Michigan's *Escanaba Press* ridiculed "Joisey" accents.[12] The *Tampa Times* described Ruppert as a "hiding" place for a fight, not even "accessible to residents of midtown Newark."[13] Even Rocky, while expressing gratitude to Jersey for allowing him to make a living, felt the magnitude of the event deserved a grander stage. It was, according to the parochial Rock, like fighting "in some back alley."[14] Things were not helped when a foul smell—like a "dead rat"—wafted over the stadium shortly before

11. Newark Grudge Match

the main event. Someone did not get the memo about the big fight and was burning piles of garbage over the outfield wall.[15] Ruppert Stadium was constructed next door to a garbage dump, and it was not uncommon for events there to be delayed by foul odors.[16]

At 9:50 p.m. referee Cavaliere checked his appearance in the mirror, straightened his bow tie, and headed toward the ring.

The preliminary fighters kept things on schedule. Paterson's Billy Kilroy (real name Ramoth), a Navy vet and all-service middleweight champion, knocked out Charlie Zack at 9:57 p.m. Kilroy and Zack would fight two months later in Pennsylvania with Zack suffering a cerebral hemorrhage. Zack was paralyzed and never fought again (Zack retired with a record of thirty-four wins versus only four losses).[17] Kilroy went on to become a movie stuntman. In any event, the timing of Kilroy's Newark knockout was convenient because the main event was scheduled to go on at 10:00 p.m.

Graziano was the first of the combatants to appear, emerging from the visitor's dugout. He was dressed in a green sweater over a white robe. Contrary to protocol, Rocky entered the ring first. Zale entered the ring seconds later, wearing a pair of trousers under his white robe.[18] Both fighters received a rousing reception from the crowd, but the Rock's support seemed louder. Referee Paul Cavaliere entered the brightly illuminated square moments later.

The fighters had to endure an elaborate and lengthy prefight ceremony. Joe Moran sang the Star Bangled Banner. Dapper Johnnie Addie, a.k.a. Giovanni Addonizio, was imported from Madison Square Garden to serve as master of ceremonies. Zale seemed to handle the agonizing delay better than Graziano, who shifted nervously.[19] Impatient by nature, the Rock understandably wanted to get on with it. The *Ring*'s Nat Fleischer, serving in an official capacity as knockdown timer, found Graziano's demeanor "cocky" during the introductions.[20]

After Addie covered the basics, including the fighters' weights, Cavaliere called the principals to the center of the ring and gave the men their instructions. Undoubtedly these two veterans knew the score. The fighters returned to their respective corners, removed their robes, and shadowboxed to keep warm as they awaited the bell for the first round.

The question of whether the fight would be televised was not resolved until the very last minute. Yankees announcer Mel Allen, handling the radio broadcast, stated at 7:15 p.m. that indeed the fight would not be broadcast over the new upstart medium. This should have been

Brick City Grudge Match

the end of it because Allen was expected to handle both the radio and the television broadcast. However, Newark taverns, seeking to draw and hold patrons at their watering holes, continued to insist the fight would be televised. In one downtown "television bar," the TV screen flashed that the feature "boxing match" was about to come on right at 10:00 p.m. Drunken cheers quickly turned to groans when a message from the New York State Boxing Commission appeared on the screen. Angry customers insisted the barkeep turn off the television and instead crank on the radio, full volume.[21] It was one of the first times in this era that a major bout was not televised.

Over at Ruppert, timekeeper Bill Buileck struck the bell and the fight began. Graziano and Zale approached each other in classic poses. Rocky circled to his left and pawed with a couple of nondescript lefts. Zale watched Graziano intently, waiting for an opening. It did not take long. Zale leapt into Graziano, firing lefts to the Rock's jaw and body followed by a two-fisted barrage as Graziano backed against the ropes. Rocky fought his way off the ropes as the two engaged at close quarters. Zale again leapt into Graziano but overshot a left hook. Zale's left hand and forearm were now wrapped around the Rock's neck. Zale grabbed and pinned down Rocky's left arm and, at close quarters, uncorked a nasty left uppercut that found the mark on Graziano's jaw. Rocky sagged.

Cavaliere separated the fighters and Graziano began backing off. Zale again jumped at Graziano and nailed Rocky with a perfect left hook high on Graziano's right cheek. Rocky crumbled in a heap barely one minute into the fight. Zale took a good look at Graziano as he lay prone on the canvas. "A sudden hush" overtook the crowd and then, "bedlam."[22] As Rocky "waivered under the glare of the lights," "a wild yelp came up" from the fans.[23] Graziano said the spectators at Ruppert Stadium were every bit as loud as at the first two fights.[24]

Graziano was up at the count of two or three but was not himself. He had a cut on his forehead near his right eye.[25] More troubling, Rocky was not fighting like Rocky. Sportswriter Red Smith of the *New York Times* was stunned by the Rock's uncharacteristic lack of aggression. Smith thought Graziano was foolishly trying to outbox Zale when slugging was all the Rock understood.[26] Far from confusing Zale with slickness and guile, Graziano reminded Smith of a lumbering water buffalo.[27] Jimmy Cannon agreed. He thought Graziano's pawing lefts were absurd and made the Rock look silly.[28] Rocky reminded Jimmy Powers of the *Daily News* of a confused drunk searching for something by

11. Newark Grudge Match

rummaging through a glove compartment.[29] Rocky's strategy appeared to be to hang on until Zale's thirty-five-year-old legs gave out.[30]

Frivolity had no place in a boxing ring with Tony Zale. He performed in a theater of pain, not at a comedy club. Zale was not amused by Rocky's poor imitation of a fancy dan boxer. And he was not about overthinking. Zale looked Graziano over and proceeded with "rapid and to the point" execution.[31] He unleashed the full arsenal on the Rock for the remainder of the first round. The ex-champ put on a body punching clinic, slamming a series of hard rights to Graziano's side and back. Zale later wrote Graziano's "face turned pale" while letting out audible groans.[32] Watching the film decades later, it still hurts to look at it. Graziano's "mouth was open and so was his defense."[33]

Things got worse for the Rock toward the end of the first round. With spectators screaming their heads off, the fighters and referee did not hear the bell ending the first round. Timekeeper Buileck said later that the throng of ringside photographers prevented him from giving the bell a good whack with his hammer. The fighters kept exchanging punches after the end of the round. Willie Ratner did not think the

Zale stands over a prostrate Graziano after a first-round knockdown as referee Cavaliere moves in. Ringside spectators erupt in bedlam (Anonymous/AP/Shutterstock).

Brick City Grudge Match

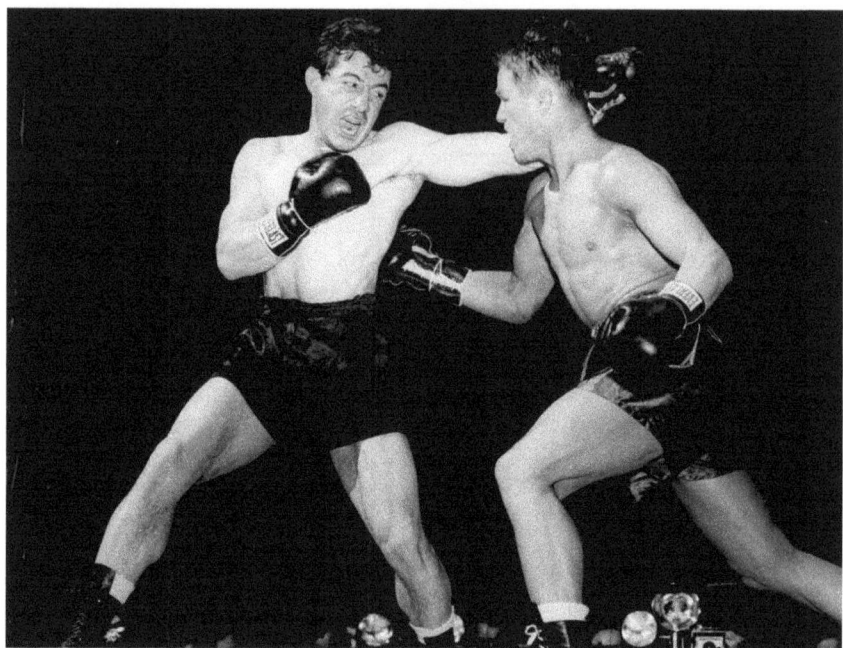

An aggressive Zale lands a body shot as Graziano misses with a left (AP Photo/File).

extracurricular activity amounted to much. But Nat Fleischer of the *Ring* disagreed. He timed eight full seconds of postbell fighting and counted several serious blows landed by Zale. One clout in particular—a "murderous right" under the Rock's heart—"undoubtedly played a part" in the ultimate outcome.[34] Anthony Marenghi counted "two solid blows" landed by Zale after the bell.[35] James Dawson of the *New York Times* felt Zale's extracurricular blows, especially "a crushing right to the heart," "unquestionably had an effect" on Graziano. The overtime fighting did not stop until Graziano's seconds jumped into the ring and Cavaliere separated the fighters.

Oddly, Rocky's cornermen felt their strategy was working just fine. Between the first and second rounds, Graziano's trainer Whitey Bimstein recommended continued use of the left. As if watching a different fight, Bimstein thought Rocky was confusing Zale.[36]

At the opening of the second round, Graziano again emphasized his left. Zale didn't seem particularly impressed but at the same time failed to show the aggression he displayed in the first frame. The fighters spent the first half of the round circling each other and trading relatively ineffectual punches from long range. Zale then connected with a straight right to Rocky's jaw. This—finally—woke up the Rock. He came off the ropes throwing his famous overhand right and followed up by shoving Zale into the corner. Graziano unleashed a two-fisted attack that repeatedly snapped Zale's head back. Zale went into a full-scale retreat and was staggered at least once. His face began to take on the haggard look of Chicago. It "suddenly appeared as if Graziano had the situation in hand."[37] Zale pulled himself together at the end of the round with another hard right to the Rock's midsection and a nice left hook to Graziano's head. There was no fighting after the bell this time. Both fighters retreated to their corners for their one minute of rest. Willie Ratner detected a "worried look on [Zale's] face and looking his years."[38] Graziano rooters were heard rumbling "Zale has run out of gas," and "Tony has shot his bolt."[39]

Heading into the third round, the ultimate outcome was by no means certain. Zale undoubtedly had the better of Graziano so far, knocking him down and landing more punches and heavier blows. But given the Rock's rally in the second frame, the battle was even on the score card. Rocky's surge reminded some of his comeback in Chicago.[40] Just about everyone assumed Graziano had more endurance than Zale, who had expended a lot of energy. Some of Zale's fans "began to fear" he had "erred in not going after Graziano more aggressively in the first."[41]

In Zale's corner, his brain trust assumed Graziano would try to build on his rally in the prior frame by coming out aggressive. They advised Zale to not wait around. When the bell rang Zale bounded off his stool and met the Rock at center ring. The fighters circled each other with Rocky pawing again at long range. Zale then launched his favorite combination: a right to the body followed by a left hook to the jaw. Both blows landed cleanly. Graziano started backing away. Zale then stepped in and landed a classic left hook, spinning the Rock's head on its axis. "A properly thrown hook is the physically most complicated punch in the boxing textbook. It can also be the most lethal. Its circular trajectory comes in from the periphery, and so is harder to see than a straight punch. When it lands the brain twists on its stem and crashes against the jagged inner part of the skull. That kind of trauma can kill a man."[42]

Rocky was in real trouble this time. He stumbled back into the ropes, slack-jawed, and tried to cover up. Zale instantly sensed that he had his man ready to go. Cool as a cucumber, as if he were "dead sure of himself,"[43] Zale measured his groggy opponent and unleashed a vicious two-fisted barrage. Graziano, getting smashed in the face and desperate

Brick City Grudge Match

Zale moves in as a badly hurt Rocky sags against the ropes (Bettmann, via Getty Images).

to get away, slid down the ropes as if he were about to sit on an invisible chair. Zale jumped back for fear of hitting his opponent while on the canvas—grounds for a disqualification.

The dazed Rock then righted himself—which did nothing but invite more pile-driving punches from the Man of Steel. Hard rights to Graziano's side were followed by more lefts to the head. At one point Zale cuffed Rocky's head with his left and then slammed a straight right to Graziano's face. A geyser of blood squirted from Rocky's nose and headed north. It left a crimson crease up the side of his nose running over Graziano's forehead "as if it had been made with lipstick, straight and clean."[44] Zale backed away and the Rock came off the ropes. Graziano threw a lazy, looping overhand right that Zale easily blocked while stepping in with a right to the heart followed by a blindingly

11. Newark Grudge Match

Zale finishes Graziano with a crushing left hook. Referee Cavaliere looks on as an unconscious Rock crashes to the canvas, slamming his head against the ring floor (Bettmann, via Getty Images).

fast left hook, which exploded on Rocky's jaw. Graziano crashed to the canvas.

What followed would fix the image of Zale as a devastating fighter. Rocky, gutsy as always, dragged himself to the ropes and pulled himself upright. Graziano got to his feet at the count of seven, but then slid to his right as if he were about to fall.* No question the ropes kept him up. Referee Cavaliere grabbed Rocky's gloves and wiped them against his own shirt. With Graziano appearing to be virtually out on his feet, Cavaliere may have considered stopping the fight. But this was a championship bout, and Cavaliere knew Rocky had rallied in Chicago and in other fights.[45] Cavaliere waved in Zale, who was on Rocky in a flash as Graziano tried to cover up on the ropes. Zale used his left as a battering ram to clear away Rocky's feeble attempts at blocking Zale's punches. Another well-aimed barrage of lefts and rights by Zale, mostly to the Rock's head, followed. Graziano then landed a left hook that Zale partially blocked, although the punch had enough steam to back off Zale. Rocky then staggered backward toward the center of the ring. Pitiless,

---

*The foregoing sequence may have been used as inspiration by Sylvester Stallone in his Academy Award–winning film *Rocky* (1976).

117

Brick City Grudge Match

Zale bounced off the ropes and calmly strolled toward Graziano as if taking a walk in the park. The coup de grâce—a "grisly conclusion"[46]—came with a cruel right to the Rock's back, followed by another left hook to Graziano's jaw that "stiffened Rocky on his heels and sent him toppling like a falling tree."[47] A "cascade of sound blasted ... out of the night."[48]

Rocky was out before he hit the floor. His head slammed into the hard canvas. The resounding crack reminded Jimmy Cannon of the sound of an auctioneer's mallet when striking the sound block.[49] Graziano's left leg folded under him, only to pop out straight once he was fully prone. Fighters have broken their legs in similar knockdowns.[50] Graziano did not move a muscle other than the heaving of his stomach. Referee Cavaliere bent over and ripped out Rocky's mouthpiece. Zale, proudly carrying "seventeen years of ring warfare,"[51] calmly moved to a neutral corner. Cavaliere picked up the count from the timekeeper. Zale's manager Art Winch watched with impatience and finally blurted out: "Hurry up!" Cavaliere completed the ten count. There was no need to rush. He could have counted to one hundred and the Rock would not have stirred.[52]

And so ended the violent trilogy of Zale and Graziano.

12

Postfight Analysis

Referee Cavaliere left the ring and returned to his dressing room where he met his son. He washed Rocky's blood from his hands and face and changed.[1] Wire reports of the fight's result were quickly transmitted and announced over the PA systems at major league ballparks throughout the country.[2]

The boxing fans in attendance were stunned yet energized by the explosive conclusion. As the buzzing crowd flooded out onto Wilson Avenue, a morbid rumor swept the throng: it was said that Tony Zale had killed Rocky Graziano in the ring.[3]

Rocky was still breathing, but badly hurt and severely concussed. Dr. Max Stern of the New Jersey Athletic Commission, who had examined both fighters before the fight, entered the ring to attend to Rocky. His cornermen splashed water on Graziano's face attempting to revive him. They carried the Rock to his corner where he slowly regained consciousness. He "smiled sheepishly." The "palsied, badly beaten" Graziano needed assistance making it to his dressing room.[4]

It is remarkable how quickly the image of a fighter can change. George Plimpton wrote how Smokin' Joe Frazier looked like an indestructible tank rolling into the ring with George Foreman in Kingston, Jamaica. Minutes later Frazier was rendered foolish and brutally dethroned. Graziano, a huge favorite coming into the ring in Newark, resembled "a hurt, bewildered boy" on the way out.[5] The prospects for the young power puncher went from a long and lucrative championship reign to the "road to oblivion, maybe"[6] in less than three rounds.

Rocky said he only came to his senses in the locker room.[7] He found himself lying naked on the dressing room table being sponged down and given smelling salts. Graziano's managers locked out the press until they felt Rocky could handle some questions.[8] Finally, they dressed Graziano and called in the press. The result: a public relations disaster and minor controversy.

Brick City Grudge Match

The press found a confused and even panicked Graziano, with his "eyes still glazed."[9] The *Newark Star Ledger*'s Anthony Marenghi saw Rocky "in a dazed condition" from Zale's powerful blows.[10] Along with the reporters, Dr. Vincent Nardiello made it into the dressing room. Rocky knew the doctor from Nardiello's role as the New York State Athletic Commission physician. Dr. Nardiello, who had no official standing in New Jersey, proceeded to examine Rocky in front of the press. Rocky could not remember the physician's name in response to Nardiello's inquiries. The following was splashed across the nation's newspapers the next day:

> ROCKY: "Sure I know you; you're the doc."
> NARDIELLO: "That's right. But what's my name?"
> ROCKY: "I know. I know. Gimme time; I know; I'll get it."
> NARDIELLO: "Come now. You've known me for a long time. You should know my name."
> ROCKY: "Something's wrong with me, doc. I can't think. Something must be wrong with me."

Dr. Nardiello finally calmed Graziano and then proceeded to offer an impromptu, but unofficial, diagnoses of the ex-champion for those present. "Definite concussion," offered the doctor. The beating Graziano had taken may have caused "serious" damage, offered Nardiello. "His reflexes were gone temporarily."[11] Dr. Nardiello, again without any official sanction, ordered Graziano to go to bed as soon as possible and keep ice packs on his head.[12] The befuddled Rocky and his ineffectual management sat there, stone faced.

Then Graziano was subjected to a grilling by the press. Some reporters were surprised they were allowed to question Rocky so soon after a devastating knockout.[13] Graziano did his best to explain what happened in Ruppert's ring. "I couldn't get off," said Rocky—fighter talk meaning he could not let his hands go and punch with the abandon for which he was famous. "I seemed cold." Graziano claimed that he went blank after the knockdown in the first round, explaining his "arms went numb."[14] "I didn't feel as if I had my strength after the first knockdown. I hardly knew I was in a fight." "I don't know if I had him hurt. I don't remember. I just fought."[15]

As the cobwebs cleared, more forthright explanations were offered. Like others before him, Rocky admitted he underestimated Zale: "I didn't think this fellow would come back like he did. I was surprised he still had a good punch." He admitted buying into the prefight narrative that Zale was washed up. And Graziano admitted he made another,

12. Postfight Analysis

more egregious strategic blunder: "I tried to be too cute and box him."[16] New Jersey Boxing Commissioner Abe Greene, so instrumental in helping Graziano get back into the ring, offered Rocky solace that he gone out like a champion and had given the crowd a good fight.[17]

Paul Cavaliere, Jr., was in the locker room Rocky shared with his father. Graziano had to walk past the Cavalieres to exit. Over seventy-three years later, Paul Jr. retained a vivid memory of the scene, "as if it happened yesterday." The Rock, still groggy and being supported by men to each side of him, shuffled slowly past. Graziano had a protruding knot on his forehead the size of an egg.[18]

Zale's dressing room was, not surprisingly, more upbeat. But Zale was the same as ever, quiet and happy, but completely composed.[19] "I knew I had him in the first round," said the taciturn warrior.[20] Otherwise, Zale was content to let his legendary trainer Ray Arcel do the talking. "Our man made himself the boss with his first left hook. That settled the matter," said Arcel.[21]

Meanwhile, phones were ringing off the hook at Newark's newspapers. Was it true, frantic callers asked, that Rocky was dead?[22] The rumor had spread like wildfire to the point where both the *Newark Evening News* and the *Newark Star Ledger* felt compelled to run stories debunking the canard.[23] Some of these stories had a darkly humorous bent ("It's official: Graziano is alive"[24]; "ALL POINTS NOTICE. There have been rumors all day that Rocky Graziano is either dead, or in a serious condition in a hospital. We have been in close touch with him. He is alive and well in his home."[25]). The rumor persisted, however, and Rocky's management felt compelled to arrange for Graziano to be photographed with his young daughter.[26] An AP wire photo ran in papers two days after the fight with a caption explaining the Rock "was very much alive despite rumors of mortal injury." The photo and an interview the next day with Rocky helped put the urban legend to rest. While depressed, Graziano vigorously denied suffering any brain injury. "I feel fine. There is nothing wrong with me a good steak won't cure."[27] The Rock offered "no alibis" and praised his eternal rival "as great a fighter and sportsman as is to be found in this world."[28]

In the days following the fight the New Jersey Boxing Commission was taken to task for allowing the Empire State's Dr. Nardiello to opine on Rocky's condition. Rocky's manager Irving Cohen belatedly went into a tirade because Nardiello's lack of official standing should have barred him from commenting on Graziano's condition.[29] Dr. Stein, who had rushed to Rocky's aid in the ring, was slow to get to Graziano's locker room. The Rock recognized him, and Dr. Stein offered his opinion that Graziano had "suffered nothing more than any boxer suffers as the result of the average knockout."[30] Subsequent examinations by Graziano's own physician and by Newark's David A. Flicker, M.D., who examined the Rock before fight, found Graziano had suffered a concussion, but "no neurological impairment."[31] But these more upbeat diagnoses were drowned out by Dr. Nardiello's unofficial pronouncements in the immediate aftermath of the fight.

Rocky's condition aside, the press coverage was all hail Zale. The grizzled boxing scribes finally recognized what they had in Tony Zale. No longer just "respected but colorless," they saw Zale for what he was: a great fighter and a greater champion. Two years prior, before the first Zale Graziano fight, Willie Ratner of the *Newark Evening News* wrote that Zale had done nothing "that stamps him an extraordinary fighter." After the third fight he was fulsome in his praise: the pulverizing victory now marked "the ex-steel worker one of the outstanding ringmen of all time." Zale had given an awesome "exhibit of boxing skill, punching power, gameness and endurance. ... [T]hough he hardly needed it, [Zale] raised himself in the estimation of the boxing public."[32] Gene Ward of the *Daily News* wrote that Zale had given Graziano "as thorough a beating as any man can be given."[33] To James Dawson of the *New York Times*, Zale proved that he, not Rocky, was the rightful heir to Stanley Ketchel's throne. Dawson praised Zale as "[b]igger than ever in stature"[34] and a "remarkable" champion whose "slashing," "destructive," and "battering" style reminded him of the great Ketchel.[35] Jack Dempsey felt Zale's constant conditioning set him apart and that Rocky never recovered from Zale's first left hook.[36]

The day after the fight, the front page of the *Newark Star Ledger* ran a banner headline: "ZALE KOS GRAZIANO IN 3RD"; "Rocky hurt, suffers bad concussion"; "21,497 watch Rocky take a bad beating." Anthony Marenghi wrote that Zale, "the ex-steel worker with the iron clad heart," "strode into Queensbury's Hall of Fame, a magnificent champion in a brilliant fight."[37] The *Ring*'s Nat Fleischer wrote Zale's smashing triumph placed him "among the Immortals in the middleweight division."[38] Zale, wrote Fleischer, was "a great fighter" who retrieved "his lost laurels in as sensational a knockout" ever in a middleweight title fight.[39]

The third Zale Graziano fight was clearly the least competitive of the trilogy. Nevertheless, reviews of the event were overwhelmingly positive. The *Ring* labeled the result the "most thrilling knockout" since

12. Postfight Analysis

Joe Louis crushed Max Schmeling in their rematch in 1938.[40] The *Ring* considered the bout "equally as furious as its predecessors," even if of shorter duration.[41] Jack Cuddy of the *Greenville News* (South Carolina) considered the fight "one of the most savage clashes witnessed in any ring, despite its brevity."[42] Harry Keck of the *Pittsburgh Sun-Telegraph* observed that he had "never a seen a man of Zale's size do so much damage on sheer punching in such a short time."[43] The *Newark Star Ledger* opined that the fans at Ruppert "saw a brawl which was as spectacular in explosion but lacking the competition of the two other bouts."[44]

The day after the fight, Zale traveled into Manhattan to pick up his $60,000 check from the promoter's office at 1630 Broadway.[45] Then he held a press conference. The writers observed that he was unmarked and in a good mood.[46] Zale expressed surprise and puzzlement, as had ringside observers, at Rocky's strategy in attempting to outbox Zale. "I don't know why he tried to box ... [m]aybe he was forced into trying something new. He fought the way I wanted him to."[47] Graziano had "played into my hands,"* said Zale.[48] Zale had privately expressed confidence before the fight that he had "figured out" the Rock and knew how to end it early.[49] The new champion doubted Rocky's claim that he "blacked out" after the first knockdown, noting how well Graziano fought in the second round.[50]

Zale's future would not include another Graziano fight. Rocky's lack of competitiveness led to doubts a fourth fight would draw.[51] Anthony Marenghi agreed that the two should not fight again, but his rationale was different: Zale and Graziano were such hard punchers that pitting them against each other again could ruin both men. The New Jersey Boxing Commission had barred a third fight between Gus Lesnevitch and Frankie Caras for the same reason.[52] Sugar Ray Robinson and Marcel Cerdan were mentioned as potential challengers for Zale.[53] He was obligated to risk his reclaimed title at least once for the same promoter.[54] For his part, Zale said, "I don't care who I fight."[55] Zale was convinced he had found the fountain of youth: "I feel like I'm going the other way—back to youth."[56]

The Newark fight was a success as a business venture. Promoter TOC received wide praise for doing a "splendid job."[57] President of TOC, Ben Bodne, expressed delight with how the affair went off and praised

---

*Rocky's trainer, Whitey Bimstein, who had devised the disastrous plan to emphasize Graziano's left in the mistaken belief it would confuse Zale, absolved himself by blaming his own fighter for the loss. "He seemed petrified when he got into the ring ... I just can't understand it." A. Del Greco, *Record*, 6/11/48.

city officials and the Newark Police Department. The police did a commendable job keeping traffic moving, and there were plenty of ushers on hand and no one had a problem finding a seat.[58] Bodne felt the event proved "businessmen could promote a boxing show in a business like manner." He also dropped any pretense that TOC's decision not to televise the fight was based on anything other than dollars and cents: "I am in business to make a reasonable profit." He would have televised the fight if doing so would not have harmed gate receipts.[59] Films of the fight were quickly distributed to theaters throughout the country, reaching Honolulu by air express five days after the fight.[60] Lawton Carver of the *Record* lodged one of the few complaints about how the show was handled: some "Row A" tickets were actually at least twenty rows from ringside—an old trick used by unscrupulous promoters.[61]

The numbers backed up Bodne's upbeat assessment. The attendance was 21,497, and the receipts and expenses broke down as follows:

Revenue

Ticket Sales:	$335,646
Broadcast Rights:	$45,000
Motion Picture Rights:	$25,000
Total Revenue:	$405,646

Expenses

Graziano Guaranty:	$120,000
Zale Guaranty:	$60,000
Taxes:	$101,000
Promotional Expenses:	$60,000
Charities:	$30,000*
Total Expenses:	$371,000
Total Profit:	$34,646[62]
	($380,785.42 in 2021 dollars)

The new (and old) champion, who was being bombarded with congratulatory telegrams, boarded a train in Newark's Penn Station for his trip home.[63] "I'll be back in Gary in time to drop something in the

---

*The widow of fighter, manager, and promoter James J. Johnston received $10,000; the Essex County VFW received another $10,000; the Damon Runyan Children Cancer Fund received $5,000; the Heart Fund of New Jersey received $2,500; and the New Jersey Camp for Blind Children received the final $2,500.

12. Postfight Analysis

collection plate at church."[64] Zale undoubtedly would have been comfortable with the familiar ritual. It was not to be. Hoosier politicians wanted to bask in the glow of Zale's triumph. And the working people of his hometown wanted to express their pride in his achievement and their identification with all that he represented. The reception would overwhelm the quiet man.

Zale disembarked from the train in Gary at 10:09 a.m. on Sunday, June 13,[65] to a stunning scene. He was greeted by a throng of five thousand cheering onlookers. Members of a Polish American–affiliated club lifted Zale on their shoulders and carried him to his new car. Another fifteen thousand admirers lined the route through Gary. The parade was led by a band perched on a truck. The procession ended at the Kosciusko American Legion Hall where Zale was a member. He was greeted by Indiana Governor Ralph F. Gates and Gary Mayor James Schwartz. Zale was presented with the key to the city.[66] The origins of the ceremony date back to medieval times when cities were enclosed by walls and locked gates. The granting of the key symbolized the blue-collar city's bond with its fighting champion, a trusted and respected friend who could come and go as he pleased.

After the politicians were done with their speeches, the man of honor was asked to say a few words. All Zale could muster was a barely audible mumble. "I never expected anything like this. Thanks."[67]

13

Last Round in Jersey City

On September 21, 1948, an early fall evening, 19,272 boxing fans poured into Jersey City's Roosevelt Stadium to watch the first championship match of any international import since the second Louis Schmeling fight. As spectators filled their seats, they had little reason to think they were about to watch the swan song of a legendary champion.

Tony Zale's opponent was European champion Marcel Cerdan, "The Tiger of France." Although his record as a fighter was excellent, Cerdan was known more for his flamboyant and unconventional lifestyle. Despite being married with three children, he carried on a very public affair with French singer Edith Piaf. Zale, in contrast, put the "straight" in straightlaced. The bout was promoted by the same outfit that promoted the Newark fight, The Tournament of Champions, Inc. Frenchman Georges Carpentier, Jack Dempsey's opponent in the "million dollar gate" fight at Boyle's Thirty Acres in Jersey City, flew in to promote the fight.

When Cerdan climbed through the ropes, he held a record of 108 victories against only 3 defeats. The three losses were by way of closely contested decisions, so arguably Cerdan was undefeated in over one hundred fights. Perhaps because of lingering doubts about the strength of Cerdan's competition, or the immense respect earned by Zale over the years, or simple American chauvinism, most of the boxing press expected Zale to tear Cerdan apart. Zale had won sixteen of his previous seventeen bouts, all by knockout—often exhibiting stunning displays of punching power. The Man of Steel still basked in the glow of his pulverizing performance in Newark three months prior. The bookies installed Zale as an 8.5-to-5 favorite over the foreigner.[1]

Zale had never seen Cerdan fight. He'd heard that Cerdan was an aggressive fighter who tended to wade in and throw a lot of punches. "That's just what I like," said Zale in typically minimalist but somehow menacing fashion. Zale always preferred facing sluggers rather

13. Last Round in Jersey City

than fancy boxers.² Sluggers usually sacrificed defense to land their big shots, and very few fighters in his own weight class could stand up to the power of Zale's punches.

Cerdan had certainly earned more respect than he was given. Doubts about the quality of his opponents should have been dispelled by the Frenchman's convincing victories over respected American veterans Holman Williams, Harold Green, and Georgie Abrams. The boxing press assumed Cerdan would buckle under Zale's power. No one seemed to notice that Cerdan had never been knocked out.

In his prefight comments, Zale blithely dismissed the threat posed by Cerdan.³ He had no plans to retire and in fact was busy mapping out the next steps in his career, including a planned title defense against Sugar Ray Robinson.⁴ His crushing win over Rocky in Newark convinced Zale that, despite his advanced age of thirty-five years, he had recovered his prewar form and remained at his peak.⁵

There were signs, however, that something was amiss. At the press event formally announcing the Cerdan fight on August 26, some scribes professed shock at "startling changes" in Zale's appearance. Just two months prior in Newark Zale had exuded robust health. Now he appeared "wrinkled" and "graying."⁶ Unknown to the press, turmoil ruled Zale's personal life. His failing marriage undoubtedly weighed on Zale.⁷

Moreover, some in the boxing press were unwilling to ignore lingering doubts about Zale's advanced age and history of taxing fights. The *Newark Star Ledger*'s Anthony Marenghi was concerned that Zale's legs might fail if the fight went past the fifth round.⁸ Marenghi had noticed something others had missed at the ballpark in Newark: "Even as [Zale] stood by the ropes watching the count over Grazzy, [Zale's] own legs were shaking from the terrific strain of the pace he set."⁹ Willie Ratner of the *Newark Evening News* added notes of caution about Zale's prospects versus Cerdan: "Zale is no longer as durable as in the years before the war. Tony will have to win quickly, at least within eight rounds."¹⁰ The fight was scheduled to go fifteen rounds, a distance Zale had not traversed in over seven years.

The fight took place in Jersey City's Roosevelt Stadium, just five miles as the crow flies from Ruppert Stadium. Perched on the edge of Newark Bay, Roosevelt Stadium was a more modern facility than Ruppert, having been constructed in 1937 under the watchful eye of long-serving Jersey City mayor, Frank "I Am the Law" Hague. Although geographically close to Newark, Jersey City was distinctly more conservative and Catholic than Newark. As late as 1956, Jersey City canceled a rock-n-roll show at Roosevelt Stadium over concerns about the alleged harmful effects of the music on young people.[11] While culturally distinct, Jersey City gave Newark a run for its money in terms of political corruption. Mayor Hague, who never made more than $8,500 annually while serving for thirty consecutive years as mayor, reportedly was worth over $10 million when he left office.[12] During a dry run for the fight, the hands-on Hague took a shot at his neighbor: "This is not Newark! This is next to the largest city in the country! Let's put on a big league show!"[13] Indeed, one reason the promoter chose Jersey City over Newark for Zale Cerdan was a rash of break-ins and petty theft from the cars parked at Ruppert Stadium during Zale Graziano III.[14]

The night of the fight a steady and raw breeze blew in from Newark Bay.[15] Pictures of spectators in *Life* magazine show men in long overcoats, topped off with fedoras. As was customary, Cerdan, the challenger, came first into the ring to the sound of polite applause. When the champion appeared making his way to the ring, the crowed stood and let out an approving roar.

The first round set the pattern for the fight. While Zale exhibited uncharacteristic caution ("he seemed nervous"[16]), Cerdan was an aggressive whirlwind, beating Zale to the punch and outboxing him. Throwing punches from all angles, Cerdan's right in particular repeatedly found the mark. Darting in and out, Cerdan made himself difficult to hit. The aggression, balance, and precision Zale had exhibited in Newark were replaced in Jersey City by indecision, awkward lunges, and the waste of inaccuracy.

Zale, sensing his title slipping away, stepped up his attack in the third round. He caught the Frenchman with a right to the jaw, and Cerdan staggered but remained upright. The fourth round was the last Zale would ever win. He landed a blockbuster right under Cerdan's heart—the punch that turned the tide for Zale in in his first fight with Al Hostak and brought Zale national attention. Cerdan's knees sagged, he "winced and blinked his eyes," and he looked "anxiously to his corner."[17] A Zale right to the jaw rocked Cerdan, but again Zale could not follow up and the challenger rode out the round.[18] Cerdan said later that he knew he had the fight won when he survived Zale's best in that frame. By the fifth stanza, Cerdan had recovered and took the round on the strength of his more active and accurate punching, "punishing [Zale] ... badly on the head and body."[19]

The result then was a forgone conclusion. Zale's punches lost their

13. Last Round in Jersey City

steam. His legs grew weary. His eyes at first registered exasperation and then dulled into resignation.[20] Increasingly asserting his dominance, Cerdan lost his fear of Zale's power and waded in with blinding combinations. Zale punched less and clinched more—telltale signs of an aging fighter.

The tragic story is as old as boxing itself. We see the once great fighter suddenly rendered vulnerable and then defenseless. Rocky Marciano knocking out Joe Louis. Larry Holmes battering Muhammad Ali. The hero stays too long and gets consumed by the very thing that made them great. It is hard to watch. You just want it to end.

The ringside scribes told the story at Roosevelt Stadium: Zale had become a "remnant of the devastating fighter" who twice seized the middleweight crown; "a lifeless shadow" of the man who had crushed Graziano three months previous.[21] Zale was an "impotent, helpless old man."[22] James Dawson of the *New York Times* wrote that Zale was "pitiful" and "putty in the hands" of Cerdan.[23] Frank Graham of the *New York Journal-American* wrote that, suddenly, the "savage" had disappeared, replaced by a washed-up pug.[24]

The finish came at the end of the eleventh round, after Zale had absorbed a series of barrages from Cerdan.[25] A left hook by Cerdan immediately before the bell clanged stunned Zale who, with his back to the ropes, slowly collapsed to his knees. His seconds rushed to Zale's aid and dragged the battered champion back to his corner.

A hush came over the crowd as the realization sank in that the end was near.[26] They had seen Zale mount improbable—almost miraculous—comebacks in the past. They must have wondered if the old lion had hidden reserves and would roar once again.

Not this time. Zale "had gone to the well once too often."[27] He had nothing left to give. The man closest to the action was referee Paul Cavalier, the same ref who oversaw Zale Graziano III. Between rounds Cavalier strolled slowly over to Zale's corner. He examined Zale's "haggard features" and waved his arms, the signal that the fight was over.[28] The spectators "gaped on unbelievingly."[29] Roosevelt Stadium became a tomb of silence except for the celebration in Cerdan's corner. Cavalier later told his son that Zale had the look of a washed-up fighter and it was remarkable Zale lasted as long as he did. Cavalier surmised that the power in Graziano's fists had ultimately ruined Zale, as they had done to so many others.[30]

The postfight analysis finally gave Cerdan his due as a fighter. The Newark writers also paid tribute to the erstwhile champion. The "old,

Brick City Grudge Match

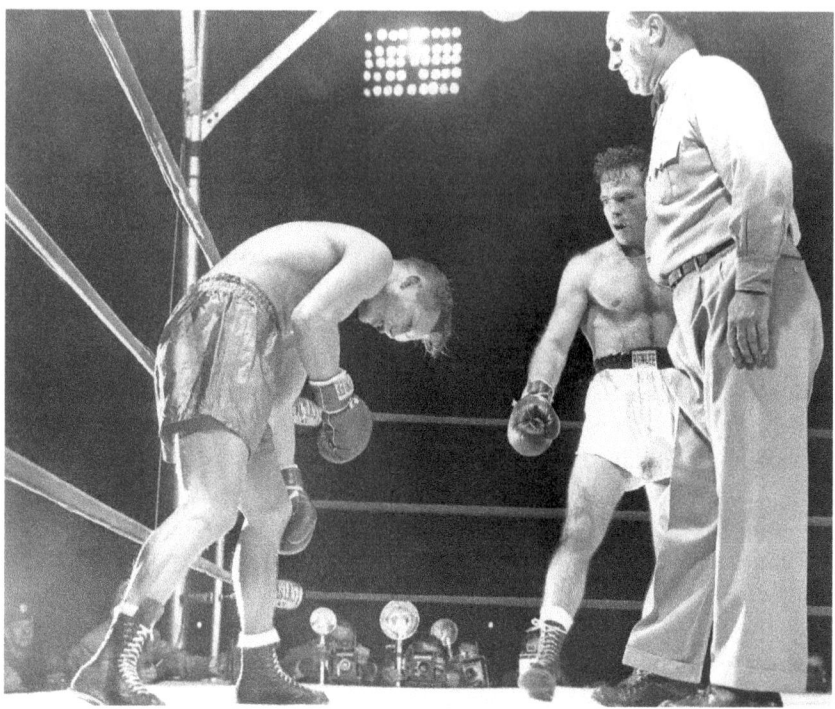

A battered and exhausted Zale collapses at the end of the eleventh round as Cerdan and referee Cavaliere look on (Gamma-Keystone, via Getty Images).

bone-weary champion" had always given it his all.[31] Zale, who only "lost when nature deserted him," "in defeat is deserving of the highest praise."[32]

In postfight interviews, Zale was confused and forgetful. His trainer Ray Arcel was forced to complete his half-baked responses to reporters' questions. Zale chalked up the defeat to "just not having it," rather than his age. But Zale offered up the lament of the aging athlete: "I knew what I wanted to do but couldn't do it."[33] Zale said he had no plans to retire.[34] He exercised his option for a rematch, and it was scheduled to take place in the Polo Grounds on June 21, 1949.[35] He convinced himself that he lost to Cerdan because of overtraining.[36] Oddly, Zale insisted he would have won the fight easily if it had been held one day prior.[37]

But Zale's management had a different view. They were concerned about his health.[38] Most of the sportswriters agreed Zale should retire.[39]

13. Last Round in Jersey City

A movement even started among the regulatory bodies to take away Zale's license to fight as a way of protecting Zale from himself.[40] Zale finally bowed to reality and announced his retirement on April 26, 1949. Tony Zale, who had been fighting since 1931 (since 1934 professionally) admitted that quitting the sport was not an easy thing for him.[41] He undoubtedly experienced apprehension leaving the thing he loved for an uncertain future. Zale said until the day he died that the biggest regret of his boxing career was losing his last fight.[42]

When Marcel Cerdan signed for the fight, he stated that his highest aspiration was to be as great a champion as Tony Zale. Cerdan would go on to lose the title to Jake LaMotta in his first defense. The colorful Frenchman died in a plane crash returning to the United States for his rematch with LaMotta. Almost half a century later, five members of Cerdan's family flew from France to Indiana to pay their respects at the funeral of the Man of Steel.[43]

14

Trial of the Redhead

On October 18, 1948, the citizens of Newark were abuzz in anticipation of North Jersey's most sensational murder trial in decades. The case had it all: a high-profile victim; lethal violence committed in the nerve center of the city's most important precinct; and sexual betrayal. Looming was the potential exposure of police corruption, as defendant Ann Powers let it be known that she had explosive testimony to offer about the Newark Police Department and others as well (the testimony of the "titian haired" seductress "will contain enough dynamite to blast officials in departments other than Newark.").[1] The drama was heightened by the uncertainty of the outcome because the prosecution's case had plenty of holes. All that was required for an acquittal was to raise the specter of reasonable doubt.

Anticipating an unprecedented demand for seats, the trial was assigned to the large second-floor courtroom in the Essex County Courthouse.[2] Seating would be on a first come, first served basis. Although the trial was not set to start until 10:00 a.m., spectators began lining up three hours early.[3] Family members, witnesses, and members of the press (twenty-three reporters provided daily coverage[4]) received preferential seat assignments, leaving only twelve spots for the public.

Despite the limited seating, an overflow crowd of 350—overwhelmingly women—showed up looking for access.[5] Mrs. Helen Mobley explained that, as a married woman, she had no sympathy for Powers but like most observers was curious to "see her under fire."[6] Anticipation of spicy testimony about Powers's relationship with Rowe was catnip to some felines. One impertinent gate-crasher tried to scam his way in by flashing a hunting license, which he claimed was a press pass.

The explosive case was assigned to the mild-mannered Honorable Joseph E. Conlon, judge of the Superior Court of New Jersey. Conlon, a former prosecutor, had a reputation for keeping a firm grip on proceedings in his courtroom. Determined to prevent the case from turning

14. Trial of the Redhead

into a circus, he let it be known to lawyers and spectators alike that he would insist on "orderliness and decorum."[7]

Essex County Prosecutor Duane E. Minard tapped his assistant Richard J. Congleton to try the case. The forty-three-year-old Congleton would go on to succeed Minard as the Essex County prosecutor and then to a successful career as an insurance executive. Tall and blond, Congleton was a deliberate, tenacious, and effective advocate.[8]

The defendant retained general practitioner Frank Metro to represent her. Metro, who had previously represented Powers in a civil auto accident case, reluctantly took the case.[9] Powers had no money to pay her legal bills. Metro finally agreed to serve as Powers's trial lawyer once he convinced another attorney to assist in the defense pro bono. Pelligrino "Peter" Rodino was a rising star in New Jersey legal circles. He also had political aspirations. A Rutgers Law grad, Rodino was on the ballot that fall as the Democratic candidate for the Tenth District congressional seat. President Harry Truman, facing an uphill reelection himself, campaigned in Newark and endorsed Rodino a couple of weeks before the trial. Rodino went on to win his race, served for decades in the House of Representatives, and earned fame as the House judiciary chairman during President Richard Nixon's impeachment proceedings.

But in this courtroom drama the judge and the lawyers ranked as mere supporting cast; the undoubted star was defendant Ann Powers, a.k.a. Ann Neff. Everyone was eager to see the mysterious femme fatale, ceaselessly portrayed by the press as a combination of smoldering sexuality and an object of terminal lust, and at the same time an icy manipulator. Ineligible for bail, Powers had gone unseen by the public for some time. Now, all eyes were on her as she entered the courtroom for jury selection.

The woman they saw was tall and trim, stylishly dressed, and remarkably self-possessed. Powers had a "detached casualness" as if she was lounging on a park bench.[10] Her pale face, "devoid of makeup," projected stolid coolness and nonchalance. Powers frequently spoke to her lawyers, Metro and Rodino, during jury selection, and even laughed during humorous moments.[11] She appeared nothing like the "vengeful woman" enraged by Rowe's rejection, as portrayed by the prosecution.

Fourteen jurors would ultimately be selected (two of which were alternates if any jurors could not make it to the end of the trial).[12] The lawyers conducted a vigorous voir dire (i.e., probing questions to detect bias or other unsuitability of the potential jurors, including questions about what they had read about the case).[13] Many were excused because of the hardship it would cause to their families. The final pool of jurors included two women, including Rita Noonan, a secretary with the prominent law firm Riker Emery & Danzig.[14] Judge Conlon ordered the jury to be sequestered at the Robert Treat Hotel for the duration of the trial, which was expected to last two weeks.

The charge against Powers was second-degree murder. The state had the burden of proving, beyond a reasonable doubt, the elements of the crime: that she had shot and killed Rowe "willfully, feloniously and with malice of aforethought." The crime carried a maximum sentence of thirty years.

The state had the first opportunity to present its case to the jury. Prosecutor Congleton laid out an explanation that was entirely circumstantial but certainly plausible. Rowe was shot, according to Congleton, during a quarrel that erupted when Rowe told Powers that he was cutting off the relationship. Powers was the only person alive with Rowe in his office when he was shot, and Rowe's dying declaration pointed the finger at Powers ("The bitch got me"). Congleton also claimed that Powers had confessed.[15] In sum, the prosecution described Powers as a "profane, hardened woman" who killed Rowe in a drunken rage when the police captain jilted her.[16]

Defense counsel Frank Metro's opening advanced the theory that the shooting resulted from a suicide attempt or an accident. He emphasized the couple's marathon drinking binge and pub crawl, which preceded the shooting, bolstering Powers's claim that she had fallen asleep in Rowe's office only to be awakened by the shot. Metro also launched into an aggressive attack on the Newark Police and the victim to boot. Rowe had a troubled marriage, bragged about his many girlfriends, and "tried to make every woman he met."[17] Metro recounted the previous shooting incident involving Rowe and his twenty-two-year-old girlfriend. Rowe, according to Metro, was in love with Powers and was chasing her; they had traveled together to Washington, D.C., and Pittsburgh. And Rowe had serious health problems and openly discussed committing suicide and had actually attempted suicide—an attempt thwarted by Powers.

Metro told the jury that "never was there such a miserable murder investigation as in this case." Police "blundering" made it impossible to determine whether Rowe committed suicide. The police had allowed Rowe's family to take home the clothes he was wearing at the time of his death, only to retrieve them later to test for powder burns. Metro reasonably asked what happened to the clothes in the interim. The cops

14. Trial of the Redhead

had also washed Rowe's hands—supposedly to take his fingerprints ("a lame excuse")—which could have removed traces of gun powder.[18] To Metro the real reason Rowe's hands were washed was obvious: either to "protect someone or hamper the defense." Finishing his opening with a flourish, Metro proclaimed the homicide squad should be on trial, not Powers.[19]

The state's first witness was county medical examiner Dr. Harrison Martland. Perching on the edge of his seat, Martland testified that Rowe could not have shot himself because there were no powder burns on Rowe's shirt.[20] In other words, the gun was fired from a distance that precluded a self-inflicted wound. When Rowe's bloody shirt was introduced into evidence, the two female jurors "paled," but Powers did not "bat an eyelash."[21]

Defense counsel Metro's cross-examination of Martland was disjointed but effective. "Scattering his cross-examination questions like buckshot pellets," Metro got Martland to admit that he would have to change his opinion on suicide if Rowe had been wearing a jacket at the time of the shooting. The state had introduced a suit jacket but had failed to identify it as Rowe's. Martland was forced to admit the washing of Rowe's hands was improper and may have removed powder.[22] Martland pushed back on Metro's assertion that Rowe's postdeath handwash precluded an effective paraffin test (designed to show gunshot residue). Martland dismissed the paraffin test as "inconclusive and discredited."[23]

The prosecution attacked the suicide theory in other ways. The state produced a physician who testified that Rowe suffered from coronary thrombosis, but the condition was quite common: 75 percent of all men over forty-five years of age supposedly had the same condition (in response to this testimony, "several gray haired members of the jury shifted uncomfortably in their chairs"[24]). In short, Rowe's health was not so bad as to prompt a suicide attempt.

With the expert testimony out of the way, the prosecution moved to proving the facts of the shooting. The state recreated the scene of the alleged crime: Rowe's desk, two chairs, and a coatrack, upon which Rowe's suit jacket was hung. A police lieutenant with a piece of chalk outlined the position of Rowe's body on the floor.[25] In addition to the macabre exhibits, the prosecution offered up the witness closest to the shooting, Detective Raymond Poquette, who walked the jury through key events. Poquette recounted the repartee between Rowe and Powers before Rowe closed the door to his office. He continued with the bloody scene after the shot, including Rowe's profane dying declaration casting blame on Powers ("The bitch got me"). Poquette also added important details that didn't make it into initial news reports and, to some extent, contradicted those reports. Instead of attempting to escape, as first conveyed, Powers had cradled Rowe's head in her arms and proclaimed: "I did it. I did it."[26] Poquette's testimony about Powers's alleged confession was corroborated by jail keeper Alfred Merkle, but oddly not by Lt. Henry Ville, the man who seized Powers.[27] The testimony about Powers's alleged confession surprised some because the police had originally contended the defendant always denied culpability.[28]

Poquette filled in other details. Over objection, he identified the clothes Rowe was wearing at the time of the shooting. Poquette identified Powers as the woman who accompanied Rowe. And Poquette identified the gun. The drama was heightened when Prosecutor Congleton asked Poquette to leave the witness stand and place the gun on Rowe's desk where he found it.[29] Defense counsel Metro's cross-examination focused on undermining Poquette's testimony about Powers's alleged confession, but Poquette stood up well.[30]

The defendant remained detached. "DEATH GUN FAILS TO STIR HER ICY CALM," blared the *Newark Star Ledger*'s headline in the October 21 edition. The alleged murderess maintained nerve and controlled her emotions. She even flashed the "vivacity" that enticed the "hard-boiled" Rowe.[31]

The only evidence of a quarrel between Powers and Rowe was a small statue of an elephant that the state claimed Powers had hurled at Rowe, breaking a window and coming to rest outside on a ledge.[32] But the elephant, like the gun and Rowe's glass-topped desk, had no prints.[33] While the absence of prints clearly helped the defense, Powers's counsel was stymied by Judge Conlon when he tried to introduce evidence of the prior shooting incident involving Rowe. Judge Conlon apparently felt Metro had not sufficiently explained the relevance of the prior incident, and perhaps that the risk of prejudice outweighed any probative value.[34] This was a major blow to the defense because Metro, in his opening, had told the jury about the previous incident, and suggested that this shooting could have been an accident as well. Any trial lawyer will tell you that failing to back up promises to the jury made during the opening will undermine counsel's credibility.

By the end of the first week, the jury looked haggard. Judge Conlon directed court attendants to go to the jurors' homes and retrieve fresh sets of clothes.[35] The judge also directed that the trial should continue

14. Trial of the Redhead

for a rare Saturday session, as a way of speeding toward conclusion. Rowe's daughter, Dorothy Scott, was expected to testify.[36]

On Saturday morning, October 23, Rowe's twenty-eight-year-old daughter, "pretty" and "hazel eyed," left her seat in the gallery to take the stand. Mrs. Scott testified that five days before the shooting, she had confronted her cheating father at midnight around the corner from the Rowe's residence.[37] The conversation took place within Powers's earshot as Ann was sitting in Rowe's car. Mrs. Scott was on the stand for an hour and described the scene in detail.

> On May 15, a week before he was killed, my husband, Andy, and I visited my parents' home. Mother was ill in bed. Shortly after 11:30 my father came in. We talked for a few minutes and Andy and I left for our home in Hillside (NJ). My husband was driving our car, and as we started down Lyons Ave., I saw Dad's car parked around the corner. I saw a person sitting in the front seat. I told Andy to pull ahead of it and park. I got out and as I started back to Dad's car, I realized it was a woman sitting there. Just then Dad came around the corner, saw me and stopped short. Before he had a chance to speak to me the woman said, "Is this your daughter?" and Dad yelled: "Jesus Christ, it is my daughter."[38]

A hush fell over the courtroom as the daughter gathered herself. Some of the women in the courtroom began crying, but Powers betrayed no emotion.[39]

After a brief pause, Mrs. Scott continued. "I sarcastically asked Dad to introduce me to her. I said, 'Come on, Dad, you know I have heard so much about her. I'd like to talk to her.'" Rowe responded that Powers was not the kind of woman his daughter should talk to. The daughter instructed her father to break off his relationship and Rowe pleaded for time. Mrs. Scott asked Rowe to "let mother get a divorce." Rowe refused and his daughter fell to the ground. Rowe picked her up, and his daughter reminded Rowe that they never minced words and issued an ultimatum to her father: she gave Rowe two weeks to end the affair with Powers or threatened Rowe was "never going to see me again—I'll be dead to you. I'll no longer be your daughter."[40] That was the last time Rowe's daughter saw him alive.[41]

The daughter stood up well to defense counsel's cross-examination. Metro tried to get Mrs. Scott to admit that no one heard the conversation other than the principals. The daughter disputed that contention because she and her father were shouting so loud neighbors opened their windows to listen to what was going on. The prosecution then called the daughter's husband to the stand to confirm the outlines of his wife's testimony. When he was done, his wife broke down crying and the judge shut down proceedings early (4:11 p.m.).[42]

The daughter's testimony supported the prosecution's theory that Rowe jilted Powers and so she shot him. Defense counsel Metro was nevertheless bulldog defiant as he left the courtroom. "Believe me, there will be no plea," he assured the assembled press.[43]

Sunday was a day of rest. After church (seven jurors attended services at the Second Presbyterian Church and four at St. John's Roman Catholic Church), Judge Conlon arranged for the jury to take a bus trip to the country.[44] The jurors probably assumed they would have to endure at least another week of testimony before rendering a verdict.

But the jury would never get the chance to decide Powers' fate. Despite her frigid façade, the testimony of Rowe's daughter rattled Powers to the core. She instructed her attorney to approach the judge about entering a non vult plea (i.e., no contest, where the defendant does not admit guilt by accepting conviction). Judge Conlon refused to accept the proposed plea. The prosecution said it would accept a guilty plea to manslaughter. Powers, over the objection of her attorney, accepted the deal.[45] Judge Conlon, in chambers outside the presence of the jury and with a court reporter taking down a stenographic transcript, got Powers to admit she shot Rowe and was pleading guilty to manslaughter.[46]

The parties then returned to open court. Veteran reporters picked up that Powers's composure had begun to slip: she "gnawed at her lower lip"; "her face white and distorted with emotion" and "fidgeted in her chair" as she waited for the judge to take the bench; and "dabbed her eyes with a sodden handkerchief." Murmurs from the gallery were heard as Judge Conlon took the bench. Conlon ordered that no one leave the courtroom and then asked defense counsel if he had a motion to make. Metro, after a "weeklong of excited courtroom histrionics," quietly moved the court to accept Powers's guilty plea to the crime of manslaughter. Conlon accepted the plea.[47]

"The tenseness of the courtroom collapsed like a punctured balloon." Rowe's widow burst into tears and was comforted by her daughter and Captain O'Neil, head of the Detective Bureau. Reporters made a mad dash to telephones and teletype machines. Judge Conlon discharged the jury and ordered his courtroom cleared. As she was led away, Ann Powers was heard screaming, "There is no justice. There is no justice."[48]

In posttrial interviews, Assistant Prosecutor Congleton revealed that he had first learned of the daughter's ultimatum to Rowe only a

14. Trial of the Redhead

couple of weeks before the trial had started.[49] His initial attempts to interview the wife and daughter were rebuffed because they were too stunned. Congleton had planned on advancing a theory that Rowe placed the gun on his desk and dared Powers to shoot herself. But Powers called Rowe's bluff and blasted Rowe.[50] In the end, Congleton felt that the guilty plea absolved the police of allegations of wrongdoing.[51]

The *Newark Evening News* was not as forgiving. The paper's editorial board indignantly bemoaned the "embarrassment to the city whose servant [Rowe] was." The cloud hanging over the leadership of the department, which had known about Rowe's reckless sexual hijinks for years but looked the other way, remained to be dispelled.[52]

Judge Conlon offered no leniency when he handed down the sentence to the unrepentant Powers. She only confessed, Conlon concluded, to avoid a conviction for second-degree murder and the potential thirty-year sentence. Judge Conlon meted out the maximum sentence for manslaughter, nine to ten years.[53]

Powers served her time at the Clinton Reformatory for Women. She was released on parole in February 1954.[54]

15

Somebody Up There Likes Me

On May 25, 1990, New Yorkers lined up at St. Patrick's Cathedral to say goodbye to one of their own. Only two miles—but a world away from his hoodlum youth on the Lower East Side—they came to pay tribute to a man who overcame the scars of his upbringing to find redemption. This simple but fascinating man would go on to captivate artistic luminaries and the public for decades.

Rocky's loss to Zale in their Newark rubber match might have broken a lesser man. The championship he had fought so hard for was gone. In many ways, the loss was embarrassing. "[T]he lowest point of my whole life," Rocky later wrote.[1] The social Rocky even made himself a hermit by locking the door and taking the phone off the hook. He lamely blamed the loss on being forced to fight in Jersey.[2] Some writers, who had obvious issues with Rocky over his war record, danced on what they thought was his professional grave ("[P]roved definitely as nothing more than an over-publicized club fighter")[3]; boxing would benefit "if the Rock … fade[d] from the premises."[4] But Rocky displayed remarkable resiliency, overcame his natural postfight funk, and instead used the ignominious defeat as a jumping-off point to a better life.

Rocky continued boxing after his Newark defeat. The record book reflects twenty-three matches post–Newark, with Rocky undefeated in all except the final two. Some of his post–Zale victories were over notable opponents, but he rarely flashed his pre–Zale fire. An exception was in his first fight after his license was restored in New York. The Rock took on Irvington's Charley Fusari at the Polo Grounds. Graziano's spirits were lifted when he attended Fusari's fight at the Garden against Vince Foster. The Rock was greeted with a standing ovation lasting five minutes.[5] Pressure started to mount on the New York licensing authorities to lift Graziano's suspension. The *Ring*'s Nat Fleischer wrote that his magazine initially supported the suspension, but "little did I then think that such punishment would be a 'life sentence.' ... [I]n the American spirit of fair play [Graziano] should be given the chance that every offender against our laws is granted to rehabilitate himself."[6]

Charley Fusari was an up-and-comer when he squared off with the Rock. Fusari entered the fight with a record of 60–4. He could punch and he could box. Plus, he was Jersey tough and established as a top contender in the welterweight division. Graziano, despite having a twelve-pound weight advantage over Fusari, was trailing on all the score cards going into the tenth and final round.[7] The Rock admitted that Fusari had "run me ragged."[8] Rocky was desperate and, like the old days, charged Fusari, throwing haymakers. Finally, the Rock landed a crushing overhand right and drove the hurt Fusari to the ropes. Charley finally slid to the canvas, only to rise at the count of nine. Wobbly, Fusari absorbed another Graziano barrage and began sliding through the ropes—similar to Zale in Chicago. The ref finally stopped the slaughter with less than a minute remaining in the fight, awarding Rocky the TKO win.[9] The sensational comeback forced Arthur Daley of the *New York Times* to admit that Graziano remained the "most colorful and exciting fighter we have."

The fascination held for Graziano by literary-minded sportswriters expanded to other types of artists. Before the legendary director Stanley Kubrick (*Spartacus* [1960]; *Dr. Strangelove* [1964]; *2001* [1968]) started his cinematic career, he worked as a photographer for *Look* magazine. In 1950, Kubrick shot a photo essay featuring Graziano. Available online today, these haunting photographs depict a man in sharp contrasts: tender family man in the morning, then—as if to prove Darwin was wrong—slowly devolving into a vicious fighter, a barely-human missing link.

The greatest actors of his generation then took their turn examining the Rock for source material. Marlon Brando befriended Rocky and channeled his mannerisms into his legendary role as ex-boxer Terry Malloy in *On the Waterfront* (1954). James Dean, initially hired to play the lead in the on-screen version of Graziano's autobiography, drew from Rocky some of the misunderstood youth angst in *Rebel Without a Cause* (1955). And Paul Newman (while working with Rocky in his portrayal of Graziano in *Somebody Up There Likes Me* [1956]), followed Rocky around for months in an effort to capture Graziano's strange combination of sullenness and excitement.[10]

Rocky's most notable match during this post–Newark phase of his career was his second-to-last fight. Rocky opened and closed his acclaimed autobiography with this bout. The fight's importance derived from the fact that it was Rocky's last chance at the middleweight championship, as well as the stature of his opponent.

For boxing fans, the name Sugar Ray Robinson evokes a response like no other. Robinson is considered by most observers to be the greatest boxer, "pound for pound," who ever lived. Robinson's record in the ring is beyond reproach, featuring, among other credentials, a ninety-one-fight unbeaten streak between 1943 and 1951; title holder in the welterweight and middleweight divisions; and winning the middleweight title five times as he repeatedly came out of retirement to reclaim the crown against younger successors. Robinson would have won the light heavyweight (160 to 175 pounds) crown against warhorse Joey Maxim if not for stifling heat in Yankee Stadium on a June night in 1952.

Robinson's performances left an indelible mark that bespoke of his greatness. Every attribute you would want in a fighter—speed, power, defense, the ability to take a punch, courage, and determination—Robinson had in abundance. All of these attributes were wrapped in a package of athletic grace and artistic style the other pugs could not hope to match. Imagine a more aggressive and stronger punching Muhammad Ali—that was Robinson. He also exuded charisma outside of the ring. The author's father-in-law was at a fight at Madison Square Garden in the 1960s, well past the time of Robinson's prime. The crowd nevertheless began to murmur, and then exploded, when Robinson—this king among men—came gracefully striding into the arena to take his reserved seat at ringside.

During his post–Newark winning streak, Rocky, who had a hard time keeping his mouth shut, began agitating in the press for another shot at the title. He even had the temerity to imply Robinson was afraid to fight him. Sugar Ray, who served as his own manager and negotiated his own deals for fights, finally grew irritated enough to phone Graziano's manager Irving Cohen and told him to set up the fight. When Cohen imparted the news, Rocky suddenly started coming up with reasons why fighting Robinson might not be a good career move. But when Cohen told Graziano how much money he would make, Rocky instructed Cohen to set it up.[11]

Graziano's last crack at the title would take place in Tony Zale's adopted hometown: Chicago. Zale himself showed up for the fight. In his autobiography, Robinson curiously invested more time analyzing Zale's behavior during the prefight introductions—ordinarily perfunctory—than his actual fight with Graziano:

15. Somebody Up There Likes Me

[Graziano] was different, and damn if Zale wasn't rooting for him. During the introduction at Chicago Stadium, their bond was obvious. Zale, his blond hair slicked back against his hard Slavic face, took a bow, then strolled over and touched my gloves. He did it quickly, unemotionally, the way hundreds of other fighters had done to me. When he got to the other corner, he grabbed Rocky's gloves and held them for several moments. He then made a fist with his right hand and clenched it in front of Rocky's face as he spoke to him. I never learned what Zale told Rocky, but his gesture seemed to be saying, "hit him like you hit me." Whatever he told him, Rocky smiled and tapped him on the jaw with a playful left jab.[12]

The fight proved to be a mismatch. Rocky stalked Sugar Ray around the ring for the first two rounds and put on a good account for himself. In the third round, a Graziano punch even caused Robinson to briefly drop to one knee—a flash knockdown. Less than one minute later it was all over.

Like many Robinson fights, the knockout came with blinding suddenness. One moment Graziano seemed to have Ray pinned against the ropes and set up for the Rock's Sunday punch, the next moment Rocky is glued to the canvas, kicking out his right leg in an odd bicycling motion, and then—like a perambulatory infant reaching for a toy beyond his reach—grasping for the ring ropes to pull himself up. Rocky got up—he always did other than when Zale knocked him out cold in Newark—but mercifully only after the ref had counted him out. One must watch the tape in slow motion to pick up on how Robinson maneuvered Rocky out of a clinch and then pistoned a jackhammer right to the jaw, sending Rocky's mouthpiece flying. Despite the lopsided result, Robinson was relieved Rocky had been counted out because, otherwise, "I would've found out what Zale had to go through."[13]

After another disappointing loss, Rocky was done with fighting. He retired and quickly transitioned to a second career as an entertainer and pitchman. Boxing constituted a major part of the primetime television lineup in the 1950s. Graziano's first gig was on ABC, where he appeared as a dim-witted straight man to comedic legend Henny Youngman, a.k.a. King of the One Liners. The live show was broadcast after the *Wednesday Night Fights*, and could last for as long as half an hour (they needed to fill more time in the event of a quick knockout). Henny's jokes stand up after all this time. They were funny and surprisingly edgy (e.g., the joke about the secret of a happy marriage remaining a secret). Or what it means to come home at night to a woman who'll give you a little love, affection, and tenderness—it means you're in the wrong house.[14]

Henny quickly moved on to other gigs leaving Rocky without a show. The public, however, loved the Rock and he quickly landed on his feet. As recounted by Rocky, the producers of *The Martha Ray Show* were looking for "a stupid guy like Rocky Graziano," to play Martha's boyfriend. Rocky suggested that he play himself. It worked. Rocky's limited ability to read paid off as he unintentionally mispronounced words in the script to great comic effect.[15]

Although barely remembered today, Martha Ray was a real talent. Think of a poor man's Lucille Ball who could sing (she had numerous hit records). Martha was a high-energy type who tended to dominate scenes, which was ideal for Rocky who knew he could only carry a supporting load.[16] Rocky's work as a comedic actor was remarkable when you consider his lack of training. In the words of author Gerald Early, the Rock "found a way to make people laugh at malapropisms without laughing at him." He "made his audiences feel superior" without looking down on Rocky.[17] And just as he understood his limitations as a fighter, Graziano knew what would sell in his role as a jokester: his authentic self. Rocky rejected out of hand Paul Newman's offer to take Rocky to a class at the prestigious Actor's Studio in Manhattan. "What for?" was Rocky's response.[18] He did not require emersion in the techniques of method acting to teach him how to be himself.

While lucrative, Rocky's TV appearances made no lasting mark on the cultural landscape. It was his autobiography, later made into a notable Hollywood film, that secured the Rock's legacy as something more than a boxer. Graziano cowrote *Somebody Up There Likes Me* (1955) with Rowland Barber, a New York journalist who was the perfect author to capture Rocky's attitude and street slang. The book received rave reviews, was an international best seller, and almost won the Pulitzer Prize.[19] The book is still considered one of the most descriptive about the "miseducation of a wayward ethnic boy written by an American."[20] The telling details about the mostly lowlife characters Rocky encountered remain.[21] But in the end it is an optimistic story because it proves "we can learn to be somebody else."[22] Even the highbrow *New York Times* reviewer Oliver Prescott loved the book: "These are the words of an honest man who had a harder battle than most people ever face, the battle with himself."[23]

The book is still jarring. Undiluted by sentimentality and self-pity, the brutal narrative is both revolting and fascinating. Thrilling descriptions of the Rock's fights only enhance the experience. Coauthor Barber undoubtedly deserves credit for the literary quality of the book. Notably, Graziano dedicated his autobiography, in part, to Abe Greene, the

15. Somebody Up There Likes Me

man more responsible than anyone for resurrecting Rocky's career and bringing the third Zale fight to Newark (Greene's "interest in my career made possible the turning of the leaf").

Hollywood's adaptation of the book was first class as directed by the supremely talented Robert Wise, known to boxing fans for *The Set-Up* (1949), a classic noir starring Robert Ryan. Wise, nominated for an Academy Award for editing *Citizen Kane* (1941), would go on to win Academy Awards for directing *West Side Story* (1961) and *The Sound of Music* (1965). The actors were also A list. James Dean was initially slotted to portray Rocky, but after Dean's death in a car accident, the part went to a young actor, Paul Newman (Rocky joked that he selected Newman because he "looked like me before I started fighting").[24] The role made Newman a star.[25] The film, although a bit dated in some respects, still holds up well today. The online movie review website Rotten Tomatoes rates the film 86 percent approval for audience score, 83 percent for critics.[26]

Rocky displayed his generous nature during the filming. His eternal rival, Tony Zale, was struggling financially. Graziano helped him out by convincing Wise and Newman to allow Zale to play himself in the movie. Bad idea. While filming the climatic fight scene, Zale landed a serious punch to Newman's midsection, causing the actor to collapse to the canvas withering in pain. Rocky described what happened next: "I jump up in the ring and grab the Polack. I yell at 'im. 'What the fuck you doin?'" Zale explained himself by claiming Newman was trying to "knock his block off." Newman demanded Zale be replaced and that was the end of Zale's involvement.[27] Court Shepard, a local New York bartender and former boxer, got the role playing Zale.

Graziano remained in the public eye for decades. Major corporations and, later, local businesses found him to be a reliable pitchman. The products he peddled ranged from cereal (Raisin Bran) and yogurt (Maharishi Yogurt), to auto mufflers (Lee Myles Transmissions).[28] Boxing referee Arthur Mercante did a radio commercial with the Rock for a pool-cleaning agent—Super Chlorination—which the Rock pronounced as "Super-Urinantion."[29] After the recording, Mercante walked with Rocky to a restaurant. Mercante recounted the reaction of everyday New Yorkers to Rocky—"the cops, the hardhats, the doormen, and even the pretty young girls," years after his fighting prime, still swarmed the champ.[30] Mercante expressed the wish that after his death he would come back as Rocky Graziano.

Intellectual types eventually grew weary of Rocky's act. Reviewers trashed his second book, *Somebody Down Here Likes Me Too* (1981), as a "shallow, show-biz narrative," where the Rock "sounds like a bad Groucho Marx, a lower East Side Italian trying to sound like a lower East Side Jew."[31] Progressive types loved the story of Rocky the reformed criminal, but not so much the story of Rocky the mercenary and capitalist. But the general public still loved Rocky. His work as a pitchman made him a multimillionaire.[32]

The reasons for Graziano's enduring popularity are easy to understand. Everyone loves a comeback story, and Rocky came back about as far as anyone could travel. In many ways Rocky was the archetypical American. He took what God gave him and through his own wherewithal transformed himself from a social misfit and retrograde into a material success and admirable person. The evolution of the Rock's character is more impressive than his material success. The scars of childhood, which must have been deep, were somehow overcome with grace. "I love this life and this country and I thank God for everything."[33]

Unlike many boxers, Rocky always had good relationships with the fairer sex. He enjoyed forty-seven years of marital bliss with Norma. By all accounts, Rocky never took advantage of his celebrity to cheat on his wife. He instinctively protected women. Graziano was pleased with the film adaptation of his life story, except for the portrayal of his family's tenement as unkempt because he thought it reflected poorly on his emotionally fragile mother.[34]

Rocky's reputation as a boxer is underrated. His record, 67–10–6, is good, with plenty of quality wins. Fifty-two of his victories (78 percent) came by way of knockout, so the Rock's reputation as a knockout artist, par excellence, is backed up in the numbers (by way of comparison, only 36 percent of LaMotta's eighty-three wins came by way of knockout). Undoubtedly, his record versus welterweights (147 pounds) is better than against full-blown middleweights (160 pounds). Being a tweener, Graziano probably would have campaigned as a junior middleweight (154 pounds) if he fought today. The Rock's reputation is probably shortchanged by his postfight career as comedic actor: his image evolved and became warm and fuzzy. And like his rival Tony Zale, Rocky is also hurt by the fact that his most impressive win—his crowning defeat of Zale at Chicago Stadium (ranked as one of the top three fights of all time in connection with the *Ring*'s seventy-fifth anniversary celebration in Atlantic City in 1997)[35]—was not captured on film. Graziano's destruction by Sugar Ray Robinson, which will live forever on YouTube, also does not help.

15. Somebody Up There Likes Me

Yet Rocky's place in the annals of boxing remains secure. The man is a preeminent example of the virtues of the sport. Graziano said himself that without boxing he would have ended up in the electric chair.[36] Although later in life he advised youngsters to avoid the sport, this man of action accepted without complaint his own fate: "I had to be a fighter to live this long and keep my place in the world."[37]

Ironically, and oddly, Graziano attributed the completion of his remarkable transformation to Zale. According to the Rock, it was Zale's Newark knockout that finally extinguished the demons of his youth: "What I didn't realize was that with that left hook in the third round, the last of Rocco Barbella had been knocked out of me. The wild kid was gone forever, the street fighter and the troublemaker."[38]

When Rocky passed, reporters sought out his eternal rival for comment. "Rocky had guts … a rough-tough fighter," said Tony Zale.[39] He might have added, as Jack Dempsey reportedly said when his rival Gene Tunney died, "Now I'm alone."

16

Brick City

The third Zale Graziano fight was arguably the biggest sporting event in Newark's history. But the dream that the fight would revive Newark's reputation as a boxing mecca rapidly faded. The promoter TOC directed its follow-up championship bout to Jersey City where Tony Zale lost his crown to Marcel Cerdan. Then the investors behind TOC bailed on the business entirely when presented with an offer they could not refuse. In May 1949, TOC was bought out by the notorious Frankie Carbo's New York–based International Boxing Club (IBC). The buyout moved Carbo and company into a monopoly position in the fight business. Big bouts moved back to the east side of the Hudson River.[1] So rather than ushering in a new golden age, Zale Graziano III coincided with the start of Newark's extraordinary downward spiral.

The story of Newark's fall is both depressing and tragic. As author Brad R. Tuttle writes in *How Newark Became Newark: The Rise, Fall, and Rebirth of an American City* (2009), "Newark experienced the perfect storm of 20th century urban troubles: deeply entrenched corruption, industrial abandonment, white flight, racial conflict, soaring crime rates, fiscal insolvency, dire poverty. Newark's saga reflects the rollercoaster ride of Everycity, U.S.A., only with a steeper rise, sharper turns, and a much more dramatic plunge."[2] Indeed, Newark's fall "stood out for the extraordinary speed, depth, and viciousness of its decline, and the monumental difficulties the city faced while attempting to dig itself out from the hole."[3]

Good-paying jobs disappeared. Newark's position as an industrial leader deteriorated after World War II as wartime contracts burned off and dried up. Manufacturers packed up and headed south and west to cities with less corruption, lower costs, and more modern infrastructure.[4] As Bruce Springsteen would write, those jobs were going, boy, and they weren't coming back.

White people disappeared along with the jobs. In the early '50s

16. Brick City

white residents began fleeing the city for the greener, adjacent suburbs, and also fifty-five miles south to Ocean County, newly opened to residential development by completion of the Garden State Parkway. Approximately one hundred thousand white people left Newark in the 1950s. Between 1940 and 1970, African Americans went from 10.6 percent of the population to 54.2 percent.[5]

Public officials, fearing declining population and the erosion of tax revenue, adopted a proactive stance. Newark, which had long suffered from a substandard housing stock, eagerly welcomed federal housing funds made available for the first time in 1949. By clearing "blighted areas" and replacing them with huge housing projects, social scientists argued the government would actually save money by eliminating the "breeding grounds" for criminals.[6] A "win–win." Entire neighborhoods would be razed. Newark built more public housing per capita than any other U.S. city.[7] These monolithic public housing projects gave Newark its new moniker, "Brick City."

The social engineers proved no more successful at solving the puzzle of governing Newark than the minimalist businessmen-politicians of the nineteenth century. Many residents resisted, not accepting bureaucratic definitions of their neighborhoods as "blighted." Nor did they take kindly to swinging wrecking balls leveling their homes—ostensibly to improve their living conditions. Among the collateral damage was the loss of Eighth Avenue, the heart of Newark's Italian American community, with restaurants elegant enough to draw DiMaggio, Jack Dempsey, Jackie Gleason, Jane Mansfield, and Marilyn Monroe.[8]

Rather than slowing or reversing the city's outmigration, the aggressive housing policy accelerated the trend. Approximately 15 percent of the First Ward's residents left the city for good after their displacement. More than half the businesses in the clearance zone ceased to exist.[9] Many of the housing projects themselves became the breeding grounds that the reformers promised to eradicate: "open-air drug and prostitution markets, lost to residents and ignored by police."[10] More than forty high-rise projects would eventually be demolished.[11]

As the city's fortunes plummeted, the tentacles of organized crime still maintained a firm grasp. Longie Zwillman remained Newark's kingpin of organized crime. But the seeds of his destruction were sown shortly after the Zale Graziano fight when Assistant U.S. Attorney Peyton Ford ordered that the FBI's files on Longie be made available to the IRS.[12] On June 25, 1952, the IRS placed a $940,471 tax lien against Longie's property. Like the fictional Michael Corlione, Longie attempted to outrun the feds by relocating his business interests to Las Vegas and Cuba.[13] He was spotted in Vegas with John "Jake the Barber" Factor, reportedly in an effort to lease the luxurious Stardust Hotel-Casino.[14] Zwillman was said to hold an interest in the Havana Riviera Casino.[15] But the walls were closing in.

Zwillman testified before the televised Kefauver Committee convened by Congress in 1950 to investigate organized crime. The agile Longie acquitted himself well before the cameras, but the experience rattled him.[16] He was trailed from the moment he left his twenty-room mansion in West Orange until he returned.[17] The pit bull Bobby Kennedy, then chief counsel to a committee investigating the mob's influence on labor unions, had a process server chasing Zwillman with a subpoena.[18] A life insurance company tracked Zwillman's associates, evaluating such persons as poor underwriting risks.[19] Placed under intense scrutiny by the IRS, he was indicted for tax evasion and forced to trial in federal court in Newark. In what seemed a bold strategy, Zwillman's lawyers offered no evidence in defense, instead relying on a legal argument that the government had failed to prove its case. But U.S. District Court Judge Jacob Wortendyke, Jr., denied the defense motion for a directed verdict of acquittal, and the case went to the jury. Observers expressed surprise when the jury came back hung.[20] Juror No. 4, Louis J. Donadio, a carpenter from Woodridge, was quoted as saying he could not recall how the jury stood as there were many votes and the count kept changing.[21]

Something was rotten. The FBI in Newark received an anonymous handwritten note that stated, in part, "WHY WAS ZWILLMAN SET FREE? ... DID Z HAVE 4 PEOPLE ON THE JURY?"[22] One of Longie's key lieutenants, Red Cohen, was overheard saying, "We had two jurors. That is how we won."[23] Later it was confirmed that Donadio and another juror had been bribed.[24] Peter D. La Placa, onetime bodyguard to Willie Moretti, and Samuel "Big Sue" Katz were charged with passing the funds. The revelation of the bribery scheme apparently broke Zwillman's resolve. He complained about the politicians who had taken his money for years and "said everything would be all right but, when I need them not one bastard is around."[25] On February 26, 1959, his wife found Longie dead in the rumpus room of their basement. Zwillman had used a plastic covered electric cord to knot a noose around his neck. He let his feet slide out from under him, tightening the noose.[26] Rumors swirled of murder, but prosecutor Brendan Byrne (elected New Jersey's governor in 1974) concluded it was suicide.[27]

16. Brick City

Newark's newspapers devoted above the fold coverage to Zwillman's career and death. The final verdict: Longie lived a "life of bold adventure and remarkable daring,"[28] but was doomed by his desire for respect and admiration in both the underworld and upperworld.[29] Ultimately, Zwillman's life was seen as a waste of talent and energy.[30] Nevertheless, reporters at the *Newark Star Ledger* bemoaned the fact that Longie's passing marked the end of his annual Christmas delivery of whiskey to the pressroom.[31]

In a tribute to the mystique he had created about himself, rumors circulated that Zwillman was still alive. A meat market clerk in Washington, D.C., claimed that Longie purchased $100 in protein products and tipped him "lavishly." FBI agents, while skeptical, ran down the rumors noting that their sainted director purchased his meat at the same market.[32] Alas, the story did not hold water. Like JFK and Elvis, Longie too was dead.

Newark's culture of official corruption, closely tied to organized crime, remained a chronic problem. In 1963, the FBI's Newark field office contributed to a report on the activities of La Cosa Nostra in the United States.[33] It turned out that Richie "The Boot" Boiardo owned the mayor, Hugh Addonizio. Elected in 1962 as a progressive and a reformer, Addonizio openly commiserated with mobsters and was eventually convicted of accepting kickbacks.[34] Assistant State Attorney General William J. Brennan, III, son of the U.S. Supreme Court Justice, acknowledged organized crime had "infested virtually every facet of public life in New Jersey."[35]

The grim history of the 1967 Newark riots is far beyond the scope of this book. Over four days, 26 people were killed, hundreds injured, and almost 1,500 arrested. Property damage was calculated at $10 million ($77 million in today's dollars). Still jarring is the cover of *Life* magazine from July 28, 1967, showing Joe Bass, Jr., bleeding out on the steaming pavement of Newark. The governor's Select Committee on Civil Disorder (known as the Lilley Commission) determined endemic poverty, lack of economic opportunity, and dissatisfaction of Newark's black community as the riot's causes. Police brutality, official corruption, and unrepresentative city government were undeniable contributors.

Caught up in the maelstrom of the riot was the family of Ida Mae Hagler. Ida was a mother of six who worked as a housekeeper and caterer. With no man around and six hungry mouths to feed, it was hard to make ends meet. The Haglers lived in a public housing project in Newark's Central Ward—ground zero for the violence. Ida's son Marvin

Brick City Grudge Match

Nathanial Hagler was a sensitive child who mostly followed his mother's hardline directives. "Being Newark, you have to be" a strict parent, reasoned Ida.[36]

Marvin was thirteen years old when Central Ward erupted. He later described the horrifying conditions engulfing the residents: "It was like the end of the world." Ida ordered her children to lay on the floor and sleep under their beds for fear of getting hit with a stray bullet. Two bullets blasted through a window and came to rest in the plasterboard over a bed. The family slid around on pillows when they needed to get food or go to the bathroom. Ida moved her family out of Newark the first chance she got, relocating them to Brockton, Massachusetts, the hometown of undefeated heavyweight champion Rocky Marciano. Her son Marvin would go on to become a legendary middleweight champion of the world, one of the best ever and a more than worthy successor to Zale and Graziano. He never forgot the town where he grew up, but his feelings were not exactly nostalgic: "You remember these things, and you remember you're glad to get out of there."[37]

In March 1968, Dr. Martin Luther King, Jr., toured Newark. He called for the election of Newark's first black mayor. Two weeks later Dr. King was shot dead in Memphis. Newark, like many urban areas, erupted in angry demonstrations. Fires consumed more Newark buildings.[38]

Kenneth Gibson took office in 1970 as Newark's first black mayor. He proved to be an honest and capable, though uninspiring, figure. But even the most talented politician and administrator would have struggled to address the problems Gibson inherited, including insolvency and labor unrest.[39] Skyrocketing crime added to the witches brew. A true low point occurred on April 1, 1971, when Mayor Gibson's own father was robbed and beaten by six assailants. Two store owners refused to allow him to use their phones to call the police. They didn't want to get involved. Their fear was understandable. Later that night, a sixty-eight-year-old Newark bus driver was shot dead trying to help a woman under assault on his bus.[40]

In 1975, *Harper's Magazine* published an article titled "The Worst American City." Newark "won" the dubious honor. The city topped nineteen of twenty-four categories, including per capita violent crime, infant death, and lowest percentage of home ownership.[41] Newark suffered population declines of approximately fifty thousand residents in the decades of the 1970s and 1980s.[42] By 1997, the population had dwindled to 259,000, a 42 percent drop-off from the 1948 peak of 450,000.[43]

16. Brick City

Newark's first signs of tangible improvement became apparent in the 1990s. Mayor Sharpe James, charismatic and persistent (albeit, corrupt), helped land the New Jersey Performing Arts Center, a beautiful facility that became a magnet for top notch entertainment and events. Mayor James achieved another milestone when a major sports arena, the Prudential Center, was built near City Hall. The NHL's New Jersey Devils host their home games at "the Rock." In 2009, the Rock hosted Newark's first championship boxing match since Zale Graziano III when Polish immigrant Tomasz Adamek squared off against Johnathan Banks for the International Boxing Federation cruiserweight championship (Adamek by TKO in the eighth round).

The intervening years fell hard on the city's once vibrant sports scene. Jackie Robinson's integration of Major League Baseball marked the death knell for the Negro leagues. Major League teams began raiding the Negro leagues for their top talent. Branch Rickey signed the Eagles' top prospect Don Newcombe to the Dodgers without any compensation, prompting Effa Manley to complain about the poaching.[44] In 1947, the Newark Eagles drew only fifty-seven thousand fans. The following year the team ran a loss of $25,000. Effa Manley and her husband sold the team's assets, including player contracts and the team bus, for $15,000. The Manleys received $5,000 for allowing Monte Irvin to sign with the New York Giants.[45]

In November 1948, the Newark Bears General Manager Parke Carroll announced the team was for sale. Attendance at Ruppert Stadium had declined from a high of 342,000 in 1932 (more than five Major League teams that season) to 88,170 in 1949. The Bears blamed "inadequate transportation to and from Ruppert Stadium" and "smoke nuisance" (i.e., air pollution). "In truth, television and integration—the former, voluntary, the latter, necessary—destroyed the Bears and Eagles, respectively."[46] The year 1949 marked the last season for the Newark Bears. The Yankees sold their Triple A affiliate to the Cubs, who moved the team to Springfield, Massachusetts.[47] Ruppert Stadium survived, at least for a while, and was rented out by the Yankees who still owned the park. In the summer of 1951, Jerry Izenberg returned to the stadium as a sportswriter to cover a stock car race for the *Newark Star Ledger*. "The outfield had been torn up and the infield paved over," he noted. "Oil stains soaked what was once the base paths. The residue of a building that had once measured the city's heartbeat now had all the charm of an unmade bed at a day-rate motel."[48]

In 1952, the Yankees announced that Ruppert Stadium would be torn down and the lot offered for sale. Instead, the Newark Board of Education, using city-backed bonds, purchased the stadium. They promised to make the park into a sports center—a "recreational showcase for the children of the city." Instead, the Board sold the lights and grandstand seats, rendering the park useless.[49]

Eventually a developer got the Ruppert Stadium site in exchange for giving the city a toxic waste dump. The city built the Ironbound Stadium on the dump, but it quickly became unusable after the federal government tested the soil and found it contaminated.[50] In 1967, the year of the riots, Ruppert Stadium finally went under the wrecking ball.

Decades later, Jerry Izenberg made an excursion to Newark's East Ward in search of the place where Tony Zale's thunderous left hook recaptured the middleweight championship. It became "a trip to nowhere through an urban maze. Streets around the stadium are gone, razor wire pockmarks the neighborhood, and an old 'Stadium Tavern' sign over a local bar" was the only link to the glorious past.[51] It is now "a landscape of chain-link fences and warehouses, factories and trucks."[52]

Newark—the city that desecrated the old burial ground of its Puritan founders—interred its most glorious sports history beneath a grim twentieth-century industrial aesthetic.

17

Requiem for a Middleweight

On March 22, 1997, undertakers at Stilinovich & Wiatrolik Funeral Home in Merrillville, Indiana, set about examining the cadaver of an eighty-three-year-old man lying on the cold slab before them. Although the deceased had suffered from Parkinson's disease and was wheelchair bound before he died, the undertakers' mouths hung agape at the chiseled specimen before them.[1] The Man of Steel had passed and gone to a better place.

Zale's triumph in his rubber match with Graziano marked the apogee of his career and a turning point for his personal life. He quickly lost his title to Frenchman Marcel Cerdan. The money Zale earned from boxing, once "expenses" for his handlers were extracted, quickly evaporated. A large and risky investment in the Tucker automobile company* wiped out the last of Zale's boxing winnings.

Most painful to Zale was the disintegration of his marriage. His wife, Adeline, proved to be emotionally unstable, promiscuous, and physically and emotionally abusive toward their children. Adeline's physical abuse of the children included slapping and choking for minor infractions (e.g., playing a note wrong on the piano).[2] The sick woman also spanked her girls to the point of bleeding.

Things came to a head when Zale discovered Adeline in a compromised position in the back seat of an automobile with one of her many paramours. Stealing a march on Tony, Adeline filed for divorce in 1949, accusing Zale of cruel and inhumane treatment.[3] The court awarded Adeline custody of the children, and she kept the girls from seeing their father. Zale's younger daughter believed her mother's second husband killed himself when he realized who he had married.[4]

---

*See Jeff Bridges in *Tucker: The Man and His Dream* (1988), directed by Francis Ford Coppola.

Brick City Grudge Match

Zale spent years trying get custody of his children, to no avail.[5] He lacked the funds to mount a serious legal challenge. Once booted out of the marital home, Zale moved to a tenement house in Chicago. The landlord gave him a starter pistol, which shot blanks, to chase away vagrants. The flat had no running water or heat.[6] Anyone who has been to Chicago in the winter can easily imagine the harshness of Zale's existence at this time.

Too proud to ask for help, Zale struggled to find a second career. He offered his services as a boxing referee, but lacked a car and had to hitchhike to events outside Chicago. He tried his hand at sportswriting, but his prose fell flat. Absurdly, he even made a run as an insurance salesman.

Zale tried to trade on his fame by greeting diners at a restaurant bearing his name. That venture failed when he chased out the nocturnal prostitutes and wiseguys. Even the cops suggested that he look the other way.[7] A plum gig fell into Zale's lap when his generous rival Rocky Graziano convinced the producer of Graziano's autobiographical film, *Somebody Up There Likes Me* (1956), to allow Zale to play himself. The role fell through when star Paul Newman, after being roughed up by Zale in a boxing sequence, came to fear Zale and demanded he be replaced.[8]

Zale eventually found steady work as a boxing instructor and mentor to disadvantaged and troubled youngsters through the Catholic Youth Organization (CYO). But none of his boys amounted to much in the professional ranks. They weren't like him. "They'd rather play than fight."[9] The *New York Times* found Zale broke and living alone in a four-story walk-up over a gym. He had not seen his daughters in years and only heard a rumor that one of them had married. Although the *Times* headline made Zale sound bitter ("For Tony Zale, Yesterday's Cheers Take on a Hollow Echo"), the old fighter actually seemed content. "I've had other jobs in between but nothing worked out. This is where I belong anyway. It's the only thing I know."[10] This hard man was not one for self-pity, and he worked to keep a positive attitude.[11]

Zale's approach to training wayward youth mimicked his approach to everything else: old school. Zale's credo: "keep kids off the street and in the gyms."[12] In the swinging '60s, Zale still advised his charges to attend church, obey their parents, and avoid premarital sex.[13] "Take off your hat and show me your report card." A trove of letters from boys he helped put on the straight and narrow testify to Zale's good works.[14] As

17. Requiem for a Middleweight

did the dozens who showed up at Zale's funeral services acknowledging they would have ended up dead on the streets without his fatherly guidance.[15] Neither of his girls attended his funeral, despite being offered free flights from California.[16]

Not everyone accepted Zale's throwback style. When he upbraided another boxing coach for using profanity around the kids, the man dropped an F-bomb and took a swing at Tony. Zale, who remained in excellent shape the rest of his life, decked the creep. The slow learner evidently realized taking on Zale without a weapon was a fool's errand. A month later, Zale was jumped unawares in a gym shower and beaten senseless with baseball bat. CYO staff found him unconscious and bleeding from one of his ears (he suffered a 90 percent hearing loss in that ear).[17]

While Zale's postboxing work paid peanuts, the esteem to which he was held by the boxing world remained. Muhammad Ali himself generously responded to Zale's request for boxing equipment to help the kids. The Greatest even appeared with Zale at the grand opening of a Chicago Parks boxing training area.[18]

The boxing press made pilgrimages to see Zale and get his take on the sport's current state. Zale took a dim view of fighters of the 1960s, now considered one of the best eras ever for boxing talent. He found them soft and overpaid. "I fought because I liked it and I had to live. In the Depression, I got $6 a match and glad of it. Now times are good; things are easy; kids are spoiled."[19] Zale felt the postwar affluence limited the talent pool: "A kid don't need to get his head punched all night to make a dollar. Besides, his parents give him whatever he wants."[20]

When Jake LaMotta, who admitted he took a dive to advance his career, wrote an article claiming "[h]onest fighters finish last," Zale felt compelled to respond with a written piece for *Boxing Illustrated*.[21] Zale acknowledged up front that "a guy like me," who "was used to answering with his fists," "might not always know the right words." Zale then unloaded on LaMotta, pointing out that men like Rocky Graziano "didn't get to the top by taking a dive along the way." Zale made no bones about his disgust for boxers who sold their soul for a few "sawbucks." "It's a tired old story, this bit about the world being a rotten place, where you've got to be rotten to get ahead." Zale ridiculed LaMotta's root-cause theory that his poverty-stricken youth led him to throw the fight: "Jake was not a hungry kid when he threw that fight to Billy Fox in 1947." In a shot aimed at LaMotta's midsection, Zale added, "And

Brick City Grudge Match

by the way, Jake, those beatings Ray Robinson gave you didn't look like fixes to me."[22] Zale's warrior code would never allow him to forgive a boxer for throwing a fight, regardless of the circumstances.*

For most Americans, Zale only reappeared in public view in 1968, twenty years after his Newark bout with Graziano. As an observant Catholic, Zale took pride in John F. Kennedy's election to the highest office in the land. It reinforced Zale's instinctive patriotism and belief that America was the land of opportunity. Zale was devastated when JFK was shot down on the streets of Dallas.[23]

In 1968, Bobby Kennedy asked for Zale's help with his presidential campaign. Zale's hometown of Gary, Indiana, had undergone a similar trajectory as Newark with steel mills being shuttered and racial tension rising. Establishment figures within the Democratic Party like RFK were alarmed at the strength exhibited in the northern primaries by George Wallace, Alabama's segregationist governor.[24] Catholics, who had embraced the New Deal and were a key part of the Democratic coalition, treated Wallace like he was a "rock star"[25] and were straying to Richard Nixon's GOP.[26]

In an effort to heal growing rifts within the party, RFK wanted to ride through the streets of Gary in a convertible with Zale—still a hero to working-class white people and Catholics—and Richard Hatcher, Gary's first African American mayor.[27] Zale agreed as he saw it as his duty to help calm the racial strife tearing his country apart. The event drew nationwide television coverage. Zale, other than his blonde hair giving way to a bleached gray, appeared to viewers remarkably unchanged from his fighting prime. RFK won the Indiana primary. The strategy of the car ride through Gary as a symbol of unity between black and working-class white people is still cited fondly by Democratic Party strategists as a model to be emulated.[28]

By the late '60s, Zale had reconnected with his daughters, but he rarely saw them. His personal life was arid. Even the Man of Steel needed companionship and intimacy. By this time, Zale had drank from the bitter cup of loneliness for two decades.

Then in June 1970 Zale met the woman who would become his

---

*Some LaMotta fans have argued that Zale ducked LaMotta. Review of the *Ring*'s rankings of the era consistently show LaMotta as the number one contender. At the time, it was widely accepted that Zale's decision to fight Rocky rather than the Raging Bull was based on Rocky's greater gate appeal—meaning more money for Zale. But reading Zale's acerbic words in *Boxing Illustrated*, it is possible Zale felt that a man like LaMotta did not deserve at shot at Zale's precious title.

17. Requiem for a Middleweight

second wife, Philomena Gianfrancisco—a true case of opposites attract. Philomena was a notable athlete in her own right, starring as an outfielder in the 1940s in the All-American Girls Professional Baseball League (see *A League of Their Own* [1992]). An attention junkie, Philomena saw in Zale the opportunity to promote her own name and accomplishments.[29]

Controlling, abrasive, and often rude, Philomena was a real character who went on a mission to promote Zale's accomplishments. Zale, never one to toot his own horn, let Philomena gather laurels for him. Although many found Philomena's antics off-putting (even Zale referred to her as "Mighty Mouth"), the squeaky wheel began a relentless search for some grease.

Irritated that Zale's rival Graziano had been granted a seat with the King of Late Night Comedy Johnny Carson, Philomena hauled Zale to a live showing of *The Tonight Show* where she proceeded to berate Carson from the audience. Carson, shocked by her outbursts, meekly slinked away and declined to acknowledge Zale's presence.[30]

During the taping of a documentary commemorating the Zale-Graziano fights, Philomena became enraged when the gregarious Rocky kept talking over her taciturn husband. She threatened to knockout the stunned Graziano.[31]

In a bizarre episode, national newspapers ran a story that Zale had died of a heart attack in a trailer park in Yuma, Arizona. In truth, the deceased was a local drunk who pretended to be Zale, filching drinks by regaling bar patrons with stories of the real Zale's ring exploits. A bewildered Zale fielded inquiries about plans for his own funeral.[32]

In 1981, Zale attended Marvelous Marvin Hagler's title defense against Mustafa Hamsho in Rosemont, a village outside Chicago. After Hagler's victory, Zale made his way to Hagler's dressing room to offer congratulations. Hagler, who frequently spoke with pride about the history of the middleweight division, was thrilled. Zale felt equally impressed by Hagler.[33] Zale must have seen a kindred spirit in his heralded successor, from their deprived and fatherless childhoods and their love of their coveted title, to their spartan approach to training and their similar, aggressive fighting styles. When the Marvelous One passed in 2021, his obituaries noted that Hagler's reign as middleweight champ was the second longest ever, only outdone by the first reign of Tony Zale.

Philomena's promotional efforts eventually bore fruit. President Ronald Reagan graciously wrote to Zale, praising his good works outside the ring to help the youth of America.[34] In 1990, President George

Brick City Grudge Match

H. W. Bush awarded Zale the Presidential Citizen's Medal, the nation's second highest civilian award.[35] Philomena, never bashful or restrained in offering her opinions, told 41 that he was better looking in person than on television.

Zale's health declined in a predicable but nevertheless sad pattern. He suffered from Parkinson's and perhaps dementia toward the end of his life. Philomena, without advising the Zaleskis, placed Zale in a nursing home.[36] Toward the end Zale, unable to keep up his beloved workout regimen and confined to a wheelchair, showed signs of depression. When visited by a family member, Zale confessed that he viewed his life as a failure because he had lost his family.[37]

By the time Zale died in 1997, memories had faded. Zale's obituary in the *Washington Post* was so perfunctory that legendary sportswriter Shirley Povich felt compelled to write his own tribute, chastising his own paper for how Zale was "atrociously shortchanged."[38] The Zaleski family had a hard time finding anyone to write Zale's biography, with Zale's nephew Ted finally undertaking the task.[39]

Boxing afficionados rate Zale on the cusp of the top ten middleweights of all time. His matches with Graziano are still cited as among the greatest of boxing trilogies. Zale's ranking is well deserved. He had many convincing victories over top-flight competition. Time and again, contemporary observers consistently rated Zale as one of the toughest boxers they had ever seen. His opponents always acknowledged his conditioning, toughness, and punching power. For three years running—1946, 1947, and 1948—Zale's matches were deemed the "Fight of the Year." His lifetime record of sixty-seven wins (forty-five by knockout, versus eighteen losses) is misleading because of the poor start of his professional career. He lost only four fights in his last ten years of fighting (against thirty-nine victories), when his competition was at its best (three of his four losses—to Conn, Graziano, and Cerdan—were to Hall of Famers; the other loss was to Billy Soose who once owned a piece of the middleweight crown).

Zale also lost four years of what should have been his prime through his honorable service during World War II. As a result, he never really had a prime. In 2003, the *Ring* ranked the top one hundred punchers of all time (all weight classes), and ranked Zale forty-first. Graziano, in eighty-three professional bouts, was KO'd only three times—twice by Zale and the other by the great Sugar Ray Robinson. Zale's reputation, however, is harmed by the lack of film of his matches—most notably his first two battles with Rocky. A YouTube search reveals little more than

17. Requiem for a Middleweight

the Newark fight with Graziano and the pounding Zale took from Marcel Cerdan in Jersey City where he lost his title.

In a sad postscript, the most tangible legacy of Zale's ring triumphs—his priceless championship belts—were stolen from the International Boxing Hall of Fame in Canastota, New York. The cowardly thief, as if seeking to erase all remaining traces of the legend of the Man of Steel, absconded into the night. An FBI investigation yielded no solid leads and the case is cold. This stolen valor remains stolen. Deborah Zale, the wife of Tony Zale's nephew Ted, spoke to me about the emotional devastation wrought by the loss of the belts. Despite his post-boxing financial struggles, Zale had taken care to preserve what he had earned with his blood. Now all the Zale family has left are the empty velvet-lined cases that once housed the precious family heirlooms.

One of the belts—awarded to Zale by the *Ring* for his Newark victory—is suitably impressive to the man and the time. Filled with

The championship belt awarded to Zale for his Newark victory by *Ring* magazine. This belt along with five others (another Zale belt plus four belts won by middleweight champ Carmine Basilio) were stolen from the International Boxing Hall of Fame in 2015. They have not been recovered (courtesy Ted Zale Family).

patriotic iconography, a golden bald eagle sits at the crest, topping multiple shields of the Stars and Stripes. Engravings on the master plate speak to an enduring truth: on June 10, 1948, Tony Zale knocked out Rocky Graziano in the third round at Ruppert Stadium to reclaim the title to which he brought nothing but honor: middleweight champion of the world.

Few remain who saw with their own eyes the Man of Steel perform in his natural habitat. But those few, even across time, remember. Like the referee's son Paul Cavaliere, Jr., who sat ringside when Zale reclaimed his title in Newark.

Zale Graziano III (Barry Thompson).

"He knew only one way to fight; to hit and be hit," wrote sportswriter Frank Graham. "His punches rocked your head and raked your body, and the harder you hit back, the harder he fought. Boxers could avoid him and spear him with their own punches ... but in stand-up fights, he was something to see, and having seen him, you would never forget him."[40]

Appendix: Career Records of Tony Zale and Rocky Graziano

Tony Zale—Professional Record

Won	67 (KOs 45)
Lost	18 (KOs 5)
Drawn	2
Bouts	87
Rounds	501
KOs	51.72%

Date	Opponent	Location	Result	Rounds
6/11/34	Eddie Allen	Chicago, IL	W PTS	4/4
6/15/34	Johnny Simpson	Chicago, IL	W PTS	4/4
6/21/34	Bobby Millsap	Chicago, IL	W KO	1/4
6/25/34	Johnny Liston	Chicago, IL	W KO	3/4
7/2/34	Ossie Jefferson	Chicago, IL	W KO	3/4
7/9/34	Lou Bartell	Chicago, IL	W PTS	4/4
7/16/34	Einar Hedquist	Chicago, IL	W TKO	4/4
7/30/34	Bobby Millsap	Chicago, IL	W PTS	4/4
8/7/34	Bruce Wade	Peoria, IL	W KO	3/8
8/13/34	Billy Hood	Chicago, IL	L PTS	6/6
8/15/34	George Black	Milwaukee, WI	W PTS	6/6
8/27/34	Wilbur Stokes	Chicago, IL	W PTS	8/8
9/3/34	Mickey Misko	Chicago, IL	L PTS	8/8
9/17/34	Mickey Misko	Chicago, IL	W KO	4/8

Appendix

Date	Opponent	Location	Result	Rounds
10/8/34	Young Jack Blackburn	Chicago, IL	W PTS	8/8
10/22/34	Frankie Misko	Chicago, IL	W KO	6/8
10/29/34	Jack Schwartz	Milwaukee, WI	W TKO	4/6
11/5/34	Jack Charvez	Chicago, IL	W PTS	8/8
11/26/34	Kid Leonard	Peoria, IL	L PTS	10/10
12/17/34	Jack Gibbons	Chicago, IL	L PTS	10/10
12/28/34	Joey Bazzone	Chicago, IL	L PTS	6/6
2/25/35	Young Jack Blackburn	Chicago, IL	W PTS	6/6
3/11/35	Max Elling	Chicago, IL	W PTS	8/8
3/27/35	Roughhouse Glover	Cincinnati, OH	L TKO	9/10
5/6/35	Johnny Phagan	Chicago, IL	L KO	6/8
7/2/35	Dave Clark	Chicago, IL	L PTS	5/5
4/13/36	Jack Moran	Chicago, IL	D PTS	5/5
7/26/37	Elby Johnson	Chicago, IL	W PTS	4/4
8/16/37	Manuel Davila	Chicago, IL	L PTS	4/4
9/17/37	Elby Johnson	Chicago, IL	W TKO	3/4
10/11/37	Billy Brown	Chicago, IL	W KO	1/4
10/18/37	Bobby Gerry	Chicago, IL	W KO	2/4
11/1/37	Nate Bolden	Chicago, IL	L PTS	5/5
11/10/37	Leon Jackson	Chicago, IL	W PTS	6/6
11/22/37	Nate Bolden	Chicago, IL	W PTS	5/5
1/3/38	Nate Bolden	Chicago, IL	W SD	8/8
1/24/38	Henry Schaft	Chicago, IL	W PTS	8/8
2/21/38	Jimmy Clark	Chicago, IL	L KO	1/8
3/28/38	King Wyatt	Chicago, IL	W PTS	8/8
5/16/38	Bobby LaMonte	Chicago, IL	W TKO	5/8
6/13/38	Jimmy Clark	Chicago, IL	W TKO	8/8
7/18/38	Billy Celebron	Chicago, IL	D PTS	10/10
8/22/38	Billy Celebron	Chicago, IL	L PTS	10/10
10/10/38	Tony Cisco	Chicago, IL	W UD	10/10
10/31/38	Jimmy Clark	Chicago, IL	W KO	2/8
11/18/38	Enzo Iannozzi	Chicago, IL	W PTS	6/6

Career Records of Tony Zale and Rocky Graziano

Date	Opponent	Location	Result	Rounds
1/2/39	Nate Bolden	Chicago, IL	L PTS	10/10
5/1/39	Johnny Shaw	Chicago, IL	W KO	5/8
5/23/39	Babe Orgovan	New York, NY	W PTS	6/6
8/14/39	Milton Shivers	Chicago, IL	W KO	3/10
10/6/39	Sherman Edwards	Chicago, IL	W TKO	3/6
10/31/39	Al Wardlow	Youngstown, OH	W KO	3/10
11/13/39	Eddie Meleski	Chicago, IL	W TKO	1/10
12/8/39	Babe Orgovan	Chicago, IL	W KO	3/8
1/29/40	Al Hostak	Chicago, IL	W UD	10/10
2/29/40	Enzo Iannozzi	Youngstown, OH	W KO	4/10
3/29/40	Ben Brown	Chicago, IL	W KO	3/10
6/12/40	Baby Kid Chocolate	Youngstown, OH	W KO	4/10
7/19/40	Al Hostak	Seattle, WA	W TKO	13/15
8/21/21	Billy Soose	Chicago, IL	L UD	10/10
11/19/40	Fred Apostoli	Seattle, WA	W PTS	10/10
1/1/41	Tony Martin	Milwaukee, WI	W TKO	7/10
1/10/41	Steve Mamakos	Chicago, IL	W PTS	10/10
2/21/41	Steve Mamakos	Chicago, IL	W KO	14/15
5/28/41	Al Hostak	Chicago, IL	W KO	2/15
7/23/41	Ossie Harris	Chicago, IL	W KO	1/10
8/16/41	Billy Pryor	Milwaukee, WI	W KO	9/10
11/28/41	Georgie Abrams	New York, NY	W UD	15/15
2/13/42	Billy Conn	New York, NY	L UD	12/12
1/7/46	Bobby Giles	Kansas City, MO	W KO	4/10
1/17/46	Tony Gillo	Norfolk, VA	W KO	5/10
2/7/46	Oscar Boyd	Des Moines, IA	W KO	3/10
2/26/46	Bobby Claus	Houston, TX	W KO	4/10
4/12/46	Ira Hughes	Omaha, NE	W KO	2/10
5/2/46	Eddie Rossi	Memphis, TN	W KO	4/10
9/27/46	Rocky Graziano	Bronx, NY	W KO	6/15
2/3/47	Deacon Logan	Omaha, NE	W TKO	6/10
2/12/47	Len Wadsworth	Wichita, KS	W KO	3/10

Appendix

Date	Opponent	Location	Result	Rounds
3/20/47	Tommy Charles	Memphis, TN	W KO	4/10
4/1/47	Al Timmons	Kansas City, KS	W TKO	5/10
5/8/47	Cliff Beckett	Youngstown, OH	W TKO	6/10
7/16/47	Rocky Graziano	Chicago, IL	L TKO	6/15
1/23/48	Al Turner	Grand Rapids, MI	W KO	5/10
3/8/48	Bobby Claus	Little Rock, AR	W KO	4/10
3/19/48	Lou Woods	Toledo, OH	W KO	3/10
6/10/48	Rocky Graziano	Newark, NJ	W KO	3/15
9/21/48	Marcel Cerdan	Jersey City, NJ	L TKO	12/15

Rocky Graziano—Professional Record

Won	67 (KOs 52)
Lost	10 (KOs 3)
Drawn	6
Bouts	83
Rounds	410
KOs	62.65%

Date	Opponent	Location	Result	Rounds
3/31/42	Curtis Hightower	Brooklyn, NY	W TKO	2/4
4/6/42	Mike Mastandrea	New York, NY	W KO	3/4
4/14/42	Kenny Blackmar	Brooklyn, NY	W KO	1/4
4/20/42	Godfrey Howell	New York, NY	D PTS	4/4
4/28/42	Charles Ferguson	Brooklyn, NY	L PTS	4/4
5/4/42	Eddie Lee	New York, NY	W KO	4/4
5/12/42	Godfrey Howell	Brooklyn, NY	W TKO	4/4
5/25/42	Lou Miller	New York, NY	D PTS	6/6
6/11/43	Gilberto Ramirez Vasquez	Brooklyn, NY	W KO	1/6
6/16/43	Joe Curcio	Elizabeth, NJ	W TKO	4/6
6/24/43	Frankie Falco	Brooklyn, NY	W KO	5/6
7/8/43	Johnny Atteley	Brooklyn, NY	W RTD	2/6
7/22/43	George Stevens	Brooklyn, NY	W KO	1/6

Career Records of Tony Zale and Rocky Graziano

Date	Opponent	Location	Result	Rounds
7/27/43	Randy Drew	Queens, NY	W KO	1/6
8/12/43	Charley McPherson	Brooklyn, NY	W PTS	6/6
8/20/43	Ted Apostoli	New York, NY	W PTS	4/4
8/24/43	Tony Grey	Queens, NY	W KO	6/6
9/10/43	Joe Agosta	New York, NY	L PTS	6/6
9/21/43	George Wilson	Brooklyn, NY	W PTS	8/8
10/5/43	Freddie Graham	Brooklyn, NY	W KO	1/8
10/13/43	Jimmy Williams	Elizabeth, NJ	W PTS	6/6
10/27/43	Charley McPherson	Elizabeth, NJ	D PTS	6/6
11/12/43	Steve Riggio	New York, NY	L PTS	6/6
11/30/43	Freddie Graham	Jersey City, NJ	W PTS	8/8
12/6/43	Charley McPherson	New York, NY	W PTS	6/6
12/27/43	Milo Theodorescu	Newark, NJ	W TKO	1/8
1/4/44	Harold Gray	Jersey City, NJ	W PTS	8/8
1/7/44	Jerry Pittro	New York, NY	W TKO	1/6
1/18/44	Phil Enzenga	White Plains, NY	W TKO	5/8
2/9/44	Steve Riggio	New York, NY	L PTS	6/6
2/24/44	Nick Calder	Highland Park, NJ	W KO	4/6
3/4/44	Leon Anthony	Brooklyn, NY	W KO	1/8
3/8/44	Harold Gray	Elizabeth, NJ	W PTS	6/6
3/14/44	Ray Rovelli	Brooklyn, NY	W PTS	8/8
4/10/44	Bobby Brown	Washington, D.C.	W KO	5/10
5/9/44	Freddie Graham	Washington, D.C.	W KO	3/8
5/29/44	Tommy Mollis	Washington, D.C.	W TKO	7/10
6/7/44	Larney Moore	Brooklyn, NY	W TKO	2/8
6/27/44	Frankie Terry	Queens, NY	W TKO	6/8
7/21/44	Tony Reno	Brooklyn, NY	W PTS	8/8
8/14/44	Jerry Fiorello	Queens, NY	W SD	8/8
9/15/44	Frankie Terry	New York, NY	D PTS	8/8
10/6/44	Danny Kapilow	New York, NY	D PTS	10/10
10/24/44	Bernie Miller	Brooklyn, NY	W TKO	2/8
11/3/44	Harold Green	New York, NY	L UD	10/10

Appendix

Date	Opponent	Location	Result	Rounds
12/22/44	Harold Green	New York, NY	L MD	10/10
3/9/45	Billy Arnold	New York, NY	W TKO	3/8
4/17/45	Solomon Stewart	Washington, D.C.	W KO	4/10
5/25/45	Al "Bummy" Davis	New York, NY	W TKO	4/10
6/29/45	Freddie "Red" Cochrane	New York, NY	W KO	10/10
8/24/45	Freddie "Red" Cochrane	New York, NY	W KO	10/10
9/28/45	Harold Green	New York, NY	W KO	3/10
1/18/46	Sonny Horne	New York, NY	W UD	10/10
3/29/46	Marty Servo	New York, NY	W TKO	2/10
9/27/46	Tony Zale	Bronx, NY	L KO	6/15
6/10/47	Eddie Finazzo	Memphis, TN	W TKO	1/10
6/16/47	Jerry Fiorello	Toledo, OH	W TKO	5/10
7/16/47	Tony Zale	Chicago, IL	W TKO	6/15
4/5/48	Sonny Horne	Washington, D.C.	W UD	10/10
6/10/48	Tony Zale	Newark, NJ	L KO	3/15
6/21/49	Bobby Claus	Wilmington, DE	W KO	2/10
7/18/49	Joe Agosta	Springfield, MA	W KO	2/10
9/14/49	Charley Fusari	New York, NY	W TKO	10/10
12/6/49	Sonny Horne	Cleveland, OH	W MD	10/10
3/6/50	Joe Curcio	Miami, FL	W KO	1/10
3/31/50	Tony Janiro	New York, NY	D SD	10/10
4/24/50	Danny Williams	New Haven, CT	W KO	3/10
5/9/50	Vinnie Cidone	Milwaukee, WI	W TKO	3/10
5/16/50	Henry Brimm	Buffalo, NY	W KO	4/10
10/4/50	Gene Burton	Chicago, IL	W KO	7/10
10/16/50	Pete Mead	Milwaukee, WI	W KO	3/10
10/27/50	Tony Janiro	New York, NY	W UD	10/10
11/27/50	Honeychile Johnson	Philadelphia, PA	W KO	4/10
3/19/51	Reuben Jones	Miami, FL	W KO	3/10
5/21/51	Johnny Greco	Quebec, Canada	W KO	3/10
6/18/51	Freddie Lott	Baltimore, MD	W KO	5/10

Career Records of Tony Zale and Rocky Graziano

Date	Opponent	Location	Result	Rounds
7/10/51	Cecil Hudson	Kansas City, MO	W TKO	3/10
8/6/51	Chuck Hunter	Boston, MA	W DQ	2/10
9/19/51	Tony Janiro	Detroit, MI	W TKO	10/10
2/18/52	Eddie O'Neill	Louisville, KY	W TKO	4/10
3/27/52	Roy Wouters	Minneapolis, MN	W TKO	1/10
4/16/52	Ray Robinson	Chicago, IL	L KO	3/15
9/17/52	Chuck Davey	Chicago, IL	L UD	10/10

Source: Boxrec.com

Chapter Notes

Abbreviations for Frequently Used Sources
AP—Associated Press
DN—*Daily News* (New York)
NEN—*Newark Evening News*
NSL—*Newark Star Ledger*
NYT—*New York Times*
UPI—United Press International

Preface

1. Attributed to Red Smith.
2. Attributed to Shirley Povich.
3. S. Dorfman, *NSL*, 6/8/48.

Chapter 1

1. *NEN*, 10/19/48.
2. *NEN*, 5/21/48.
3. *NEN*, 10/19/48.
4. *NSL*, 5/22/48.
5. *Ibid.*
6. *Ibid.*
7. *NEN*, 5/21/48; *NSL*, 10/22/48.
8. *NEN*, 5/21/48.
9. *NYT*, 5/22/48.
10. *NSL*, 5/22/48.
11. *NSL*, 5/21/48.
12. *DN*, 5/22/48.
13. *NEN*, 5/22/48.
14. *NSL*, 5/21/48.
15. *Ibid.*
16. *NEN*, 5/26/48.
17. *NYT*, 5/22/48.
18. *NSL*, 5/21/48.
19. *NSL*, 10/17/48.
20. *Ibid.*
21. *Ibid.*
22. *NSL*, 6/9/48.
23. *NSL*, 6/8/48.
24. *Ibid.*
25. *NSL*, 10/17/48.
26. *Ibid.*
27. *NSL*, 10/28/48.
28. *Ibid.*
29. *NSL*, 5/21/48, 6/9/48.
30. *NSL*, 6/4/48.
31. *NSL*, 5/23/48.
32. *NSL*, 6/3/48.
33. *NSL*, 6/5/48.
34. *NEN*, 5/30/48.
35. *NSL*, 10/17/48.
36. *NEN*, 5/26/48, 6/8/48.
37. *NEN*, 6/4/48.
38. *NEN*, 6/24/48.
39. *NEN*, 5/30/48.
40. *NEN*, 5/28/48.
41. *NSL*, 6/2/48.
42. *Ibid.*
43. *NSL*, 6/3/48.
44. *NSL*, 5/28/48, 5/30/48, 6/4/48.
45. *NSL*, 5/26/48.
46. *Ibid.*
47. *NSL*, 5/29/48.
48. *NSL*, 6/3/48.
49. *NSL*, 5/31/48.
50. *NL*, 5/29/48.

Chapter 2

1. Brad R. Tuttle, *How Newark Became Newark: The Rise, Fall, and Rebirth of an*

Notes—Chapter 2

American City (New Brunswick, NJ: Rivergate Books, an Imprint of Rutgers University Press, 2011), 115.
2. *Ibid.*, 15–16.
3. *Ibid.*
4. *Ibid.*, 17.
5. *Ibid.*, 22.
6. *Ibid.*
7. *Ibid.*, 33.
8. *Ibid.*, 36.
9. *Ibid.*
10. *Ibid.*
11. *Ibid.*, 37.
12. *Ibid.*, 38.
13. *Ibid.*, 44.
14. *Ibid.*, 48.
15. *Ibid.*, 63.
16. *Ibid.*, 72.
17. *Ibid.*, 84.
18. *Ibid.*, 75.
19. *Ibid.*, 84.
20. *Ibid.*, 7–8.
21. Scott M. Deitche, *Garden State Gangland: The Rise of the Mob in New Jersey* (Lanham, MD, Boulder, CO, New York, London: Rowman & Littlefield, 2018), 1–2.
22. *Ibid.*
23. *Ibid.*, 71.
24. *Ibid.*, 5–6.
25. *Ibid.*, 6–7.
26. *Ibid.*, 42; see also *NYT*, 11/4/30.
27. Deitche, *Garden State Gangland*, 42.
28. *Ibid.*, 8.
29. *Ibid.*, 21–31.
30. *Ibid.*, 26–27.
31. FBI Memo by J. E. Hoover, 11/6/35, in Federal Bureau of Investigation, *Abner "Longie" Zwillman—The FBI Files*, Vol. 1 (Minneapolis, MN: Filiquarian Publishing, LLC/Quontro, 2021) (hereafter cited as "FBI Memo").
32. FBI Memo, 11/6/35.
33. FBI Memo, 1/28/57.
34. Richard Ben Cramer, *Joe DiMaggio: The Hero's Life* (New York: Simon & Schuster, 2000), 141.
35. *Ibid.*, 142.
36. Robert P. Kalter, "A Man of Many Faces," *NSL*, 2/27/59.
37. Joe Carragher and Richard O. Shafer, "Despondent Zwillman Ends It All," *NSL*, 2/27/59.
38. See, e.g., Helen Warden Erskine, "Zwillman as Host Has a Long Memory," *NSL*, 1/3/56, describing a lunch at Jack Dempsey's Restaurant in Manhattan with Zwillman who startled the author with his conservative dress and classy demeanor.
39. "The Editor's Opinion," *NSL*, 2/27/59, describing Zwillman as "the brightest and the most nearly successful human product of the Prohibition Era."
40. Cramer, *Joe DiMaggio*, 141.
41. Deitche, *Garden State Gangland*, 25–26.
42. Carragher and Shafer, "Despondent Zwillman Ends It All."
43. *Ibid.*
44. Deitche, *Garden State Gangland*, 25–26.
45. Cramer, *Joe DiMaggio*, 142.
46. FBI Memo, 4/3/54, 11.
47. See, e.g., Erskine, "Zwillman as Host Has a Long Memory."
48. Carragher and Shafer, "Despondent Zwillman Ends It All."
49. *Ibid.*
50. Deitche, *Garden State Gangland*, 34.
51. *Ibid.*, 35.
52. FBI Memo, 1/15/58.
53. Carragher and Shafer, "Despondent Zwillman Ends It All."
54. Deitche, *Garden State Gangland*, 34.
55. *DN*, 10/19/35.
56. Dietche, *Garden State Gangland*, 35.
57. *DN*, 10/29/35.
58. FBI Memo, 4/3/54, 8.
59. Deitche, 36; Tuttle, *How Newark Became Newark*, 112.
60. Tuttle, *How Newark Became Newark*, 112.
61. FBI Memo, 8/12/57.
62. FBI Memo, 3/12/56.
63. *Ibid.*
64. FBI Memo, 9/3/58, 3.
65. Tuttle, *How Newark Became Newark*, 125.
66. *Ibid.*, 147–48.
67. Cramer, *Joe DiMaggio*, 143.
68. *Ibid.*, 183.
69. See, generally, Ronald A. Mayer,

The 1937 Newark Bears: A Baseball Legend (New Brunswick, NJ: Rutgers University Press, 1994).
70. See, generally, Frederick C. Bush and Bill Nowlin, eds., *The Newark Eagles Take Flight: The Story of the 1946 Negro League Champions* (Phoenix, AZ: Society for American Baseball Research, Inc., 2019).
71. "Berra, Doby Hoping New Name Is a Sign Old Rift Is Healed," *Star-Ledger*, 5/9/01.
72. Jerry Izenberg, *Through My Eyes: A Sport's Writer's 58-Year Journey* (Haworth, NJ: St. Johann Press, 2009), 13.

Chapter 3

1. Thad "Ted" Zale and Clay Moyle, *Tony Zale: The Man of Steel* (Iowa City, IA: KO Publications, 2014), 17–20.
2. Paul Niemark, "Honest Fighters Finish First," *Boxing Illustrated*, July 1961.
3. *Ibid.*
4. Zale and Moyle, *Man of Steel*, 30.
5. *Ibid.*, 27.
6. *Ibid.*, 33–34.
7. *Ibid.*, 34.
8. Niemark, "Honest Fighters Finish First."
9. Zale and Moyle, *Man of Steel*, 273.
10. *Ibid.*
11. *Ibid.*, 37–38.
12. *NYT*, 8/4/82.
13. Springs Toledo, *Murderers' Row: In Search of Boxing's Greatest Outcasts* (self-published, 2017), 181; see also Huge Fullerton, Jr., AP Special News Service, 11/27/41.
14. Niemark, "Honest Fighters Finish First."
15. *Ibid.*
16. Zale and Moyle, *Man of Steel*, 41.
17. *Ibid.*
18. Niemark, "Honest Fighters Finish First."
19. W. Ratner, *NEN*, 6/15/48.
20. Niemark, "Honest Fighters Finish First."
21. *Ibid.*

22. B. Mee, *Independent* (London), 3/24/97.
23. John Jarrett, *Champ in the Corner: The Ray Arcel Story* (Stroud, Gloucestershire, UK: Stadia, 2007), 189.
24. *Ibid.*, 196.
25. Quoting Zale opponent Billy Soose.
26. Niemark, "Honest Fighters Finish First."
27. *Ibid.*
28. Zale and Moyle, *Man of Steel*, 74.
29. *Ibid.*, 52.
30. *DN* (AP), 7/20/40.
31. W. Ratner, *NEN*, 6/15/48.
32. Zale and Moyle, *Man of Steel*, 74.
33. *DN* (UPI), 2/22/41.
34. *Ibid.*
35. *DN* (UPI), 5/29/41.
36. *Ibid.*
37. Zale and Moyle, *Man of Steel*, 78.
38. *NEN*, 9/26/46.
39. Jimmy Cannon, *Nobody Asked Me, But...: The World of Jimmy Cannon* (New York: Holt, Rinehart and Winston, 1978), 107.
40. J. Murray, *Los Angeles Times*, 9/8/91.
41. W. Ratner, *NEN*, 5/21/48.
42. M. Hirsely, *Chicago Tribune*, 3/21/97.
43. Cannon, *Nobody Asked Me, But...*, 107.
44. Zale and Moyle, *Man of Steel*, 288.
45. *Ibid.*, 96.
46. *Ibid.*, 96.
47. Jarrett, *Champ in the Corner*, 190.
48. *DN*, 11/29/41.
49. Jeffrey Sussman, *Rocky Graziano: Fists, Fame, and Fortune* (Lanham, MD, Boulder, CO, New York, London: Rowman & Littlefield, 2018), 71.
50. Zale and Moyle, *Man of Steel*, 90.
51. Arthur Daley, *NYT*, 9/21/48.
52. W. Ratner, *NEN*, 11/29/41.
53. *DN*, 11/29/41.
54. *Ibid.*
55. Ken Blady, *The Jewish Boxer's Hall of Fame* (New York: Shapolsky Publishers, Inc., 1988), 253–57.
56. W. Ratner, *NEN*, 11/29/41.
57. *DN*, 11/29/41.
58. Jarrett, *Champ in the Corner*, 189.

Notes—Chapter 4

59. Cannon, *Nobody Asked Me, But...*, 106.
60. *Ibid.*, 105.
61. W. Ratner, *NEN*, 11/14/42.
62. Jarrett, *Champ in the Corner*, 187.
63. Zale and Moyle, *Man of Steel*, 36.
64. S. Fider, *Daily Oklahoman*, 6/9/48.
65. Zale and Moyle, *Man of Steel*, 94.
66. *Ring*, February 1947, 3.
67. W. Ratner, *NEN*, 6/15/48.
68. S. Povich, *Washington Post*, 3/3/97.
69. Zale and Moyle, *Man of Steel*, 99–108.
70. Jarrett, *Champ in the Corner*, 191.
71. *Ibid.*

Chapter 4

1. Sussman, *Rocky Graziano*, 1.
2. *Ibid.*, 3.
3. *Ibid.*, 2.
4. Rocky Graziano with Rowland Barber, *Somebody Up There Likes Me* (New York: Simon and Shuster, Inc., 1955), 79; N. Ward, "How Rocky Graziano Became Boxing's Greatest Muse," *Deadspin*, 1/18/16.
5. Sussman, *Rocky Graziano*, 4.
6. Graziano and Barber, *Somebody Up There Likes Me*, 48.
7. *Ibid.*, 47.
8. *Ibid.*, 195.
9. *Ibid.*, 5–6.
10. *Ibid.*, 7, 24.
11. *Ibid.*, 34.
12. *Ibid.*, 35.
13. *Ibid.*, 36.
14. *Ibid.*, 37–40.
15. *Ibid.*, 57, 75.
16. *Ibid.*, 69–71.
17. *Ibid.*, 75.
18. *Ibid.*, 85.
19. *Ibid.*, 105.
20. *Ibid.*, 106.
21. *Ibid.*
22. *Ibid.*
23. *Ibid.*, 113.
24. *Ibid.*, 114.
25. *Ibid.*, 118.
26. *Ibid.*, 124.
27. *Ibid.*, 128.
28. *Ibid.*, 132.
29. *Ibid.*, 134–35.
30. *Ibid.*, 7.
31. *Ibid.*, 9.
32. Jonathan Eig, *Luckiest Man: The Life and Death of Lou Gehrig* (New York: Simon and Schuster, Inc., 1955), 325.
33. Graziano and Barber, *Somebody Up There Likes Me*, 158.
34. Eig, *Luckiest Man*, 342.
35. Graziano and Barber, *Somebody Up There Likes Me*, 162–65.
36. *Ibid.*, 168.
37. *Ibid.*, 175–76.
38. Sussman, *Rocky Graziano*, 11.
39. Graziano and Barber, *Somebody Up There Likes Me*, 178–87.
40. *Ibid.*, 199.
41. *Ibid.*, 200–01.
42. *Ibid.*, 205–06.
43. Sussman, *Rocky Graziano*, 13.
44. *Ibid.*, 14.
45. Graziano and Barber, *Somebody Up There Likes Me*, 219–20.
46. Sussman, *Rocky Graziano*, 15.
47. *Ibid.*, 20–25.
48. Graziano and Barber, *Somebody Up There Likes Me*, 258.
49. Sussman, *Rocky Graziano*, 31–44.
50. S. Siciliano, *Asbury Park Press*, 5/28/48.
51. Sussman, 48.
52. *Ibid.*, 49.
53. *Ibid.*, 52–53.
54. *Ibid.*, 54–55.
55. A. Marenghi, *NSL*, 8/25/45.
56. *Ibid.*
57. Sussman, *Rocky Graziano*, 55.
58. *Ibid.*, 46–47.
59. A. Marenghi, *NSL*, 9/29/45.
60. *NEN*, 6/24/46.
61. Sussman, *Rocky Graziano*, 60.
62. *Ibid.*
63. A. Marenghi, *NSL*, 3/30/46.
64. Sussman, *Rocky Graziano*, 61.
65. C. Adams, *NSL*, 3/27/46; A. Marenghi, *NSL*, 3/30/46.
66. S. Povich, *Washington*, 5/25/90.
67. *NSL* (AP), 9/27/46.
68. W. Ratner, *NEN*, 7/24/46.
69. *DN*, 9/28/46.
70. Zale and Moyle, *Man of Steel*, 127.

Notes—Chapters 5 and 6

Chapter 5

1. Ben Yagoda and Kevin Kerrane, eds., *The Art of the Fact: A Historical Anthology of Literary Journalism* (New York: Simon & Schuster, Inc., 1997), 115.
2. *DN*, 9/28/46.
3. *NEN*, 9/28/46.
4. *Ibid.*
5. "Rocky Meets His Master," *Ring*, December 1946.
6. J. Dawson, *NYT*, 9/28/46.
7. *NYT*, 10/1/46.
8. W. Ratner, *NEN*, 9/28/46; A. Marenghi, *NSL*, 9/28/46.
9. Graziano and Barber, *Somebody Up There Likes Me*, 298.
10. A. Marenghi, *NSL*, 9/28/48.
11. *DN*, 9/28/46.
12. Zale and Moyle, *Man of Steel*, 128.
13. Graziano and Barber, *Somebody Up There Likes Me*, 297.
14. *NEN*, 9/28/46.
15. *NSL*, 9/28/46.
16. W. Ratner, *NEN*, 9/28/46.
17. Graziano and Barber, *Somebody Up There Likes Me*, 297.
18. W. Ratner, *NEN*, 9/28/46.
19. A. Marenghi, *NSL*, 9/28/46.
20. Graziano and Barber, *Somebody Up There Likes Me*, 297.
21. W. C. Heinz, *The Professional* (Cambridge, MA: De Capo Press, 2001), 237.
22. *Ring*, December 1946, 11.
23. A. Marenghi, *NSL*, 9/28/46.
24. Cannon, *Nobody Asked Me, But...*, 108.
25. "Rocky Meets His Master," *Ring*.
26. W. Ratner, *NEN*, 9/28/46.
27. Graziano and Barber, *Somebody Up There Likes Me*, 298.
28. A. Marenghi, *NSL*, 9/28/46.
29. *Ring*, December 1946, 9.
30. *Ibid.*, 35.
31. Zale and Moyle, *Man of Steel*, 131.
32. Jarrett, *Champ in the Corner*, 192.
33. *Ring*, December 1946, 9.
34. Graziano and Barber, *Somebody Up There Likes Me*, 298–99.
35. W. Ratner, *NEN*, 9/28/46.
36. Jarrett, *Champ in the Corner*, 192.
37. Zale and Moyle, *Man of Steel*, 133.
38. *Ibid.*, 137.
39. *DN*, 9/28/46.
40. *Ibid.*
41. Jarrett, *Champ in the Corner*, 192.
42. *DN*, 5/24/90.
43. *Ring*, February 1947.
44. H. Goldberg, *NEN*, 7/16/47.
45. Zale and Moyle, *Man of Steel*, 136–37.
46. *Ring*, February 1947.
47. Cannon, *Nobody Asked Me, But...*, 107.
48. *NEN*, 9/28/46.
49. Sussman, *Rocky Graziano*, 100.
50. A. Daley, *NYT*, 6/9/48.

Chapter 6

1. Zale and Moyle, *Man of Steel*, 128.
2. *Ibid.*, 124 (citing *Walla Walla Union Bulletin*, 7/18/46); see also *NEN*, 4/3/46 (Zale acknowledged he agreed to fight Graziano because of Rocky's "proven box office appeal"); *NEN*, 7/16/47.
3. T. Carroll, "Golden Boys of Boxing," *Ring*, February 1947, 30.
4. *NEN*, 9/28/46.
5. *NSL*, 9/28/46.
6. Jarrett, *Toy Bulldog*, 184.
7. *Ring*, February 1947.
8. Toledo, *Murderers' Row*, 241.
9. J. Flaherty, "The Woeful Life of Jake LaMotta," *Inside Sports*, January 1981.
10. *Ring*, November 1946, 16–17.
11. *Ibid.*
12. *Ring*, December 1946, 17.
13. N. Fleischer, *Ring*, April 1947.
14. *Ring*, December 1946, 16, 38.
15. See, generally, Toledo, *Murderers' Row*.
16. *Ring*, December 1946, 16.
17. *Ibid.*
18. *Ibid.*; *Ring*, February 1947, 12.
19. A. Marenghi, *NSL*, 5/21/48.
20. *NYT*, 7/15/47.
21. *NYT*, 10/1/46.
22. *Ibid.*
23. *Ring*, March 1947, 53.
24. Graziano and Barber, *Somebody Up There Likes Me*, 300–01.
25. *Ibid.*, 305.
26. *Ibid.*, 307.

27. *Ring*, April 1947, 3.
28. Graziano and Barber, *Somebody Up There Likes Me*, 306.
29. John Jarrett, *Toy Bulldog: The Fighting Life and Times of Mickey Walker* (Jefferson, NC, London: McFarland & Co., Inc., 2013), 191–92.
30. Sussman, *Rocky Graziano*, 85–87.
31. W. C. Heinz, *The Top of His Game: The Best Sportswriting of W. C. Heinz*, ed. Bill Littlefield (The Library of America, 2015), 521.
32. *Ibid.*, 524.
33. *Ring*, April 1947, 3, 43.
34. Zale and Moyle, *Man of Steel*, 146.
35. *Ring*, April 1947, 3.
36. Graziano and Barber, *Somebody Up There Likes Me*, 315.
37. *Ring*, April 1947, 3.
38. See, e.g., Smith quoted in Graziano and Barber, *Somebody Up There Likes Me*, 319.
39. *NEN*, 2/3/47.
40. "Honest Fighters Finish First," *Boxing Illustrated*, July 1961.
41. Zale and Moyle, *Man of Steel*, 147.
42. *NEN*, 2/3/47.
43. Zale and Moyle, 154.
44. *Ibid.*, 153.
45. *Ibid.*, 172.
46. Heinz, *Top of His Game*, 528.
47. Sussman, *Rocky Graziano*, 102.
48. Graziano and Barber, *Somebody Up There Likes Me*, 322.
49. Heinz, *Top of His Game*, 528.
50. Graziano and Barber, *Somebody Up There Likes Me*, 322.
51. Heinz, *Top of His Game*, 529.
52. Zale and Moyle, *Man of Steel*, 155.
53. *NEN*, 7/16/47.
54. Graziano and Barber, *Somebody Up There Likes Me*, 324.

Chapter 7

1. *NSL* (AP), 7/17/47.
2. *NEN*, 7/17/47.
3. Cannon, "Tony Zale: Working Man," in *Nobody Asked Me, But...*, 109.
4. *NSL* (AP), 7/17/47.
5. *Ibid.*
6. *Ibid.*
7. *Ibid.*
8. Graziano and Barber, *Somebody Up There Likes Me*, 324.
9. J. Cannon, "The Graziano Zale Fight," *New York Post*, 7/17/47.
10. *NSL*, 7/17/47.
11. Graziano and Barber, *Somebody Up There Likes Me*, 324.
12. N. Fleischer, "Graziano Turns the Tables on Zale," *Ring*, September 1947, 7.
13. Graziano and Barber, *Somebody up There Likes Me*, 325.
14. *Ibid.*
15. *Ibid.*
16. *Ibid.*
17. *NEN*, 7/17/47.
18. Graziano and Barber, *Somebody Up There Likes Me*, 326.
19. *NSL* (AP), 7/17/47.
20. *Ibid.*
21. *Ibid.*
22. Graziano and Barber, *Somebody Up There Likes Me*, 326.
23. J. Cannon, *New York Post*, 7/17/47.
24. *Ring*, September 1947, 7.
25. *NSL*, 7/17/47.
26. *Syracuse Herald Journal*, 7/17/47.
27. *NEN*, 7/17/47.
28. Graziano and Barber, *Somebody Up There Likes Me*, 326.
29. *NEN*, 7/17/47.
30. *NSL* (AP), 7/17/47.
31. *Ring*, September 1947, 7.
32. *Ibid.*
33. *Ibid.*
34. See D. Daniel, "New York Salons Hold the Fistic Bag," *Ring*, November 1947, describing Graziano as "the standout figure in world boxing."
35. *Ring*, October 1947.
36. *Kingsport Times*, 9/15/47.
37. J. Cannon, "Those Honest Pugilists Are All Blood and Guts," *New York Post*, 7/18/47.

Chapter 8

1. "Boxing," *Britannica*, www.Britannica.com, accessed on July 3, 2020.
2. Barak Y. Orbach, "Prizefighting and the Birth of Movie Censorship," *Yale*

Journal of Law & the Humanities (2009): 269.

3. *Ibid.*, 263, citing "Trials of Sullivan, McCleester, and Kensett," *New York Herald*, 11/27/1842.

4. *Ibid.*

5. N. Fleisher, *Ring*, April 1946, 12.

6. See Hurley Boxing Law, named for Assemblyman Joseph Hurley.

7. Orbach, "Prizefighting and the Birth of Movie Censorship," 262n50, citing *New York Daily Mirror*, 2/19/25.

8. *NYT*, 2/28/18.

9. Attributed to John Lardner.

10. *NYT*, 7/3/21.

11. *Passaic Daily News* (AP), 7/5/21.

12. Cannon, *Nobody Asked Me But...*, 105.

13. Orbach, "Prizefighting and the Birth of Movie Censorship," 257–59, 279.

14. "Boxing," *Film Reference*, Filmreference.com, accessed July 6, 2020.

15. See, e.g., "Boxing and Cinema: Day of the Fight and Killer's Kiss," John Woodbridge & Sons Makers, Ltd., https://john-woodbridge.com, accessed August 2, 2020.

16. See, generally, Eddie Muller, "Noir 101," noiralley.tcm.com.

17. See, e.g., James M. Cain, *The Postman Always Rings Twice* (1934) and *Double Indemnity* (1943); Raymond Chandler, *The Big Sleep* (1939) and *Farewell, My Lovely* (1940); and Dashiell Hammett, *The Maltese Falcon* (1930).

18. *Ibid.*

19. Jarrett, *Toy Bulldog*, 4.

20. *Ibid.*, 5.

21. Boxraw (boxraw.com) "Toy Bulldog: The Unique Life of Mickey Walker, 7/11/22 (accessed on 10/1/22)

22. Jarrett, 48–49.

23. *Ibid.*, 136.

24. Max Schmeling, with George Von der Lippe, *Max Schmeling: An Autobiography* (Chicago: Bonus Books, 1998), 22.

25. Jarrett, *Toy Bulldog*, 201–02.

26. *Ibid.*, 204-05.

27. Schmeling, 195.

28. *Ibid.*, 184.

29. *Ibid.*, 211.

30. *Ibid.*, 209–12.

31. H. Bright, "Jersey Jolters," *Ring*, June 1947, 19.

32. J. Murray, *Los Angeles Times*, 8/8/91.

33. Jack Cavanaugh, *Tunney: Boxing's Brainiest Champ and His Upset of the Great Jack Dempsey* (New York: Random House, 2006), 97.

34. Cannon, *Nobody Asked Me But...*, 107–08.

35. Cavanaugh, *Tunney*, 97.

36. J. Izenberg, *Star-Ledger*, originally posted on 2/25/09, updated on 4/2/19.

37. Robert F. Fernandez, Sr., *Boxing in New Jersey, 1900–1999* (Jefferson, NC: McFarland & Co., Inc., 2014), 43.

38. Philip Roth, *Philip Roth at 80: A Celebration* (A Library of America Special Publication, 2014).

39. *Ibid.*

40. Curt Smith, "Ruppert Stadium," in Frederick C. Bush and Bill Nowlin, eds., *The Newark Eagles Take Flight: The Story of the 1946 Negro League Champions* (Phoenix, AZ: Society for American Baseball Research, Inc., 2019), 168.

41. Kevin Mitchell, *Jacobs Beach: The Mob, The Garden & The Golden Age of Boxing* (Boston: Hamilcar Publications, 2019), 73, suggesting something was fishy with the referee.

42. See, e.g., *NYT*, 7/30/41.

43. *Ibid.*

44. *Jacques Cousteau Odyssey: Diving for Roman Plunder* (documentary, 1978).

Chapter 9

1. T. Carroll, "Rocky Road to Ring Royalty," *Ring*, October 1947.

2. "Ring Ratings for the Month," *Ring*, October, 1947, ratings ending August 10, 1947.

3. Graziano and Barber, *Somebody Up There Likes Me*, 328.

4. Mitchell, *Jacobs Beach*, 15.

5. Attributed to Budd Schulberg.

6. Attributed to Jimmy Cannon.

7. T. Carroll, "Sable Sockers to the Fore," *Ring*, March 1947.

8. *Ibid.*

9. A. Marenghi, *NSL*, 5/21/48.

10. Frederick V., *The Golden Age of Boxing on Radio and Television: A Blow-by-Blow History from 1921 to 1964* (New York: Carrel Books, 2017).
11. Jeffrey T. Sammons, *Beyond the Ring: The Role of Boxing in American Society* (Urbana, Chicago: University of Illinois Press, 1990), 131.
12. *Ibid.*, 140.
13. Travis Vogan, *The Boxing Film: A Cultural and Transmedia History* (New Brunswick, NJ: Rutgers University Press, 2021), 60.
14. Sammons, *Beyond the Ring*, 132.
15. *Ibid.*, 133.
16. Vogan, *The Boxing Film*, 60.
17. *DN*, 9/28/46.
18. Mitchell, *Jacobs Beach*, 90.
19. Sammons, *Beyond the Ring*, 136.
20. *Ibid.*
21. *NSL* (AP), 1/22/48.
22. *NSL* (International News Service), 1/24/48.
23. *NSL* (AP), 1/26/48.
24. *NSL* (AP), 1/28/48; *NSL*, 2/17/48.
25. *NSL* (AP), 1/26/48.
26. *DN*, 1/29/48.
27. *NSL* (AP), 2/6/48.
28. Mitchell, *Jacobs Beach*, 83.
29. *Ibid.*
30. *DN*, 2/2/48.
31. *NSL* (AP), 2/17/48.
32. A. Marenghi, *NSL*, 3/4/48.
33. *NSL* (International News Service), 3/27/48.
34. *Ibid.*
35. *NSL* (AP), 3/26/48.
36. A. Marenghi, *NSL*, 3/14/48.
37. *NYT*, 2/24/50.
38. Mitchell, *Jacobs Beach*, 78.
39. *Ibid.*, 80–81.
40. A. Marenghi, *NSL*, 3/4/48.
41. Mitchell, *Jacobs Beach*, 81.
42. *NSL*, 3/22/48.
43. *NSL*, 3/28/48.
44. *NSL*, 4/1/48.
45. *NSL*, 4/2/48.
46. *NSL*, 4/6/48.
47. Zale and Moyle, *Man of Steel*, 181.
48. Graziano and Barber, *Somebody Up There Likes Me*, 329.
49. *NSL* (AP), 4/6/48.
50. Graziano and Barber, *Somebody Up There Likes Me*, 331.
51. A. Marenghi, *NSL*, 4/9/48.
52. Vince Guerrieri, "Toots Shor," Society for American Baseball Research, 7/9/20, SABR.com.
53. Larry Rosler, "Me and My Homeboy, Jackie Gleason," *Medium*, medium.com, 2/22/19.
54. FBI Memo, 6/18/58.
55. Cramer, *Joe DiMaggio*, 113.
56. A. Del Greco, *Record*, 4/9/48.
57. Cramer, 304–05.
58. A. Marenghi, *NSL*, 4/9/48.
59. *Ibid.*
60. F. Casale, *NSL*, 4/9/48.
61. A. Marenghi, *NSL*, 4/9/48.
62. Sammons, *Beyond the Ring*, 136.
63. A. Del Greco, *Record*, 4/9/48.
64. A. Marenghi, *NSL*, 4/9/48.
65. *NSL*, 4/10/48.
66. *Ibid.*
67. A. Marenghi, *NSL*, 4/9/48.
68. Cavanaugh, *Tunney*, 171–72.
69. *Ibid.*
70. *Ibid.*; see also F. Casale, *NSL*, 4/12/48.
71. F. Casale, *NSL*, 4/9/48.
72. *Ibid.*
73. A. Marenghi, *NSL*, 4/30/48.
74. A. Marenghi, *NSL*, 4/24/48.

Chapter 9

1. F. Casale, *NSL*, 4/10/48.
2. *NSL* (AP), 4/19/48.
3. *NSL*, 4/26/48.
4. W. Ratner, *NEN*, 5/23/48.
5. *Ibid.*
6. *NSL*, 6/6/48.
7. *Ibid.*
8. *NSL* (AP), 5/8/48.
9. *Ibid.*
10. *Ibid.*
11. Graziano and Barber, *Somebody Up There Likes Me*, 332.
12. Cavanaugh, *Tunney*, 268.
13. *NSL*, 5/21/48; *Pottsville Republican* (PA), 6/8/48.
14. F. Casale, *NSL*, 5/24/48.
15. *Ibid.*
16. *Ibid.*

Notes—Chapter 9

17. *NYT*, 5/3/48.
18. *NSL*, 5/9/48.
19. *NSL*, 5/20/48.
20. W. Ratner, *NEN*, 5/21/48.
21. Zale and Moyle, *Man of Steel*, 184.
22. A. Marenghi, *NSL*, 6/3/48.
23. *Ibid.*
24. Paul Niemark, "Honest Fighters Finish First," *Boxing Illustrated*, July 1961.
25. F. Casale, *NSL*, 6/1/48.
26. F. Casale, *NSL*, 6/3/48.
27. A. Marenghi, *NSL*, 6/3/48.
28. *Ibid.*
29. F. Casale, *NSL*, 6/3/48.
30. *Ibid.*; see also A. Marenghi, *NSL*, 6/3/48.
31. *Ibid.*
32. *NSL*, 5/20/48.
33. *Ring*, September 1947, 4–6.
34. F. Casale, *NSL*, 6/3/48.
35. *Ibid.*
36. *Ibid.*
37. A. Marenghi, *NSL*, 6/3/48.
38. A. Del Greco, *Record*, 6/7/48.
39. Jarrett, *Champ in the Corner*, 194.
40. *NSL*, 6/7/48.
41. *NSL*, 6/4/48.
42. *NSL*, 6/5/48.
43. Jarrett, *Champ in the Corner*, 191.
44. *Ibid.*
45. *NSL*, 6/7/48.
46. *NSL*, 6/6/48.
47. *NSL*, 6/8/48.
48. *NSL*, 6/5/48.
49. *NSL*, 6/7/48.
50. *NYT*, 6/5/48.
51. *NSL*, 6/6/48.
52. *NYT*, 6/5/48.
53. *NSL*, 6/6/48.
54. *NYT*, 6/7/48.
55. *NSL*, 6/8/48.
56. *Ibid.*
57. *NYT*, 6/8/48.
58. *NSL*, 6/9/48; *NEN*, 5/28/48.
59. *NEN*, 6/6/48.
60. *NSL*, 6/11/48.
61. J. Beer, *NEN*, 6/11/48.
62. *Ibid.*
63. *NSL*, 6/11/48.
64. H. Goldberg, *NEN*, 6/6/48.
65. F. Casale, *NSL*, 6/11/48.
66. *Ibid.*
67. *Ibid.*
68. *NEN*, 6/9/48.
69. F. Casale, *NSL*, 6/10/48.
70. Romano, *The Golden Age of Boxing*, 210.
71. H. Goldberg, *NEN*, 6/6/48.
72. *NSL*, 6/9/48.
73. *Evening Sun* (PA), 6/5/48.
74. *NSL*, 6/10/48.
75. *NEN*, 6/9/48.
76. *NSL*, 6/10/48.
77. J. Beer, *NEN*, 6/11/48.
78. F. Casale, *NSL*, 6/11/48.
79. H. Goldberg, *NEN*, 6/6/48.
80. *NSL*, 5/23/48.
81. *NSL*, 5/29/48.
82. *NSL*, 6/1/49.
83. *NSL*, 6/3/48.
84. *NSL*, 6/4/48.
85. *NSL*, 6/5/48.
86. *NEN*, 6/8/48.
87. *NSL*, 6/8/48.
88. *NSL*, 6/10/48.
89. J. McDowell, *NSL*, 6/10/48.
90. *NSL*, 6/2/48.
91. *NSL*, 5/24/48.
92. Schmeling and Von der Lippe, *Max Schmeling*, 189.
93. *NSL*, 5/24/48.
94. *NSL* (AP), 5/28/48.
95. *NSL*, 6/10/48.
96. *NSL*, 6/6/48.
97. F. Casale, *NSL*, 6/10/48.
98. *NEN*, 6/9/48.
99. F. Casale, *NSL*, 6/11/48.
100. *NEN*, 6/9/48.
101. F. Casale, *NSL*, 6/10/48.
102. *DN*, 6/8/48.
103. *Ibid.*
104. N. Cocchia, *NSL*, 6/5/48.
105. *NSL*, 6/10/49.
106. A. Marenghi, *NSL*, 6/10/48.
107. *NSL*, 6/10/48.
108. *Ibid.*
109. *NEN*, 6/9/48.
110. *NSL*, 6/10/48.
111. F. Casale, *NSL*, 6/10/48.
112. *NSL*, 6/10/48.
113. *Ibid.*
114. *Ibid.*
115. Ed Sullivan, *DN*, 6/10/48.
116. *NSL*, 6/11/48.
117. F. Casale, *NSL*, 6/11/48.

118. *NSL*, 6/10/48.
119. S. Burick, *Dayton Daily News*, 6/10/48.
120. *NSL*, 6/10/48.
121. *NSL*, 5/28/48.
122. B. Corum, *Muncie Evening Press*, 6/9/48.
123. *NSL*, 6/8/48.
124. *Ibid.*
125. *NSL*, 6/9/48.
126. *Ibid.*
127. W. Ratner, *NEN*, 6/9/48.
128. A. Del Greco, *Record*, 6/9/48.
129. *Ibid.*
130. Jimmy Powers, *DN*, 6/8/48.
131. *Ibid.*
132. *NSL*, 6/11/48.
133. *Ibid.*
134. *Ibid.*

Chapter 11

1. Interview with Paul Cavaliere, Jr., 8/27/21.
2. Paul Cavaliere Biography, NJ Boxing Hall of Fame, www.njboxinghof.org.
3. Edward Brennan, "Paul Cavaliere Boxing's First Third Man," *Boxing Illustrated*, December 1961.
4. *Ibid.*
5. *Ibid.*
6. *Ibid.*
7. *NSL*, 6/11/48.
8. J. Beer, *NEN*, 6/11/48.
9. Interview Paul Cavaliere, Jr., 8/27/21.
10. Cramer, *Joe DiMaggio*, 131.
11. A. Daley, *NYT*, 6/9/48.
12. J. Ward, *Escanaba Daily Press*, 6/10/48.
13. *Tampa Times*, 6/8/48.
14. Graziano and Barber, *Somebody Up There Likes Me*, 333.
15. *NSL*, 6/11/48.
16. Smith, "Ruppert Stadium," in Bush and Nowlin, *The Newark Eagles Take Flight*, 170.
17. Jordon Schwartz, "Kilroy Was Here: The Story of Boxer and Stuntman Billy 'Kilroy' Ramoth," *Clifton Merchant Magazine*, February 2008.
18. J. Beer, *NSL*, 6/11/48.
19. A. Marenghi, *NSL*, 6/11/48.
20. "Zale Thrills in Kayo Role," *Ring*, August 1948.
21. *NEN*, 6/11/48.
22. A. Marenghi, *NSL*, 6/11/48.
23. *Ibid.*
24. Graziano and Barber, *Somebody Up There Likes Me*, 333.
25. W. Ratner, *NEN*, 6/11/48.
26. Red Smith, "The Zale–Graziano Wars," in *The Red Smith Reader* (New York: Random House, 1982), 284.
27. *Ibid.*
28. Cannon, *Nobody Asked Me, But...*, 110.
29. *DN*, 6/11/48.
30. *Ibid.*
31. W. Ratner, *NEN*, 6/11/48.
32. *NSL*, 6/11/48.
33. W. Ratner, *NEN*, 6/11/48.
34. *Ring*, August 1948, 12.
35. A. Marenghi, *NSL*, 6/11/48.
36. Graziano and Barber, *Somebody Up There Likes Me*, 333.
37. W. Ratner, *NEN*, 6/11/48.
38. *Ibid.*
39. J. Powers, *DN*, 6/11/48.
40. A. Marenghi, *NSL*, 6/11/48.
41. *Ibid.*
42. Toledo, *Murderers' Row*, 48.
43. W. Ratner, *NEN*, 6/11/48.
44. J. Powers, *DN*, 6/11/48.
45. Interview Paul Cavaliere, Jr., 8/27/21.
46. A. Marenghi, *NSL*, 6/11/48.
47. J. Dawson, *NYT*, 6/11/48.
48. Gene Ward, *DN*, 6/11/48.
49. Cannon, *Nobody Asked Me, But...*, 111.
50. Fernandez, *Boxing in New Jersey*, 158.
51. "Zale Thrills in Kayo Role," *Ring*, August 1948, 50.
52. *Ring*, August 1948, 12.

Chapter 12

1. Edward Brennan, "Paul Cavaliere Boxing's First Third Man," *Boxing Illustrated*, December 1961.
2. See, e.g., *St. Louis Star and Times*, 6/9/48 (announcement at Sportsman

Notes—Chapter 13

Park); D. Young, *DN*, 6/11/48 (Forbes Field).
3. A. Marenghi, *NSL*, 6/12/48.
4. *Ibid.*
5. *NSL*, 6/11/48.
6. W. Ratner, *NEN*, 6/12/48.
7. Graziano and Barber, *Somebody Up There Likes Me*, 334.
8. A. Marenghi, *NSL*, 6/11/48.
9. *Ibid.*
10. A. Marenghi, *NEN*, 6/11/48.
11. *NSL*, 6/11/48.
12. *Ibid.*
13. A. Marenghi, *NSL*, 6/12/48.
14. H. Goldman, *NSL*, 6/11/48.
15. *NSL*, 6/11/48.
16. H. Goldman, *NSL*, 6/11/48.
17. *Ibid.*
18. Interview Paul Cavaliere, Jr., 8/27/21.
19. H. Goldman, *NSL*, 6/11/48.
20. H. Goldman, *NEN*, 6/11/48.
21. J. Beer, *NEN*, 6/11/48.
22. *NEN*, 6/11/48.
23. *Ibid.*
24. A. Marenghi, *NSL*, 6/12/48.
25. *Ibid.*
26. *NSL*, 6/12/48.
27. A. Marenghi, *NSL*, 6/12/48.
28. *NSL*, 6/11/48.
29. A. Marenghi, *NSL*, 6/12/48.
30. *Ibid.*
31. *NSL*, 6/12/48, 6/14/48; W. Ratner, *NEN*, 6/12/48.
32. W. Ratner, *NEN*, 6/11/48.
33. *DN*, 6/11/48.
34. J. Dawson, *NYT*, 6/12/48.
35. J. Dawson, *NYT*, 6/11/48.
36. R. Johnson, *Tennessean*, 6/14/48.
37. A. Marenghi, *NSL*, 6/11/48.
38. "Zale Thrills in Kayo Role," *Ring*, August 1948, 12.
39. *Ibid.*, 13.
40. *Ibid.*, 12.
41. *Ibid.*
42. *Greenville News* (SC), 6/11/48.
43. H. Keck, *Pittsburgh Sun-Telegraph*, 6/12/48.
44. A. Marenghi, *NSL*, 6/11/48.
45. *NEN*, 6/11/48.
46. A. Marenghi, *NSL*, 6/12/48.
47. *Ibid.*
48. *NSL*, 6/11/48.
49. Interview with Ted Zale, 9/19/21.
50. A. Marenghi, *NSL*, 6/13/48.
51. A. Marenghi, *NSL*, 6/12/48.
52. *Ibid.*
53. W. Ratner, *NEN*, 6/12/48; J. Beer, *NEN*, 6/11/48.
54. A. Marenghi, *NSL*, 6/12/48.
55. A. Marenghi, *NSL*, 6/13/48.
56. *Fort Worth Star-Telegram* (AP), 6/11/48.
57. *Ring*, August 1948, 12.
58. *NEN*, 6/11/48.
59. W. Ratner, *NEN*, 6/12/48.
60. *Honolulu Star-Bulletin*, 6/17/48.
61. L. Carver, *Record*, 6/11/48.
62. *NEN*, 6/11/48.
63. *NEN*, 6/14/48.
64. W. Ratner, *NEN*, 6/12/48.
65. *Ibid.*
66. *NEN*, 6/14/48.
67. *Ibid.*

Chapter 13

1. A. Marenghi, *NSL*, 9/21/48.
2. Zale and Moyle, *Man of Steel*, 216.
3. *Ibid.*
4. *Ibid.*, 202.
5. *Ibid.*, 208.
6. F. Casale, *NSL*, 8/27/48.
7. Zale and Moyle, *Man of Steel*, 209–13.
8. A. Marenghi, *NSL*, 9/21/48.
9. A. Marenghi, *NSL*, 9/23/48.
10. W. Ratner, *NEN*, 9/20/48.
11. *Time*, 7/23/56.
12. "Hague's End," *Time*, 5/23/49.
13. J. Powers, *DN*, 9/22/48.
14. *DN*, 9/3/48.
15. A. Marenghi, *NSL*, 9/22/48.
16. *NSL*, 9/22/48.
17. *Ibid.*
18. J. Dawson, *NYT*, 9/22/48.
19. W. Ratner, *NEN*, 9/22/48.
20. A. Marenghi, *NSL*, 9/22/48.
21. *Ibid.*
22. G. Ward, *DN*, 9/22/48.
23. J. Dawson, *NYT*, 9/22/48.
24. Jarrett, *Champ in the Corner*, 196.
25. W. Ratner, *NEN*, 9/22/48.
26. A. Marenghi, *NSL*, 9/22/48.
27. W. Ratner, *NEN*, 9/22/48.

28. A. Marenghi, *NSL*, 9/22/48.
29. *Ibid.*
30. Interview with Paul Cavaliere, Jr., 8/27/21.
31. *Ibid.*
32. W. Ratner, *NEN*, 9/22/48.
33. J. McCulley, *DN*, 9/22/48.
34. *NSL* (AP), 9/23/48.
35. *NEN* (AP), 4/26/49.
36. Jarrett, *Champ in the Corner*, 196.
37. *Ibid.*
38. *NSL*, 12/31/48.
39. See, e.g., A. Marenghi, *NSL*, 9/23/48.
40. Zale and Moyle, *Man of Steel*, 232.
41. *NEN* (AP), 4/26/49.
42. Jarrett, *Champ in the Corner*, 196.
43. Interview with Ted Zale, 9/19/21.

Chapter 14

1. *NSL*, 10/16/48
2. *NEN*, 10/13/48.
3. *NSL*, 10/22/48.
4. *NSL*, 10/21/48.
5. *Ibid.*
6. *NSL*, 10/22/48.
7. *NEN*, 10/17/48; *NSL*, 10/17/48.
8. *NSL*, 10/20/48.
9. *NSL*, 10/19/48.
10. *Ibid.*
11. *Ibid.*
12. *Ibid.*
13. *Ibid.*
14. *Ibid.*
15. *Ibid.*
16. *NSL*, 10/20/48.
17. *Ibid.*
18. *Ibid.*
19. *NSL*, 10/19/48.
20. *NSL*, 10/20/48.
21. *Ibid.*
22. *Ibid.*
23. *Ibid.*
24. *Ibid.*
25. *DN*, 10/21/48.
26. *NSL*, 10/21/48.
27. *NEN*, 10/21/48.
28. *NSL*, 11/12/48.
29. *NSL*, 10/21/48.
30. *NEN*, 10/21/48.
31. *NSL*, 10/21/48.
32. *NEN*, 10/22/48.
33. *NSL*, 10/23/48.
34. *Ibid.*
35. *NSL*, 10/22/48.
36. *NSL*, 10/23/48.
37. *DN*, 10/24/48.
38. *Ibid.*
39. *Ibid.*
40. *Ibid.*
41. *NSL*, 10/25/48; *NEN*, 10/23/48.
42. *DN*, 10/24/48.
43. *Ibid.*
44. *NEN*, 10/23/48.
45. *NEN*, 10/25/48.
46. *Ibid.*
47. *NSL*, 10/26/48.
48. *Ibid.*
49. *Ibid.*
50. *NSL*, 11/12/48.
51. *NSL*, 10/26/48.
52. *NEN*, 10/25/48.
53. *NEN*, 12/12/48.
54. *NEN*, 1/10/54; *Herald News*, 2/24/54.

Chapter 15

1. Graziano and Barber, *Somebody Up There Likes Me*, 334.
2. *Ibid.*, 332–33.
3. B. Grayson, *Statesville Daily Record* (SC), 6/16/48.
4. L. Carver, *Record*, 6/11/48.
5. Graziano and Barber, *Somebody Up There Likes Me*, 336.
6. *Ring*, August 1948, 50.
7. *NYT*, 9/15/49.
8. Graziano and Barber, *Somebody Up There Likes Me*, 337.
9. Fernandez, *Boxing in New Jersey*, 92.
10. Gerald Early, "The Romance of Toughness," *The Antioch Review* 45, no. 4 (Autumn 1987): 385–408.
11. Sussman, *Rocky Graziano*, 124.
12. Sugar Ray Robinson with Dave Anderson, *Sugar Ray* (Boston: Da Capo Press, 1994), 166–67.
13. *Ibid.*
14. "Youngman, Henny," BrainyQuote, www.brainyquote.com, accessed December 26, 2019.

Notes—Chapter 16

15. Sussman, *Rocky Graziano*, 154.
16. *Ibid.*, 158–59.
17. Early, "The Romance of Toughness," 403.
18. Nathan Ward, "How Rocky Graziano Became Boxing's Greatest Muse," *Deadspin*, 1/18/19.
19. Sussman, *Rocky Graziano*, 163–65.
20. Early, "The Romance of Toughness," 401.
21. *Ibid.*
22. *Ibid.*
23. O. Prescott, *Books of the Times*, *NYT*, 3/21/55, 23.
24. Arthur Mercante, with Phil Guarnieri, *Inside the Ropes* (Ithaca, NY: McBooks Press, 2006), 131.
25. Sussman, *Rocky Graziano*, 169–70.
26. Rotten Tomatoes, www.rottentomatoes.com, accessed on December 27, 2019.
27. Sussman, *Rocky Graziano*, 172.
28. *Ibid.*, 162.
29. Mercante and Guarnieri, *Inside the Ropes*, 132.
30. *Ibid.*, 134.
31. Early, "The Romance of Toughness," 402.
32. *Ibid.*
33. Graziano and Barber, *Somebody Up There Likes Me*, 349.
34. Rocky Graziano, with Ralph Corsel, *Somebody Down Here Likes Me Too* (New York: Stein & Daily, 1981), 132.
35. *NYT*, 3/9/97 (D. Anderson), Section 8, Page 3.
36. D. Mullen, "Wake for Graziano at Manhattan Funeral Home," UPI, 5/24/90.
37. Graziano and Barber, *Somebody Up There Likes Me*, 344.
38. *Ibid.*, 334–35.
39. B. Jauss, "Graziano Was All Blood and Guts," *Chicago Tribune*, 5/24/90.

Chapter 16

1. Sammons, *Beyond the Ring*, 138.
2. Tuttle, *How Newark Became Newark*, 11.
3. *Ibid.*, 8.
4. *Ibid.*, 154.
5. C. O'Dea, "Newark Before the Comeback: A City Marked by White Flight, Poor Policy," *NJ Spotlight*, 9/4/19.
6. Tuttle, 124–25.
7. *Ibid.*, 126–27.
8. *Ibid.*, 131.
9. *Ibid.*, 134.
10. "Newark's Residents Hope to Replace Demolished Housing Project Park, Gardens," *Star-Ledger*, 4/1/19.
11. Tuttle, *How Newark Became Newark*, 228.
12. FBI Memo, 10/5/48.
13. "Zwillman Probes to Go on Despite Suicide," *NSL*, 3/2/59.
14. *Ibid.*
15. *Ibid.*
16. Deitche, *Garden State Gangland*, 40.
17. "Despondent Zwillman Ends it All," *NSL*, 2/27/59.
18. FBI Memo, 2/10/58.
19. FBI Memo, 1/14/59.
20. *NSL*, 2/24/56, 2/28/56, 3/2/56.
21. *NSL*, 3/2/56.
22. FBI Memo, 9/25/56.
23. FBI Memo, 1/21/59.
24. *NSL*, 2/21/59.
25. FBI Memo, 3/3/59.
26. *NSL*, 2/27/59.
27. Deitche, *Garden State Gangland*, 45–46.
28. R. Kalter, "A Man of Many Faces," *NSL*, 2/27/59.
29. "The Editor's Opinion," *NSL*, 2/27/59.
30. *Ibid.*
31. FBI Memo, 1/12/60.
32. FBI Memo, 5/1/59.
33. Deitche, *Garden State Gangland*, 71.
34. *Ibid.*, 75.
35. Tuttle, *How Newark Became Newark*, 183.
36. Brian Doogan, *The Superfight* (Luton, England: Brian Dugan Media UK Ltd., 2020), 11–12, 23.
37. *Ibid.*, 12, 18–25.
38. *Ibid.*, 178.
39. *Ibid.*, 195.
40. *Ibid.*, 198.
41. *Ibid.*, 208.
42. *Ibid.*, 209.

43. *Ibid.*, 235.
44. A. Williams, "We Have No Right to Destroy Them," *NYT*, 4/14/21.
45. Smith, "Ruppert Stadium," in Bush and Nowlin, *The Newark Eagles Take Flight*, 174.
46. *Ibid.*
47. Izenberg, *Through My Eyes*, at 15.
48. *Ibid.*
49. *Ibid.*
50. *Ibid.*
51. *Ibid.*, 13.
52. Smith, "Ruppert Stadium," in Bush and Nowlin, *The Newark Eagles Take Flight*, 174–75.

Chapter 17

1. Zale and Moyle, *Man of Steel*, 15.
2. *Ibid.*, 249.
3. *Ibid.*
4. *Ibid.*, 248.
5. *Ibid.*, 252.
6. *Ibid.*, 250.
7. *Ibid.*, 266.
8. *Ibid.*, 268.
9. *NYT*, 3/4/68.
10. Zale and Moyle, *Man of Steel*, 281.
11. Interview with Ted Zale, 9/19/21.
12. Zale and Moyle, *Man of Steel*, 241.
13. *Ibid.*, 296.
14. Interview with Deborah Zale, 9/7/21.
15. Interview with Ted Zale, 9/19/21.
16. Zale and Moyle, 12.
17. *Ibid.*, 286.
18. *Ibid.*, 292.
19. *Ibid.*, 279.
20. *NEN* (UPI), 2/1/59.
21. "Honest Fighters Finish First," *Boxing Illustrated*, July 1961.
22. *Ibid.*
23. Zale and Moyle, *Man of Steel*, 274.
24. Rick Perlstein, *Before the Storm: Barry Goldwater and the Unmaking of the American Consensus* (New York: Nation Books, 2001), 321.
25. D. Polman, "A New Book Describes Hunter S. Thompson's Prescience," *Atlantic*, 12/28/18.
26. Patrick J. Buchanan, *Nixon's White House Wars: The Battles that Made and Broke a President and Divided America Forever* (New York: Crown Forum, 2017); see, generally, Chapter 8, "Converting the Catholics."
27. Zale and Moyle, *Man of Steel*, 275.
28. See, e.g., C. Matthews, "Bobby Kennedy's Humility and Willingness to Change Makes Him the Perfect Antidote to Trump," *Think*, 6/4/18.
29. Zale and Moyle, *Man of Steel*, 299, 305.
30. *Ibid.*, 314.
31. *Ibid.*, 312.
32. *Ibid.*, 328.
33. *Ibid.*, Hagler blurb on inside cover; see also *Sports Illustrated*, 3/24/86 (Hagler quoted, "Now Zale, there was one rough, tough fighter.").
34. *Ibid.*, 326.
35. *Ibid.*, 325.
36. *Ibid.*, 341–48.
37. *Ibid.*, 350.
38. S. Povich, *Washington Post*, 3/3/97.
39. Zale and Moyle, *Man of Steel*, 7–8, 358.
40. Jarrett, *Champ in the Corner*, 196.

Bibliography

Books

Blady, Ken. *The Jewish Boxer's Hall of Fame.* New York: Shapolsky Publishers, Inc., 1988.

Buchanan, Patrick J. *Nixon's White House Wars: The Battles that Made and Broke a President and Divided America Forever.* New York: Crown Forum, an imprint of the Crown Publishing Group, a division of Penguin Random House LLC, 2017.

Bush, Frederick C., and Bill Nowlin, eds. *The Newark Eagles Take Flight: The Story of the 1946 Negro League Champions.* Phoenix, AZ: Society for American Baseball Research, Inc., 2019.

Cannon, Jimmy. *Nobody Asked Me But...: The World of Jimmy Cannon.* New York: Holt, Reinhart and Winston, 1978.

Cavanaugh, Jack. *Tunney: Boxing's Brainiest Champ and His Upset of the Great Jack Dempsey.* New York: Random House, 2006.

Congdon, Lee. *Legendary Sports Writers of the Golden Age: Grantland Rice, Red Smith, Shirley Povich, and W. C. Heinz.* Lanham, MD: Rowman & Littlefield, 2017.

Cramer, Richard Ben. *Joe DiMaggio: The Hero's Life.* New York: Simon & Schuster, 2000.

Deitche, Scott M. *Garden State Gangland: The Rise of the Mob in New Jersey.* Lanham, MD: Rowman & Littlefield, 2018.

Doogan, Brian. *The Superfight.* Luton, England: Brian Dugan Media UK Ltd., 2020.

Eig, Jonathan. *Luckiest Man: The Life and Death of Lou Gehrig.* New York: Simon & Schuster, 2005.

Federal Bureau of Investigation. *Abner "Longie" Zwillman—The FBI Files*, Vol. 1. Minneapolis, MN: Filiquarian Publishing, LLC/Quontro, 2021.

Fernandez, Robert F., Sr. *Boxing in New Jersey, 1900–1999.* Jefferson, NC: McFarland, 2014.

Graziano, Rocky, with Rowland Barber. *Somebody Up There Likes Me.* New York: Simon & Schuster, 1955.

Graziano, Rocky, with Ralph Corsel. *Somebody Down Here Likes Me Too.* New York: Stein & Daly Publishing, 1981.

Heinz, W.C. *The Professional.* Cambridge, MA: De Capo Press, 2001.

Heinz, W.C. *The Top of His Game: The Best Sportswriting of W. C. Heinz.* Edited by Bill Littlefield. New York: The Library of America, 2015.

Izenberg, Jerry. *Through My Eyes: A Sports Writer's 58-Year Journey.* Haworth, NJ: St. Johann Press, 2009.

Jarrett, John. *Champ in the Corner: The Ray Arcel Story.* Stroud, Gloucestershire, UK: Stadia, 2007.

Jarrett, John. *Toy Bulldog: The Fighting Life and Times of Mickey Walker.* Jefferson, NC: McFarland, 2013.

Kahn, Roger. *A Flame of Pure Fire: Jack Dempsey and the Roaring '20s.* New York: Harcourt Brace & Co., 1999.

Bibliography

Mercante, Arthur, with Phil Guarnieri. *Inside the Ropes.* Ithaca, NY: McBooks Press, Inc., 2006.
Mitchell, Kevin. *Jacobs Beach: The Mob, The Garden & The Golden Age of Boxing.* Boston: Hamilcar Publications, 2019.
Oates, Joyce Carol. *New Jersey Noir.* New York: Akashic Books, 2011.
Perlstein, Rick. *Before the Storm: Barry Goldwater and the Unmaking of the American Consensus.* New York: Nation Books, 2001.
Robinson, Sugar Ray, with Dave Anderson. *Sugar Ray.* Boston: Da Capo Press, 1994.
Romano, Frederick V. *The Golden Age of Boxing on Radio and Television: A Blow-by-Blow History from 1921 to 1964.* New York: Carrel Books, 2017.
Roth, Philip. *Philip Roth at 80: A Celebration.* New York: A Library of America Special Publication, 2014.
Sammons, Jeffrey T. *Beyond the Ring: The Role of Boxing in American Society.* Urbana: University of Illinois Press, 1990.
Schmeling, Max, with George Von der Lippe. *Max Schmeling: An Autobiography.* Chicago: Bonus Books, 1998.
Smith, Red. *The Red Smith Reader.* New York: Random House, 1982.
Sussman, Jeffrey. *Rocky Graziano: Fists, Fame, and Fortune.* Lanham, MD: Rowman & Littlefield, 2018.
Toledo, Springs. *Murderers' Row: In Search of Boxing's Greatest Outcasts.* N.p.: Tora, 2012.
Tuttle, Brad R. *How Newark Became Newark: The Rise, Fall, and Rebirth of an American City.* New Brunswick, NJ: Rivergate Books, an Imprint of Rutgers University Press, 2011.
Vogan, Travis. *The Boxing Film: A Cultural and Transmedia History.* New Brunswick, NJ: Rutgers University Press, 2021.
Yogoda, Ben, and Kevin Kerrane, eds.. *The Art of the Fact: A Historical Anthology of Literary Journalism.* New York: Simon and Shuster, Inc. (Touchstone), 1997.
Zale, Thad "Ted," and Clay Moyle. *Tony Zale: The Man of Steel.* Iowa City, IA: KO Publications, 2014.

Newspapers

Asbury Park Press
Chicago Tribune
Daily News (*DN*, New York)
Daily Oklahoman
Dayton Daily News
Escanaba Daily Press
Escarra Daily Press
Evening Sun (PA)
Fort Worth Star Telegram
Greenville News (SC)
Herald News (NJ)
Honolulu Star-Bulletin
Independent (London)
Independent Pottsville Republican
Kingsport Times

Los Angeles Times
Muncie Evening Press
New York Journal-American
New York Times (*NYT*)
Newark Evening News (*NEN*)
Newark Star Ledger (*NSL*)
Pittsburgh Sun-Telegraph
Pottsville Record
Record (Bergen, NJ)
St. Louis Star and Times
Statesville Daily Record (SC)
Syracuse Herald Journal
Tampa Times
Tennessean
Washington Post

Magazines and Websites

The Antioch Review
Atlantic

Boxing Illustrated
Boxrec.com

Bibliography

Brainyquote.com
Britannica.com
Clifton Merchant Magazine
Deadspin
Filmreference.com
Inside Sports
John-Woodbridge.com
Medium.com
Newspapers.com

NJ Boxing Hall of Fame
NJsportlinght.com
Ring
Rottentomatoes.com
Society for American Baseball Research
Sports Illustrated
Think
Time
Yale Journal of Law & the Humanities

Interviews

Cavaliere, Paul, Jr. August 27, 2021.
Zale, Deborah. September 7, 2021.
Zale, Ted. September 19, 2021.

Index

Abrams, Georgie 28, 53, 127
Actor's Studio 144
Adamek, Tomasz 153
Adamson, Harold 99
Addie, Johnnie 111
Addonizio, Hugh 151
Aegean Sea 75
African Americans 17–18, 149
Ali, Muhammad 1, 92, 129, 157
All-American Girls Professional Baseball League 159
Allen, Mel 99, 111–112
Altman, Joseph (mayor) 83
Amateur Athletic Union 35
American Broadcast Company 143
American Dream 68
American Legion 99
American Medical Association 66
Anastasia, Albert "Mad Hatter" 13, 100
Anzalone, Ross 95
Applegate, Willie "Red" 71
Arcel, Ray 23, 30, 47, 49, 87, 95–96, 121, 130
Archer, Freddie 71
Arguello, Alexis 1
Armstrong, Henry 75
Arnold, Billy 38
Associated Press 82, 121
Atlantic City, New Jersey 82–83, 146
Australia 99

Badami, Stefano 13
Bain, Abie 71
Baker, Tommy 71
Ball, Lucille 144
Ballantine Ale 98
Bamberger's 18
Banks, Johnathan 153
Barbella, Ida (mother) 32
Barbella, Nicola (father) 32
Barber, Rowland 144
Basilio, Carmine 161
Bass, Joe 151
Bear, Max 108–109

Behr, Johnny 59–61
Belloise, Steve 78
Bellows, George 93
Berlin, Germany 99
Berlin Airlift 99
Berman, Otto "Abbadabba" 13
Berra, Yogi 19
Bettina, Melio 22, 110
Bimstein, Whitey 37, 114, 123
Black Murderers' Row 52, 100
Blue Moon (tavern) 70
Bodne, Ben 98, 123–124
Body and Soul 68
Boiardo, Richie "The Boot" 14–15, 18, 151
Boxing Illustrated 157–158
Boyle's Thirty Acres 65–66, 126
Braddock, James J. 71, 80, 108
Brando, Marlon 30, 141
Brennan, William J. 151
Brick City 148–149
Britton, Jack 69
Brockton, Massachusetts 152
Bronx, New York City 44
Brooklyn, New York City 42
Brooklyn Dodgers 19, 153
Buckley, Joseph W. 99
Bufania, Nicholas "Joe Bones" 13
Buileck, Bill 112–113
Burbank, California 80
Burley, Charley 24, 53, 75, 78
Bush, Pres. George H.W. 159–60
Butte, Montana 77
Byrne, Brendan 150

Cagney, James 67
California 94, 157
Call of the Wild 80
Calypso 75
Canada 99
Canastota, New York 161
Cannon, Jimmy 2, 27, 29, 47, 49, 58, 60, 66–67, 112, 118
Canzaneri, Tony 73
Capone, Al 69

189

Index

Caponigro, Tony "Bananas" 13
Caras, Frankie 123
Carbo, Frankie 72–73, 83–84, 110, 148
Carpentier, Georges 65–66, 84, 126
Carroll, Parke 153
Carson, Johnny 159
Cartier, Walter 67
Carver, Lawton 124
Casablanca Club 16
Casale, Frank 90, 103, 105
Castle William (military prison) 36
Catholic Church (and religion) 20, 33, 158
Catholic Youth Organization (CYO) 92, 156–157
Cavaliere, Paul 108–109, 111–113, 117–119, 121, 130
Cavaliere, Paul, Jr. (son) 108–111, 121, 162
Central Park, New York City 92, 97
Central Planning Board 17
Central Ward, Newark 73, 151
Cerdan, Marcel 53, 78, 84, 86, 101, 123, 126–127, 129–131, 148, 155, 160
Ceres, Jimmy "Peanuts" 18
Champion 68
Charles, Ezzard 23, 72, 110
Charley Burley and the Black Murderer's Row 52
Chicago, Illinois 20, 26, 58, 77, 88, 90, 92–93, 105, 115, 117, 141–142, 156, 159
Chicago Cubs 153
Chicago Parks District 157
Chicago Stadium 25–26, 56, 58, 106, 146
Chinatown, New York City 34
Citizen Kane 145
Clark, Jimmy 24
Clark, William 14
Claus, Bobby 84
Cleveland, Ohio 93
Cleveland Indians 101
Cliffside, New Jersey 95
Clinton Reformatory for Women 139
Club Miami 86
Cochrane, Freddie "Red" 40, 71, 75
Cohen, Irving 36–37, 83, 121, 142
Cohen, Red 150
Columbia Broadcast System 82
Comiskey Park 56
Communist Party 100
Congleton, Richard J. 133–134, 138–139
Conlon, Joseph E. 132, 136, 138–139
Conn, Billy 24, 29–30, 80–81, 160
Convention Hall 82
The Corbett-Courtney Fight 67
Corleone, Michael 149
Corleone, Vito 15–16
Costello, Frank 15
Cousteau, Jacques 75
Coxackie (school) 34

Crafts, Dr. Wilbur F. 66
Cuddy, Jack 123

Daily News 6, 29, 42, 106, 112, 122
Daley, Arthur 28, 110, 141
Dallas, Texas 158
Daly, Leon 19
D'Amico, Gapare 14
Damon Runyan Children Cancer Fund 124
Darthard, Jackie 57
Davids, Charles L. 74–75
Davids Stadium 75
Davis, Bummy 39
Dawson, James 45, 53, 114, 122, 129
Day of the Fight (film) 67
The Day of the Fight (magazine article) 43
Dean, James 141, 145
DeCarlo, Angelo "Gyp" 13
DeFazio, Johnny "Red" 95
Delaney, Jack 109
Delannoit, Cyrille 101
Del Greco, Al 95, 105, 123
Democratic Party 158
Dempsey, Jack 21, 38–39, 54, 65–66, 84, 93, 109–110, 122, 126, 147, 149
DeNiro, Robert 67
De Paul, Andy 95
Dewey, Thomas 16
DiMaggio, Joe 18, 86, 110, 149
Doby, Larry 19
Dr. Strangeglove 141
Donadio, Louis J. 150
Dorfman, Sid 105
Douglas, Kirk 67–68
Dowd, Bernie 95
Doyle, Jimmy 93
Dresch, Adam 3
Dublin, Ireland 79
Dumont Television Studios 98
Dunphy, Don 49
Duran, Roberto 23

Early, Gerald 144
East Orange, New Jersey 67
East Ward, Newark 1, 19, 74, 154; *see also* Ironbound Section
Edison, Thomas 67
Edwards, Edward 66
Eighth Avenue, Newark 149
Eigner, Joyce 100
Elizabeth, New Jersey 69, 73, 75, 95
Ellenstein, Meyer 17
Ellenville, New York 90
England 63, 99
Escanaba Press 110
Essex County Courthouse 97, 132
Essex County Veterans of Foreign Wars 124

Index

Factor, John "Jake the Barber" 150
Federal Bureau of Investigation 14, 17, 88, 149–151, 161
Firpo, Louis 92
First Precinct 5–7; *see also* Newark Police
First Ward, Newark 13, 15, 18, 149
Flatbush, Brooklyn 71
Fleischer, Nat 24, 30, 45, 47–48, 53, 61, 111, 114, 122, 140
Flicker, Dr. David A. 122
Flynn, Errol 67
Ford, Peyton 149
Foreman, George 72, 119
Fort Dix 36
Fort Leavenworth 37
Foster, Bob 92
Fox, Billy 84
France 99, 131
Frazier, Joe 39, 92, 119
Freehold, New Jersey 71
Fulton, Fred 98
Fusari, Charley 71, 110, 140–141

Galento, Tony 86, 108
Garden State Parkway 149
Garfield, John 68
Garfield, New Jersey 71
Gary, Elbert Henry 20
Gary, Indiana 20, 90, 100, 158
Gary Works 23
Gates, Ralph F. 125
Gavilan, Kid 72
Gehrig, Lou 35
Gellman, Charley (aka "Chuck Halper") 73
Gianfrancisco, Philomena (wife) 159–160
Gibson, Kenneth 152
Gimbel, Bernard 110
Gimbels Department Store 110
Gleason, Jackie 70, 86, 149
Glover, Frank "Roughhouse" 23
Goldberg, Hy 106
Golden Age of Boxing 2, 73
Golden Gloves 20, 22
Goldstein, Ruby 47
Gordon, Joe 19
Graham, Frank 129, 162
Grand Central Station 62
The Great Depression 1, 15, 71, 73, 109, 157
Greb, Harry 24, 69, 73
Green, Harold 40, 127
Greene, Abe 84, 88, 90, 93–94, 102, 108–110, 121, 144
Greenville News 123
Griffith Stadium 100

Hagler, Ida Mae (mother) 151–152
Hagler, Marvelous Marvin 24, 96, 151–152, 159

Hague, Frank 127
Hahne's 18
Halper, Lou 71
Hamburg, Germany 101
Hamsho, Mustafa 159
Harlow, Jean 14
Harman, Harvey 101
Harper's Magazine 152
Hatcher, Richard 158
Havana, Cuba 80
Havana Riviera Casino 150
Hawaii 99
Heart Fund of New Jersey 124
Heinz, W.C. 2, 43, 47, 54–57, 67
Hemingway, Ernest 67
Highland Park, New Jersey 73, 100
Hinkes, Max "Puddy" 13
Hoboken, New Jersey 100
Hodges, Russ 99
Hogan, Ben 101
Hogan, Frank 55
Holmes, Larry 129
Hoover, J. Edgar 14, 88
Horne, Sonny 40, 85
Hostak, Al 25, 128
Hot Springs, Arkansas 90
Hudson County Penitentiary 99
Hudson River 2, 73, 92, 98, 106, 148
Hurley, Joseph 5
Hurley Boxing Law 65

Illinois Athletic Commission 79
immigration 16–17, 20
Indiana 131, 158
Internal Revenue Service 149–150
International Boxing Club 148
International Boxing Hall of Fame 161
International Reform Bureau 66
Ironbound Section 19, 74, 154
Irvin, Monty 19, 153
Izenberg, Jerry 1, 19, 73, 153–154

Jack, Beau 72
Jacobs, Mike 79–81, 86, 109–110
James, Sharpe 153
Jeffries, Jim 80
Jersey City, New Jersey 12, 65, 85, 95, 97, 110, 126, 128, 148
Jersey City Giants 101
Jersey Shore 15, 99
Johnson, Jack 77–79
Johnston, James J. 124
Jones, James Earl 67
Jones, Roy 24

Kapilow, Danny 73
Katz, Sam "Big Sue" 13, 150
Keansburg, New Jersey 70

Index

Kearns, Jack 54
Keck, Harry 123
Keenan, John B. 102–103
Kefauver Committee 150
Keighry Head, Elizabeth, New Jersey 69
Kennedy, Bobby 150, 158
Kennedy, Pres. John F. 151, 158
Ketchel, Stanley 24, 77–78, 122
Killroy, Billy 95, 111
King, Martin Luther, Jr. 152
Kingston, Jamaica 119
Klaus, Frank 78
Konigsberg, Kayo 13
Kosciusko American Legion Hall 125
Kubrick, Stanley 67, 141

La Cosa Nostra 151
Lake Michigan 20
LaMotta, Jake 31, 52, 55, 75, 78, 84–85, 90, 100–101, 110, 131, 146, 157–158
Langford, Sam 24
Lansky, Meyer 15
La Placa, Peter D. 150
Larasso, Louis 13
Larkin, Tippy 71
Las Vegas, Nevada 150
Laurel Garden 38, 67, 73–74, 109
A League of Their Own 159
Lebkuecher, Julius 12
LeConte Brothers 13
Lee Myles Transmissions 145
Leonard, Benny 98
Leonard, Sugar Ray 1, 25
Lesnevitch, Gus 71, 84, 110, 123
Lewis, Ted "Kid" 98
Life 60, 128, 151
Lilley Commission 151
Lincoln, Abraham 12
Lindbergh kidnapping 7, 16
Livingston, New Jersey 95
London, Jack 80
Long Branch, New Jersey 99
Longo, Frank 14
Look 67
Los Angeles, California 101
Louis, Joe 22, 29, 61, 72, 79, 80–81, 109, 129
Lower East Side, New York City 33–34, 140
Lower West Side, New York City 79
Lowman, Lawrence 87
Luciano, Charles "Lucky" 15
Lytell, Bert 78

Mad Men 37
Madison Square Garden 22, 28, 30, 40–41, 53, 64, 69, 73, 79, 84, 89, 111, 140, 142
Maharishi Yogurt 145

Mailer, Norman 27
Major League Baseball 153
Malloy, Terry 141
Mamakos, Steve 25
Manasquan, New Jersey 99
Manhattan, New York City 11, 32, 73, 85, 93, 144
Manley, Effa 19, 153
Mansfield, Jane 149
Marciano, Rocky 71, 82, 129, 152
Marenghi, Anthony 2, 40, 45–46, 51, 83, 85, 103, 105, 114, 120, 122–123, 127
Marquis of Queensbury Rules 28
The Martha Ray Show 144
Martin, Whitney 82
Martland, Dr. Harrison 135
Maxim, Joey 142
Mayfair Farms 8
McCoy, Thomas 64
McLeed, Dr. Neil S. 100
Meadowbrook Bowl 74
Mercante, Arthur 145
Merchantville Township, New Jersey 71
Merkle, Alfred 136
Merrillville, Indiana 155
Metro, Frank 133–136
Miller, Charles 87
Miller, Heine 83
Milligan, Tommy 70
Milwaukee, Wisconsin 27
Minard, Duane E. 6–9, 133
Mobley, Helen 132
Monaco, Sam 13
Monroe, Marilyn 86, 149
Montgomery, Bob 72
Monzon, Carlos 24
Moore, Archie 53
Moran, Joe 111
Moretti, Willie 150
Mundt-Nixon bill 100
Murder, Inc. 16
Murderers' Row 52, 100; *see also* Black Murderers' Row
Murphy, Vincent 17, 102, 103
Mutual Network 99

Nardiello, Dr. Vincent 120–122
National Boxing Association 52, 56, 83, 88
National Broadcast Company 44, 81
Neff, George 7–6
Negro leagues 153
Neusel, Walter 101
New Brunswick, New Jersey 73, 95
New Jersey 63, 64, 68, 73, 83, 88, 93–95, 107–108, 110, 140
New Jersey Bell Telephone Company 98
New Jersey Boxing Commission 121, 123

Index

New Jersey Camp for Blind Children 124
New Jersey Heavyweight Championship 108
New Jersey Legislature 63
New Jersey Performing Arts Center 153
New Jersey State Athletic Commission 84, 119
New Jersey's Boxing Hall of Fame 95, 109
New York Boxing Writers' Association 82
New York City, New York 11, 17, 27, 91, 97
New York City Reformatory (a.k.a. Farms) 34–35
New York Daily Mirror 85
New York Giants (baseball) 153
New York Journal American 129
New York State 82–83, 93, 121
New York State Athletic Commission 28, 52, 54–56, 77, 79, 82, 120
New York State Boxing Commission 112
New York Sun 54
New York Times 28, 45, 75, 110–111, 114, 122, 129, 141, 144, 156
New York Yankees 75, 99
Newark 1–2, 11–15, 17, 67, 69, 72–73, 81, 85, 88–89, 91–92, 95, 98–99, 106, 110–112, 126–127, 132, 140–141, 143, 147–149, 151–152, 158, 161; deindustrialization 148; industrialization 11–12; organized crime 10–11, 13–14; progressive era 12; prohibition 15; Puritans 12, 154
Newark Airport 18
Newark Armory 56, 97
Newark Bay 11, 128
Newark Bears 19, 101, 106, 153
Newark Board of Education 154
Newark City Hall 13, 91, 101
Newark City Hospital 5
Newark College of Engineering (n.k.a NJIT) 104
Newark Eagles 19, 71, 101, 153
Newark Evening News 2, 5, 27, 29, 40–41, 45, 49, 83, 90, 103, 105–106, 121–122, 127, 139
Newark General Hospital 13
Newark Penn Station 106, 124
Newark Police 5, 6, 17, 100, 124, 132, 134, 136
Newark Star Eagle 75
Newark Star Ledger 2, 5, 9, 40, 45, 51, 83, 90, 95, 100, 103, 104, 120–123, 127, 136, 151, 153
Newcombe, Don 153
Newman, Paul 141, 144–145
Niederreiter, Andy 85, 91
Nixon, Pres. Richard M. 100, 133, 158

noir (fiction) 68
noir (film) 2, 68
Noonan, Rita 134

Ocean County, New Jersey 1, 149
O'Dwyer, William 16, 110
Olympics 21–22, 24
O'Malley, Gene 93
On the Waterfront 30, 141
Otty, Harry 52
Owens, Jessie 24

Pabst 27
Palace Chop House 16
Palmiero, Frank "Blinky" 72, 84
Pal's Tavern 8
Parker, Dan 85
Parkinson's Disease 71
Passaic River 11, 14, 16
Passionelle 100
Paterson, New Jersey 73, 109
Pellecchia, P. James, Jr. 9
Philadelphia, Pennsylvania 11
Philadelphia Athletics 101
Piaf, Edith 126
Pian, Sam 23, 87
Pine Barrens 36
Pittsburgh, Pennsylvania 134
Pittsburgh Sun-Telegraph 123
Plimpton, George 119
political corruption 11, 13
Polo Grounds 130, 140
Polverino, Joe "The Indian" 13
Pompton Lakes, New Jersey 29
Poquette, Raymond 5, 135–136
Port Authority, New York City 97
Povitch, Shirley 160
Powers, Ann 7–8, 99, 132–139
Powers, Henry (husband) 7
Powers, Jimmy 29, 106, 112
Prescott, Oliver 144
Presidential Citizen's Medal 160
Presley, Elvis 22, 151
The Professional 47, 67
Provenzano, Anthony "Tony Pro" 13
Prudential Center 153
Pryor, Billy 27
Pulaski Skyway 1, 97, 106

Raging Bull 84
Rahway, New Jersey 25
Raisin Bran 145
Rallie, Effie 7
Ratner, Willie 27, 29–30, 40–41, 45, 49, 83, 90, 103, 105, 122, 127
Ray, Martha 144
Reagan, Pres. Ronald 159
Rebel Without a Cause 141

Index

Record (n.k.a. *Bergen County Record*) 95, 105, 123–124
Reno, Nevada 80
Requiem for a Heavyweight (TV broadcast) 51
Rickey, Branch 153
Riker Emory & Danzig 134
Ring (magazine) 24–25, 30, 40, 45, 47, 49, 51, 53, 55, 61, 71–72, 77–80, 84, 94, 110–111, 113, 122–123, 140, 146, 160–161
Ringside Gym, Chicago 90
Risko, Johnny 70
Riviera Country Club 101
Roach, Lavern 84
Robert Treat Hotel 101, 103, 134
Robinson, Jackie 19, 153
Robinson, Sugar Ray 24, 41, 52–53, 75, 78, 84, 93–94, 110, 123, 127, 142–143, 146, 158, 160
Robson, Paul 100
Rockefeller, John D. 15
Rocky (film) 117
Rodino, Peligrino "Peter" 133
Roosevelt, Theodore 64
Roosevelt Stadium 85, 126–129
Rosemont, Illinois 159
Rosenbloom, Maxie "Slapsie" 52
Ross, Barney 110
Rosselli, Dominic "The Ape" 13
Rotando, Anthony 13
Roth, Phillip 74
Rowe, Thomas 5–6, 8, 16–17, 99, 132, 134–139
Ruggles, Charles R. 64
Rumson, New Jersey 69, 109
Ruppert Stadium 19, 74, 85, 97–98, 104, 106–107, 110–112, 123, 127–128, 153–154, 162
Russo, John "Big Pussy" 13
Russo, Louis "Babe Ruth" 14
Rutgers Law School 133
Rutgers University 101
Ruth, Babe 65
Ryan, Robert 68

St. Hedwig Catholic Church 20
St. John's Roman Catholic Church 138
St. Patrick's Cathedral 140
St. Peter's Prep 110
Salisbury, Gene 95
Schaeffer, Benjamin 10
Schmeling, Max 70–71, 80, 101
Schultz, Dutch (aka Arthur Flegenheimer) 16–17
Schwartz, James 125
Scorsese, Martin 84
Scott, Dorothy (daughter) 137–138
Seattle, Washington 25

Second Presbyterian Church, Newark 138
Servo, Marty 40–41
The Set-Up 68, 145
Shank, Reuben "Cowboy" 54
Sharkey, Jack 70, 109
Shepard, Court 145
Shor, Toots 86–87
Siegal, Bugsy 83
Simon, Abe 72
Sinatra, Frank 8, 70
Sing Sing Prison 33
Smith, Red 2, 55, 67, 112
Smith, Will 67
Somebody Down Here Likes Me Too 146
Somebody Up There Likes Me (book) 3, 144–145
Somebody Up There Likes Me (film) 141, 156
Soose, Billy 28, 110, 160
The Sopranos 68
The Sound of Music 145
Spartacus 141
Springfield, Massachusetts 153
Springsteen, Bruce 22, 71, 148
Stacher, Joseph "Doc" 13
Stardust Hotel-Casino 150
Stassi, Joe 13
Steiger, Rod 30
Stern, Dr. Max E. 92–93, 103, 119, 121–122
Stevens, Cliff 95
Stilinovich & Wiatrolik Funeral Home 155
Stillman's Gym 36, 91–92
Stoltz, Allie 71
Strauss, Sol 82
Stribling, Ken 100–101
Super Chlorination 145
Sussex Avenue Armory 98

Tampa Times 110
television 80, 98, 111–112
Theodorescu, Milo 38
Third Ward, Newark 14
Toldeo, Springs 52, 56
Tombs Jail 34
The Tonight Show 159
Toots Shor's Restaurant 85–86
Torment 100
Tourine, Charlie "The Blade" 13
Tournament of Champions, Inc. 81, 98, 123–124, 126
Troia, Joseph 14
Troia, Vincent 14
Truman, Pres. Harry 2, 16, 99–100, 133
Tucker Automobile Company 155
Tucker: The Man and His Dream 155
Tunney, Gene 49, 109–110, 147
Tuttle, Brad R. 148

Index

Twentieth Century Sporting Club 81, 86
2001: A Space Odyssey 141

Unger, Norma (wife) 37, 146
United Press 26
United States Army 36, 79
United States Navy 30
United States Steel 20
United States Virgin Islands 71
University of Wisconsin 22

Ville, Henry 5, 136

Wagon Wheel 70
Walcott, Jersey Joe 61, 71, 84
Walcott, Joe (welterweight) 71
Walker, Mickey 29, 54, 69–70
Walker Law 73, 79
Wallace, Cowboy 71
Wallace, George 158
Ward, Gene 122
Ward, Jim 110
Washington, Denzel 67
Washington, D.C. 18, 25, 100, 134, 151
Washington Post 160
Washington Senators 101
Wayne, John 67
Wednesday Night Fights 143
Weill, Al 82–83
Weiss, Emanuel "Mendy" 16
West New York, New Jersey 73
West Orange, New Jersey 8, 150
West Side Story 145
Western Union 99
Wiedenmayer's Park 74, 98

Wikipedia 2
Willard, Jess 65, 80
Williams, Holman 127
Williams, Ike 72–73
Wills, Harry 98
Winch, Art 23, 118
Wisconsin 57
Wise, Robert 145
Woods, Lou 84
Workman, Charles "The Bug" 13, 16
World Boxing Hall of Fame 25
World War I 6, 65
World War II 2, 29, 160
Wortendyke, Jacob 150
Wrigley Field 56

Yankee Stadium 41, 51, 56, 70, 80
Young, Terry 35
Youngman, Henny 143
Yuma, Arizona 159

Zack, Charlie 95, 111
Zale, Deborah 161
Zale, Ted 160
Zaleski, Adeline (wife) 27, 155
Zaleski, Josef (father) 20
Zaleski, Kataryna (mother; aka Catherine) 20
Zaleski, Joseph (brother) 20–21
Zaleski, John (brother) 20–21
Zivic, Fritzie 75
Zwillman, Abner "Longie" 14–17, 86, 149–151

www.ingramcontent.com/pod-product-compliance
Ingram Content Group UK Ltd.
Pitfield, Milton Keynes, MK11 3LW, UK
UKHW042009140426
5217IPUK00015B/1078